# Global Activism, Global Media

# Global Activism,
# Global Media

Edited by

Wilma de Jong, Martin Shaw
and Neil Stammers

Pluto Press

LONDON • ANN ARBOR, MI

First published 2005 by Pluto Press
345 Archway Road, London N6 5AA
and 839 Greene Street, Ann Arbor, MI 48106

www.plutobooks.com

British Library Cataloguing in Publication Data
A catalogue record for this book is available from the British Library

ISBN 0 7453 2196 8 hardback
ISBN 0 7453 2195 X paperback

Library of Congress Cataloging in Publication Data applied for

10 9 8 7 6 5 4 3 2 1

Designed and produced for Pluto Press by
Chase Publishing Services, Fortescue, Sidmouth, EX10 9QG, England
Typeset from disk by Newgen Imaging Systems (P) Ltd., India
Printed and bound in the European Union by
Antony Rowe Ltd, Chippenham and Eastbourne, England

# Contents

# List of Photographs

# Acronyms and Abbreviations

| | |
|---|---|
| ANC | African National Congress |
| ASF | Asian Social Forum |
| CAFOD | Catholic Agency for Overseas Development |
| CAT | Community Activist Technology |
| CND | Campaign for Nuclear Disarmament |
| END | European Nuclear Disarmament |
| ftm | female-to-male |
| GATS | General Agreement on Trade in Services |
| GCS | global civil society |
| GUF | Global Union Federation |
| IDRF | Indian Development and Relief Fund |
| IC | International Council (of the OC) |
| ICFTU | International Confederation of Free Trade Unions |
| ILGA | International Lesbian and Gay Association |
| ILO | International Labour Organisation |
| IMC | Independent Media Centre (Indymedia) |
| IMF | International Monetary Fund |
| INGO | international non-governmental organisation |
| LGBT | lesbian, gay, bisexual, transgender |
| MAI | Multilateral Agreement on Investment |
| NGO | non-governmental organisation |
| NRI | Non-Resident Indians |
| NWICO | New World Information and Communication Order |
| OC | (Brazilian) National Organising Committee (later to be the IOC, Indian National Organising Committee at WSF4) |
| OECD | Organisation for Economic Co-operation and Development |
| PT | Partido dos Trabalhadores (Brazilian Workers' Party) |
| RSS | Rashtriya Sevak Sangh (ultra right-wing Hindu organisation) |
| SMO | Social Movement Organisation |
| SMWN | Social Movements World Network |
| TAN | transnational advocacy networks |

| | |
|---|---|
| TIUI | Traditional International Union Institutions |
| TJM | Trade Justice Movement |
| TLIO | The Land Is Ours |
| TSMO | Transnational Social Movement Organisation |
| UNDP | United Nations Development Programme |
| UNESCO | United Nations Educational, Scientific and Cultural Organisation |
| VHP | Vishwa Hindu Parishad (ultra right-wing Hindu organisation) |
| WDM | World Development Movement |
| WSF (FSM) | World Social Forum |
| WTO | World Trade Organisation |

# Preface

## GLOBAL ACTIVISM, GLOBAL MEDIA: A WAKE-UP CALL

There is much talk about the impact of popular culture and the political apathy of citizens who would rather consume and be entertained than get engaged in the complex issues facing our world today. But that is only one story.

Another is almost the opposite. Our world has more social and political movements, voluntary associations and campaigning organisations than ever before. Many of these developments are neither registered nor recorded, partly because of the complexities of gaining access to the producers of mass media or, more generally, because of the contours of relations and structures of power in the contemporary world.

This book attempts to offer an overview and insight into some of these developments, the people involved in them and their attempts to communicate their views to others. While inevitably limited in its scope, this book also reminds us of the links between today's activism and the many struggles of the past. If Bauman is right in pointing out 'The culture of a consumer society is mostly about forgetting not learning' (Bauman 1998:82), then today's activism must also insist that the lessons of history must be learnt.

Another world *is* possible, but there are many complexities to working out how we get there: to address the issues of strategies and goals. Gandhi argued that one cannot take up arms and fight for peace and it is our contention that Gandhi was right to argue that ends and means can't be separated. There have already been too many histories of struggles for justice turning into their horrific opposites. There can't be a fairer world if we can't at the same time celebrate diversity and there can't be a global society without difference and dissent.

Wilma de Jong, Martin Shaw, Neil Stammers

October 2004

## BIBLIOGRAPHY

Bauman, Z. (1998) *Globalisation: The Human Consequences*, New York: Columbia University Press.

# Introduction

*Wilma de Jong, Martin Shaw and Neil Stammers*

In the first decade of the twenty-first century, politics seem to be convulsed by the violent conflicts between powerful states and armed groups that erupted after 11 September 2001. Around and behind those conflicts, however, other kinds of actors are at work in society across the world. More peaceful forms of social and political activism, informed by visions of change, permeate all areas of social life and all regions. Activism contests local and global power structures and offers alternatives to the politics of force. Activist politics spawn movements, networks, organisations and websites. They influence 'mainstream' politics over fundamental world issues like trade, gender relations and the environment as well as war.[1]

In this new period, politics *is* communication: politicians' pronouncements, terrorists' bombs and peaceful protest alike are geared to ways of communicating to people. All political conflict takes place largely within and through organised media of communication, but these are much more varied than the term 'mass media' implies. Communication may be direct, from political actor to audience in media that actors themselves define, as well as indirect, through formal media institutions. In the twenty-first century, transformations of communications technology offer many radical new possibilities.

Although both contemporary activism and mass media can be traced back over a half-century or more, they each have distinctive significance in the emerging 'global' era. National and other boundaries that constrained activism and media alike have not disappeared; but both have been transformed by expanded possibilities of interconnection. Activism appears to be 'global' in a new way, with coordinated worldwide protests for 'global justice' that involve many different strands of activity. Media appear to be increasingly globalised, as national television, press, etc. are subsumed in gigantic worldwide flows of information and ideas, symbolised by the internet which offers social and political actors new opportunities for more direct communication.

I

It should be obvious that we cannot understand activism without seeing how it communicates politically, or contemporary media without looking at how activists are both using and transforming political communication. And we cannot really look at either except in an increasingly global context. And yet studies of activism, media and globalisation are usually carried on quite discretely. The aim of this book is to offer students of these areas the chance to integrate these dimensions of contemporary social and political reality. For the first time, we bring together social movement, media and globalisation issues in one volume, offering students a wide range of authoritative writers who are thinking about these interrelated questions.

## ACTIVISTS, ACADEMICS AND DISCIPLINES

This volume therefore aims to cross two divides that are usually deeply sedimented: between academics and activists and between different academic disciplines. It was our intention from the outset that this should not be a purely academic book and we have been lucky to elicit contributions from activists and those who straddle the academic/activist divide, as well as from major scholars. We hope that this combination of academic and activist contributions gives the volume a depth and texture that is often missing from purely academic texts. We believe that it allows us to interrogate a range of fundamental questions about global activism and global media in a refreshing way.

If it is rare in the west to bring academics and activists together, it is unfortunately not uncommon to find varying degrees of mutual distrust and discomfort between them. One explanation is not difficult to discern. Activists are necessarily concerned with doing things – trying to achieve change. They are committed to the possibility of social actors being able to exercise or construct meaningful agency through their activism. In contrast academics, especially those from the social sciences, are trained to look for structural patterns in social relations across space and time. Academics often ascribe causal power to such structural patterns, often downgrading the agency of social actors and, in the most extreme cases, denying social actors the possibility of having any meaningful agency at all.

In academic circles this relationship between actors, agency and structure has been the subject of protracted conceptual debates (for an overview see McAnulla 2002). Nevertheless, there can be little doubt that how someone's understanding of agency is configured is likely to be related to a broader orientation in terms of optimism and pessimism. To believe that social actors can have meaningful agency in terms of changing things for the better implies a more optimistic outlook than a view that holds that human action and behaviour is largely a product of the interplay of structural forces. (Unless of course that interplay is expected to deliver an unqualified positive outcome: however few today hold the nineteenth-century belief in evolutionary progress.)

These tendencies can be seen in many of the contributions included here. Overall, contributions from activists appear significantly more optimistic than those from academics, some of whom are distinctly pessimistic. While the reader will make up her/his own mind as to whether particular arguments and accounts are either over-optimistic, overly pessimistic, or get it about right, this tendency raises an interesting question about the relationship between historical circumstances, the intellectual positioning taken on the actors/agency/structure issues and the psychosocial dispositions of activists and academics.

The disciplinary divisions in the academic world are much better known and talked about, at least by academics themselves! As we got together to plan this volume, one of the first issues that emerged was the extent to which such divides lead to miscommunication and significant omissions in the areas we intended this book to cover. We quickly came to the view that much academic work on activism from the disciplines of sociology, politics and international relations largely ignores the relationships between activism and media – despite the fact that much of our information and knowledge about activism is necessarily mediated through mainstream or alternative media. Similarly, work on activism within media studies often ignores the empirical and conceptual work on social movements, NGOs (global) civil society and the (global) public sphere to be found in international relations, politics and sociology.

At the beginning of the twenty-first century, it should hardly be necessary to argue the case for the importance of interdisciplinary study. Yet while the rhetoric of 'interdisciplinarity' is alive and well, we are not convinced that the reality matches this. Indeed, we suspect that recent decades have witnessed, in part at least, the raising of disciplinary barriers as a defensive reaction to the demand and increasing necessity for interdisciplinary study. We are not suggesting here that the 'depth' sometimes achieved by the disciplines should be sacrificed to the 'breadth' and 'connectivity' of interdisciplinary work, but we do argue that depth without breadth and connectivity provides, at best, impoverished forms of knowledge.

In this volume we bring together academics from all the disciplines we have mentioned. This does not make it a volume of interdisciplinary work, but it does open the door for cross-disciplinary conversations and we feel it provides many pointers and raises many questions that should be the subject of future, more fully interdisciplinary, research.

## GLOBAL CHANGE, MEDIA AND ACTIVISM

In order to understand the potentialities of global and local activism and the relation of such activism to various forms of media, our contributors address, explicitly or implicitly, a range of issues that are central to analysing the world today. They cluster in two broad areas: the nature and extent of contemporary social change and the nature of media and the mediation of activism.

### The nature and extent of contemporary social change

All of our contributors accept that some degree of substantive social change is taking place worldwide and that this is typically referred to as globalisation. But they are deeply divided as to what globalisation is and whether it marks the beginning of an epochal shift from one form of society to another. Furthermore, those who do see an epochal shift occurring are themselves divided over its trajectory and what to call it.

Similarly, there are differing views as to the main 'causal drivers' of contemporary social change. While some identify capitalism as the main driver of neo-liberal economic globalisation, others perceive information and communication technologies as the key catalyst, and one even sees political-military change as key. Some deny that a main causal driver can be identified at all. For them, globalisation comprises complex processes of interaction between political, economic, cultural and technological phenomena and, following from this, they emphasise that the trajectory and outcomes of contemporary social change are neither predetermined nor predictable.

Another important issue is how our contributors variously configure their understanding of the relationship between 'the global' and 'the local'. Can local activism be global in content, as the slogan 'think globally, act locally' famously suggested? Can it really have global impact? Some forms of global activism (such as meetings of the World Social Forum, demonstrations and protests) are necessarily spatially located, but how important are 'virtual activism' or 'cyber-activism' in bridging particular locations? In contrast to this, while the phrase 'global media' is commonly used – indeed it is in the title of this book – is it really the case that the mainstream television and press are best understood in global terms? Two of our contributors insist that mainstream media are still better comprehended as predominantly national phenomena.

A further thread that runs through almost all the contributions concerns the relationships of activism and institutionalised power structures. There are many and varied references to the problem of elite politics and institutionalised structures that serve to reproduce dominant forms of power. How deep are the problems this causes for those forms of activism that seek to engage with those institutional structures? Some authors suggest they are intractable and instead emphasise grassroots movement activism that is claimed or assumed to be more democratic, dialogic and/or participatory.

A related issue is that most people (although not necessarily activists themselves) get their information and knowledge about even the most radical grassroots activism from the mainstream media. What are the implications of this? Interestingly, contributors who examine how campaigning NGOs try to get their message across through mainstream media argue that campaign objectives *can* be achieved. In other words, institutionalised though they may be, mainstream media do not necessarily reproduce existing forms of dominant power in a simple or straightforward way. This suggests a much more complicated relationship between radical grassroots activism, semi-institutionalised activism by large, well-resourced NGOs and the mainstream media than is sometimes acknowledged by radical critics. Put simply, the denunciation of all forms of elite politics and uncritical celebration of all grassroots activism may be naïve.

However, we also know from the work of scholars such as Weber, Michels and Foucault that forms of activism that become institutionalised over time and/or focus their attentions on trying to achieve change through existing institutional structures of power, become implicated in their tendencies to preserve the status quo and maintain 'order'. This 'organisational question' is posed throughout this book in a variety of ways but there is no clear or conclusive consensus on solutions to such problems.

## The nature of the media and the mediation of activism

In this book a distinction is drawn between mainstream and alternative media. Mainstream media comprise the mass media of television, radio and the press that are corporately owned, controlled or governed (including by public corporations such as the BBC). Alternative media are those media that are produced by activists themselves. Accessing or using these different types of media require different strategies, tools and skills on the part of activists regardless of whether they are grassroots campaigners or involved in organisations such as Greenpeace or ActionAid. And of course some radical activist groups, such as Indymedia, focus principally on the production of their own media.

The role of the mainstream media, particularly news media, in fostering and sustaining democratic society has been widely debated. Media and their sources frame the news agenda, structure the debate and create what we perceive as the reality in which we live. In this sense, news media play a hegemonic role in our society – their perceptions and interpretations of the world become common sense. However, this process is continuous and creative, not static and rigid. New ideas are always entering our perception of the world, but there is 'the residue of absolutely basic and commonly agreed, consensual wisdom' (Gramsci 1971:422). It is this common sense that has to be both engaged with and challenged by those seeking to achieve social change.

Several contributions discuss how activists need to set up 'events', 'spectacles' and even 'stunts' in order to gain access to mainstream media reporting. While these accounts appear to be consistent with broader critical accounts of the media and society such as those of Baudrillard (1988) and Debord (1987), a more mundane explanation can also be posed in terms of such activism being 'outsider' rather than 'insider' activism. Research has demonstrated that activist groups and organisations do not fare well as sources for news production (Manning 2001; Cottle 2000). News producers have a hierarchy of sources with a clear preference for political, governmental and corporate institutions. In other words, activist groups are at the bottom of the pile. This hierarchy is continued amongst activist groups and organisations, with the more institutionalised and professionalised organisations having preferred access, especially if they have lobbyists in the central political arena. Among the organisations and movements discussed in this book, Oxfam and Amnesty

International would appear to have much easier access to mainstream media than the World Development Movement or The Land Is Ours.

In order to subvert this existing source hierarchy and conform to contemporary news styles, activist groups organise events and pseudo-events, perform stunts or spectacular actions to draw at the attention of news producers. Although this might not always succeed, it is both significant and ironic that, by conforming to the requirements of contemporary news production, even radical activists can sometimes get their alternative analysis and point of view across in the mainstream media.

Historically, of course, radical activists have had problematic relationships with mainstream media and public relations, both of which have been viewed as part of the machinations of consumer capitalism. Media strategies were believed to produce the inauthentic, the unreal, the fake, and their use was regarded as selling one's soul if not collaborating with the enemy. So radical activists (for example in the women's movements and green movements) created their own media and put emphasis on self-management and empowerment within what was often described as 'counterculture' or 'alternative society'. This typically consisted of the printed word in leaflets, pamphlets, magazines and newspapers.

As activists from that earlier generation, we feel something of a sea change has taken place. First, contemporary activists appear to be much more savvy with regard to mainstream media. Both the semi-institutionalised and professional NGOs (which themselves often grew out of an earlier generation of activism) and contemporary radical grassroots activists are deploying advanced media strategies in order to get their issues into the mainstream media. In part, this is perceived as a way of getting issues onto the political agenda, but it is also about influencing public opinion and gaining support. Debord returns in the sense that 'self-initiated' and 'self-managed' events, actions or spectacles mean that activists are more in control. They try to approach the mainstream media on their own terms. To an extent they succeed, deploying media strategies becomes a form self-empowerment for those involved as well as being part of their struggle for social change.

Second, the way in which contemporary radical activists have seen the potential in the new information and communication technologies and have embraced them has certainly transformed the landscape of alternative media. Take the example of our own 'local' radical weekly newsletter '*SchNEWS*', published by 'Justice? – Brighton's Direct Action Collective'. They claim to print about 3,000 hard copies of which about 650 are posted out around the world. But then they have about 10,000 email subscribers who receive the newsletter as a PDF file and are encouraged to print and circulate it in their own locality. The *SchNEWS* website also receives several thousand 'hits' weekly and is 'mirrored' on other radical websites <http://www.schnews.org.uk>. In contrast to this, as the contribution by Kavada argues, some of the more established and professionalised NGOs appear simply to use the new technologies as an extension of their traditional communications strategies.

## CONCEPTS OF SPACES AND ACTORS

As well as orientations to the issues discussed above, our authors also necessarily engage, explicitly or implicitly, with a range of important concepts. Not surprisingly, our academic contributors are more concerned with analysing these concepts in detail – whereas our activist contributors seem less concerned with their analytic coherence, using them more as a 'hook' or a form of shorthand to discuss various forms of activism and connections between them.

Yet there is no escaping from the fact that some sort of concepts have to be used, first to describe the space or spaces within which activism takes place and is reported on and interpreted by media, and second to specify types of collective social actor and particular forms of activism. There is of course much general contestation and dispute about which concepts are better and more useful and this, in turn, is often connected to the orientations of the users in terms of their ideologies, goals and approaches to organisational questions. Unsurprisingly, elements of this general contestation and dispute are reflected in this volume. Here we look at the main areas in turn, but only briefly because the first part of the book contains chapters that look at some of these concepts in detail.

### Spaces for activism and mediation

The key concepts deployed in this volume are those of civil society and global civil society on the one hand and the public sphere or the international/global public sphere on the other. While there may be thought to be considerable overlap between them – it could even be argued that really they are synonymous – it appears to us that in this volume the terms civil society and global civil society are used to denote spaces within which activism takes place, whereas the terms public sphere or international/global public sphere are used to denote an arena of communication and the mediation of information, knowledge and interpretation.

The term civil society has a long history in social and political thought. However, for our purposes, we can distinguish two main ways of talking about civil society. The first is derived from western enlightenment thought of the eighteenth and nineteenth centuries in which civil society is juxtaposed with the state. Clearly, if everything that is not part of the state is deemed to be part of civil society, then market relations and the activities of corporations and businesses are necessarily part of civil society. It was in this sense that Marx (*Das Kapital* 1867) argued that the basic anatomy of civil society was to be found in political economy. However in the twentieth century, and especially since the 1960s and 1970s (that saw an upsurge in movement activism all around the world), civil society has more often been understood as a sphere of associational life juxtaposed with both state and market. Within this understanding, then, the activities of corporations and businesses are not part of civil society and civil society cannot be reduced to market relations. Broadly speaking, neo-liberals and Marxists use civil society in its older, more traditional, formulation whereas thinkers and activists of various political persuasions use the more recent understanding of civil society.

The emergence of the term global civil society is a relatively recent phenomenon, associated with the emergence of debates about globalisation, the increasing global interconnectedness of movement activism and the orientation of recent activism aimed at changing the policies of international institutions such as the UN, the World Bank and the International Monetary Fund. Interestingly, however, the basic division in understandings of civil society described in the previous paragraphs has been largely replicated in debates about global civil society. Some authors firmly tie their analysis of activism within global civil society to developments within global economic relations, while others see global civil society as a space from which existing relations and structures of economic power can be challenged. However, what is also particularly interesting is how global civil society might relate to global political relations. In both the traditional and more recent formulations of civil society, civil society was defined in relation to the state. In terms of global civil society, do existing international political institutions 'stand in' for the state or does the discourse of global civil society signal important shifts in the nature of political power? One of us has argued elsewhere that a global state is emerging (Shaw 2000). In his chapter, Lipschutz argues that global civil society is embedded in what he calls the biopolitics of global governmentality.

Another important question left hanging in much of the debate about (global) civil society is crucial to this volume. Where do media fit in? If civil society is a sphere of associational life, should we see the mainstream media as part of civil society or more properly connected to the state (in the case of public media corporations like the BBC) or a particular element of market relations (in the case of private media corporations)? The relevance of this gap in discussions of civil society and global civil society may be illuminated further if we turn our attention to the concept of the public sphere and the international public sphere.

Like the term civil society, the distinction between 'public' and 'private' has been long debated in social and political thought. However the concept of the public sphere has been particularly associated with the work of Habermas who examined the emergence of the bourgeois public sphere in early modern Europe. Although 'public sphere' was originally linked to the more traditional understanding of the term civil society, a difference in emphasis has emerged in the uses of the two terms.[2] While civil society was always used to denote associational life, the public sphere has come more specifically to denote forms of communicational life. It is not therefore surprising that the concept of the public sphere understood as a sphere of communicational life has been especially influential in media studies. In his chapter in the first part of the book, Colin Sparks examines the concept of the public sphere from a media studies perspective. In this field, the concept of the public sphere has generated intense debates about democratic participation – or rather more often, lack of participation – in the public sphere by citizens themselves; and about the importance of the media's contribution to the democratic functioning of the public sphere. Clearly the concept remains controversial. While some argue that it is so problematic that it cannot be a useful analytical tool, others make the point that it can nevertheless be used as an evaluative tool: as a way of explaining how the media could contribute to the democratic functioning of society and should operate as a key part of the public sphere.

In this volume, the possibility of 'alternative' or 'counter' public spheres is also important. One criticism of Habermas' description of the public sphere is that it ignored historically subordinated social groups such as the working class, women and ethnic minorities. Benhabib (1992) and Fraser (1992) have sought to remedy this failing by conceptualising multiple public spheres or counter spheres. Negt and Kluge (1993) identify a proletarian public sphere as a counter public sphere. Counter public spheres comprise the communicational efforts of groups and organisations that challenge existing power relations. Habermas himself has recognised that social movements (women's, green, etc.) based in the 'lifeworld' can reshape the public sphere.

The question arises of course as to the relation between any such counter public spheres and the mainstream public sphere. While dominant forms of power may be supported and reproduced through the public sphere, this does not necessarily mean that counter public spheres are powerless. Much of this book is concerned with examining the range of ways in which activists construct and use alternative forms of communicational life and how they attempt to relate to mainstream media. So, for example, Coyer looks at the emergence and role of Indymedia in the 'anti-globalisation movement', Gaber and Willson at the media strategy of ActionAid in the 'conflict diamonds' campaign, and de Jong at the media strategies of Greenpeace in the Brent Spar conflict.

When thinking about the concept of the public sphere, it is clear that the news media play a crucial role not only as sources of information for citizens but also as a key part of the public sphere itself – the space where a diversity of opinion can be expressed and debated. For his part, Habermas, with his emphasis on the importance of face-to-face communication, does not take sufficient account of mass mediated communication – arguably the very essence of contemporary western society.

### Collective actors and forms of activism

The contributors to this volume use a wide variety of terms to describe both collective actors and the nature and forms their activism takes. Nevertheless, there do seem to be some common patterns that can be usefully identified here.

One of the central terms that many authors use is *movement*. Sometimes this is used in the context of a particular movement such as 'the peace movement' or 'anti-globalisation movement'. At other times range of prefixes are attached, giving us 'political movements', 'demonstration movements', 'grassroots movements' and last but not least, 'social movements'. The notion of movement is also implicit in the use of terms such as 'DIY politics' or 'grassroots activist networks'. What all of these terms have in common is reference to largely non-institutionalised forms of collective activism. 'Movement' implies a broader base of informal or less formally organised activism that does not rely on formally structured organisation to exist – even if formally structured organisations have significant roles. (As with civil society, we can 'globalise' this term, as in 'global social movements' or 'transnational movements', retaining the general meaning.)

The other main term widely used to describe collective actors is that of non-governmental organisation (NGO) and its 'upscaled' equivalent, international non-governmental organisation (INGO). Different chapters look at particular NGOs and INGOs such as ActionAid, Greenpeace, the World Development Movement, Amnesty International and Oxfam. The feature that NGOs share that also distinguishes them from movements (even though they may be part of a movement) is that they are formally structured organisations.

If we now turn to the nature and forms of activism examined in this volume, we find that while movements frequently make demands of political and economic institutions, a significant aspect of movement activism tends to be non-institutionally oriented and largely anti-institutional, taking for example the form of protest demonstrations and direct action. In contrast, while NGOs and INGOs are sometimes involved in demonstrations and direct action, at the same time they are more likely to be willing to engage political and economic institutions via forms of activism such as lobbying and negotiation.

Throughout this volume connections are made between, on the one hand, the different types of collective actors and their forms of activism and, on the other, the problem of elite politics and the extent to which engagement with institutionalised structures of power serves to reproduce dominant forms of power. The chapter by Stammers and Eschle examines these sorts of issues in some detail. Other contributors come to different conclusions but, as we suggested earlier, this is a complex set of issues that defies straightforward answers.

## CONCLUSION

This book aims to develop concerns that are important to all kinds of students – and practitioners – of activism and media. It aims to bring into the academic disciplines an increased awareness of this nexus of issues, so as to help change the ways that they are thought about and studied. It aims to bring to activists and other practitioners a range of academic perspectives that are relevant to their campaigning work. It has been in the nature of this book to open up areas of enquiry rather than to come to definitive conclusions. We hope that it will stimulate further thought, study and action.

Given the rate of rapid social change, the apparent reinforcement of the already enormous asymmetries of power in the world, the violent responses to these changes by groups such as Al Qaeda, and the media focus on the horrors of war and violence, it is easy to understand why so many people are pessimistic about the possibilities for future positive social change. Yet this focus on present 'events' sometimes obscures our view of longer-term social 'processes'. And we know from a longer-term, historical perspective, that people's campaigns and non-violent struggles against oppression and injustice can succeed. In other words, the activism of 'progressive' social actors has impacted positively on longer-term processes of social transformation and will do so again. From this perspective, this book engages with the often complex but vital issues and questions we have to face, not so much to demonstrate that 'another world is possible', but in order to renew the processes involved in trying to make it.

## NOTES

1  For the purposes of this volume, activism is assumed to mostly be 'progressive' and 'non-violent' in its aims, if not always its outcomes. We do not generally cover 'regressive' (e.g. right-wing and Islamist) or armed activism, although we recognise that there are important issues of definition and analysis involved in this distinction and one chapter (John Downing's) does adopt a wider frame.

2  In Habermas' later work, concepts of 'system' (especially the two steering systems of political power and money) and 'lifeworld' appear to connect most clearly to the more recent understandings of (global) civil society as the space of associational life separate from the state and market.

## BIBLIOGRAPHY

Baudrillard, J. (1988) *The Ecstasy of Communication*, New York: Semiotext
Benhabib, S. (1992) *Situating the Self: Gender, Community and Postmoderism in Contemporary Ethics*, Cambridge: Polity Press

Cottle, S. (2000) 'Rethinking theories of news access', *Journalism Studies*, 1, 3:427–48

Debord, G. (1987) *The Society of the Spectacle*, Rebel Press/Aim Publications

Fraser, N. (1992) 'Rethinking the public sphere; a contribution to the critique of actually exiting democracy', in C. Calhoun (ed.) *Habermas and the Public Sphere*, Cambridge, MA: MIT Press: 109–42

Gramsci, A. (1971) *Selections from the Prison Notebooks*, edited by Q. Hoare and G. Nowell-Smith, London: Lawrence and Wishart

Marx (1909) *Capital*, Volume 1, edited by F. Engels, Glaisher

McAnulla, S. (2002) 'Structure and agency' in D. Marsh and G. Stoker (eds) *Theory and Methods in Political Science*, 2nd edition, Basingstoke: Palgrave

Manning, P. (2001) *News and News Sources: A Critical Introduction*, London: Sage

Negt, O. and Kluge, A. (1993) *The Public Sphere and Experience: Towards an Analysis of the Bourgeois and Proletarian Public Sphere*, Minneapolis: University of Minneapolis

*SchNEWS* website at <http://www.schnews.org.uk.>

Shaw, M. (2000) *Theory of the Global State*, Cambridge: Cambridge University Press

# Part I

# Global Civil Society, Global Public Sphere and Global Activism

# 1
# Networks of Knowledge and Practice: Global Civil Society and Global Communications

*Ronnie D. Lipschutz*

Since 1990, the notion of 'global civil society' (GCS) has been the focus of a good deal of research, theorising and criticism. Much of the debate has focused on the relationship of transnational organisations to states and global governance. Another topic of conflict involves the status of social movements as well as their motivations, methods and objectives. A third line of dispute lies between those who view GCS as non-political and those who argue that it is very political. But, global civil society – by whatever of its many names we might wish to call it and however we might describe it – exists. Those agents, actors, organisations, institutions of transnational social exchange and action are there, for all to see (Lipschutz 1996; Wapner 1996; Keck and Sikkink 1998; Colas 2002). And central to the projects and activities of GCS is communication.

It is, by now, something of a cliché to note that the world has 'gotten smaller' in recent decades, due to changes in transportation and communication technologies. As a result of this process of planetary diminution, it would appear that there is now more globalised activism than ever before in human history. This might well be the case, but the role of communication in enabling transnational political activism has been central for some centuries. Gutenberg's press made possible the Protestant Reformation by facilitating the movement of the printed word. Long-distance shipping during the eighteenth century brought word of uprisings and revolutions to all continents. Even the Revolutions of 1848 came about, in part, through continent-wide communications networks consisting primarily of journals, newspapers and travellers, which spread news of uprisings from one country to the next. *Plus ça change ...*

What is not often noted is that today's communications media are of two types, and facilitate somewhat different modes of political action. The most powerful media are private conglomerates, engaged primarily in generating and supplying consumer demand for 'news' and information through lurid headlines and broadcasts 'torn from the headlines'. Less powerful media, especially the internet, provide channels for two-way communications, permitting the creation of a global epistemic context within which virtually simultaneous political activism and action can take place in widely separated locations. Whether the flow of information and knowledge is one-way or two makes a difference in terms of who that news affects, how resulting effects come about and how those affected might respond.

A central point here, as we shall see below, is that effective political action is premised upon the ability of activists to make a case for ethical-political change, to convince large numbers of people, both individually and in groups, to sign on to the project for change, and to infuse that change into the ethical-political basis of a given society. The goal here is to act collectively and effect change through a systemic strategy that seeks to instantiate transnational ethical principles in individual societies. Individual consciousness raising is not enough and, in a globalised world, even national change is not always enough. A broader reach is necessary.

In this chapter, I take on the task of examining the role of communication media in the expansion and activities of global civil society. I begin with a general discussion of historical conceptualisations of civil society and its relationship to the liberal state and link the ethical basis of the state to the particular practices of different segments of civil society. Next, I describe how global communication systems and media have helped to create GCS and foster its various activities. Finally, I discuss the relationship between communications and global governmentality.

## CONCEPTUALISING GLOBAL CIVIL SOCIETY

There are two, rather broad, conceptualisations of civil society in tradition and literature. The first is associated with the market and the private sphere (Ferguson; Smith; Marx), the second, with politics and the public sphere (Hegel; Gramsci; Colas). Although we tend to view Ferguson (1776/1995) and Smith (1776/1982) as the intellectual antagonists of Marx (1932/1970), all three understood civil society in terms of (a) a separation between state (public) and market (private) and (b) as a realm of civil association beyond the reach or authority of the state. As propagated by de Tocqueville in *Democracy in America* (1835/1966), the liberal version of civil society visible in the United States provided both public goods that the state was unable to supply as well as private goods and affiliations that could only be obtained through the market and outside the state. Marx understood civil society in much the same terms, but regarded it as the cat's paw of the bourgeoisie, which maintained a very visible line between state and market in order to fence private property off from the public grasp. In Marx's teleology, consequently, when the proletarian revolution finally arrived, not only would the state wither away, so would civil society. Moreover, with them would go private property as well as the market.

For Marx, the ethics governing society clearly arose out of the desires and interests of capital (and the bourgeoisie), and the public sphere was, in any event, at their service. For Ferguson and Smith, society's morals were primarily religious ones, whose source was transcendent and, consequently, not open to debate, challenge or alteration. Businessmen would meet and plot, and to expect otherwise would be naïve, if not downright foolish. Their activities would have to be regulated, preferably via the moral force of religion but, if not, through public regulation (although not too much of it; this is why trust is seen as so central to capitalism). Thus, civil society would also determine what activities could be privatised and which could not.

The competing version of civil society's origins is associated with Hegel (1821/1952) and Gramsci (1970; see also Adamson 1980, 1988) and elaborated more recently by Alex Colas (2002). It is, in many ways, a less prosaic explanation and, perhaps, more romantic, in keeping with its German origins. All the same, it is not, therefore, any less correct than the political economists' version. According to Hegel, the ethics that underpin actor behaviour in capitalist society originate within civil society. That is, social norms originate within certain elements of civil society, and these are infused into the state through the force and actions of civil society. Recall that Hegel's teleological view of the state was such, that it represented something like the immanent will of the nation, transformed into the transcendent *geist* of the state.

Unlike the political economists, Hegel made a clear distinction between morality and ethics. As Colas points out:

> for Hegel, morality can only become meaningful if it operates within a community, if it is given content through the individual's involvement in public

life .... [T]he associative elements of civil society take on not only a representative but an ethical role by integrating individuals into the wider community, recognizing the value of their work and educating them in the virtues of civic life. (2002:41)

Shlomo Avineri explains that Hegel distinguished between *Moralität*, which is individual, subjective morality and *Sittlichkeit*, the wider totality of ethical life. *Moralität* regulates the relations among individuals with one another *qua* individuals. But superimposed on this is the broader ethical life of the community [i.e., the State], of people relating to each other not as individuals but as members of a wider community (1972: Ch. 7).

Hegel made this differentiation clear in the *Philosophy of Right*, when he wrote

If the state is confused with civil society, and if its specific end is laid down as the security and protection of property and personal freedom, then the interest of the individuals as such becomes the ultimate end of their association, and it follows that membership of the state is something optional. But the state's relation to the individual is quite different from this. Since the state is mind objectified, it is only as one of its members that the individual himself has objectivity, genuine individuality, and an ethical life. (*Philosophy of Right*, 3.3 §258, 'Remark')

Hegel was not much interested in the sources of this ethical life – whether it originated in the family or some association in civil society – only that it be lived through the political community. Those ethics become the basis of state behaviour and are binding on civil society as well as the market. Once a set of ethics has become part of the state, in other words, it resembles a set of transcendent morals that must be followed and obeyed, whatever the individual interests of social and economic actors. However, whereas transcendent morals are fixed, ethics are not. They may differ from one state to the next and can be changed as seems appropriate and necessary.

This view of ethics becomes important in terms of understanding different forms of political activism undertaken by civil society. Colas draws on Gramsci to argue that civil society is the setting from which social movements and political activism originate, 'within the context of capitalist modernity' (2002:43). In order to reconcile the two apparently conflicting views, Colas further asserts that 'civil society has historically found expression in two predominant forms – one linked to the private sphere of the capitalist market, the other to the struggles against the all-encroaching power of the state' (2002:47). The former is populated by those organisations and actors who pursue their self-interest through the mechanisms of the market, the latter by those who seek to challenge and change the ethical structures and politics of the state. These are, of course, idealised forms: operating within the structures and strictures of economic liberalism, in which reproduction necessitates activities within the market, even the most dedicated social movement cannot survive on air alone. But note: activism through the market presumes that individuals' morality can be called upon to effect social change; activism directed toward the state seeks to change the ethics binding on all of civil society and the market.

What these two competing conceptions do not answer directly is the following question: are actors in the market, such as modern corporations, also part of civil society? The tradition of Ferguson, Smith, and Marx would say yes: the first two because it is the realm of 'freedom'; the third because it is the place where capital and the bourgeoisie control the mode of production. Hegel wrote about corporations, but not as we understand them today, since they did not exist in Hegel's time. His corporations were cities, guilds and other similar associations. Consequently, in Hegel's time 'economic actors' were either individuals or companies run by individuals. In either instance, individuals were certainly members of civil society and were, therefore, bound to act according to the ethical code of the state. By the time Gramsci wrote *The Prison Notebooks*, corporations had become widely recognised as legal individuals in their own right. Certainly, however, Gramsci's notion of civil society did not include such aggregations of capital nor the idea that capital might seek to propagate corporate morality through 'social responsibility'.

Colas, as indicated above, deals with this dilemma through the bifurcation of civil society. But this particular market-state confusion highlights a more fundamental tension in contemporary capitalist societies: how and why are the public (state) and the private (market) differentiated? In democratic market systems, civil society provides the foundational values and ethics that underpin the specific form of and limits on markets, and civil society's members expect the state to follow its dictates in this regard (not that this always happens). Not all elements of civil society are political; indeed, by the conventional definition (one shared by Locke *and*

Marx, although with differing conclusions) civil society exists in some twilight zone between state and markets, engaged in activities that constitute and reproduce the fabric of everyday social life. Civil society is not considered to include the purely private realm, such as the family or the body, even though the norms of civil society as well as the laws of the state and the practices of the market all colonise and permeate the household and the bedroom.

This limited conception of civil society is a peculiarity of capitalism as well as the methodological individualism of liberal theory and practice. Within liberalism, especially as fetishised in the United States, the only legitimate political actor is the individual which is why, paradoxically, corporations are treated as legal individuals while labour and other social movements are not. As Mancur Olson deductively argued (1966), collective action ought only to occur through the aggregation of the interests of individuals who seek a return on their investment of resources and time. Olson found it difficult to explain the facts of groups and social movements that were not motivated by such self-interest, but was nonetheless forced to acknowledge their existence. What went unsaid by him, but has been of concern to others, is that such groups might exercise unwarranted and potentially corrupting power as against the rest of society's members who, unable or unwilling to act collectively, remain individuals (e.g., Huntington 1981). Consumers exercising their individual aggregated choice in markets are perfectly acceptable; citizens exercising their collective desires in politics are not.

This is why labour unions have always been regarded as problematic within liberalism: their threat to withhold property, that is, labour in the self or 'human capital' through the strike is envisioned as the theoretical equivalent of investors colluding to prevent the free flow of capital for investment and speculation. (That this parallel is patently ridiculous and incorrect hardly makes a difference on the ideological battlefield.) In liberal theory, therefore, civil society is the realm of legitimate *non-political* collective action, of associations that are motivated neither by economic self-interest nor a search for power but, rather, by shared pleasures and pastimes such as bowling and stamp-collecting (Putnam 2000). Political action is legitimate only when exercised through the individual vote. Because these associations pose no challenge to either the political and economic order and, in fact, reproduce it on a daily basis, their existence is not a problem for that order.

Gramsci also placed civil society between state and market and outside the private sphere of family and friendship. In the context of Italian society of the period in which he wrote, however, civil society was, most decidedly, political. In Gramsci's framework, the 'corporate-bureaucratic state order with its linked capitalist economic order' (Nielson 1995:58) stood as a more or less unitary arrangement through which the hegemony of the capitalist class was both exercised and naturalised. Civil society then became 'primarily a sphere of *ethical–political* contestation among rival social groups' (Adamson 1980; Adamson 1988:325) struggling for ideological hegemony. As Kai Nielson puts it;

> In locating civil society we must look for those organizations or practices that are not directly governmental or economic but which generate opinions and goals, in accordance with which people who partake in those practices and are a part of these organisations seek not only to influence wider opinion and policies within existing structures and rules, but also sometimes to alter the structures and rules themselves. (Nielson 1995:45–6)

Under these circumstances, evidently, civil society groups can become a threat to the established order, especially if they have political objectives or 'seek to alter the structures and rules'.

These are ideal types, of course. 'Really-existing' civil society is a good deal more complicated and, in a liberal democracy, the distinction between markets and politics often becomes obscured, if not virtually meaningless. Markets are manipulated for political ends; politics comes to resemble auctions in markets. The result is that what looks 'political' may well be no more than market-based action, and groups whose goals ostensibly involve structural change may be doing no more than tinkering with certain details involving exchange and behaviour. I will return to the implications of this argument below.

## GLOBAL CIVIL SOCIETY AND GLOBAL COMMUNICATIONS

How do global communications fit into the picture drawn above? Here, I want to argue that, parallel to the bifurcation of GCS into economics- and politics-oriented actors, there is also a similar split in global media. This is hardly surprising, inasmuch as we would place media in civil society. All types of contemporary communication media have been thoroughly colonised and commodified by capitalism, and all are deeply embedded in markets, including the internet. Nevertheless, both types of media can motivate action via either politics or markets. Below, I will address in some detail how these outcomes map on to the bifurcation of civil society and the distinctions set up by Alex Colas and others. But there is a second dimension to communication media that is not captured fully by the bifurcation, as shown in Table 1.1.

*Table 1.1*   Communication media

|  | 'One way' (e.g., TV) | 'Two-way' (e.g., internet) |
| --- | --- | --- |
| Politics | 'CNN Effect' aggregated pressure | 'Stop the MAI' collective action |
| Markets | 'Save the Children' aggregated morality | 'Get Nike' aggregated preferences |

Some media are 'one-way', that is, they deliver processed and commodifed information to consumers, whose response is the aggregated sum of individual choice. Television is the primary example a 'one-way' medium. Some media are 'two-way', that is, they permit both the production and consumption of information, and its transformation into knowledge and action. Responses may be either aggregated, as above, or collective. The internet is an example of this type of medium. Here, I briefly describe each type of impact and outcome.

**The 'CNN Effect'**

This term was coined in the early 1990s, during the first years of chaos and famine in what had formerly been Somalia. The images of starving children and general disorder televised, in particular, by CNN were claimed to have generated an aggregated demand for American intervention to restore political order and social stability there. During its final weeks, the first Bush Administration sent food aid to Somalia and dispatched troops to protect those distributing the relief, and left the incoming Clinton Administration to carry on. That adventure ended badly and made policymakers much more wary of public pressures arising from television coverage of other social disasters. Note that broadcasters have no intention of generating such public pressure.

### 'Save the Children!'

In this instance, televised infomercials and documentaries are designed to elicit charitable contributions to groups and organisations working in poor and vulnerable areas of the world. Viewers' morality is challenged and they are asked to send money. No political action is demanded nor are there any challenges to the legitimacy of those institutions that might be responsible for the poverty and hunger suffered by children and others. Instead, viewers are led to believe that their individual monetary support for relief organisations can 'solve the problem'. Such groups raise hundreds of millions of dollars from individuals every year, but make no effort to change the political environment in which these problems have developed.

### 'Get Nike!'

In recent years, growing numbers of activist and non-governmental organisations have used communication media – especially the internet – to campaign against corporations that violate human rights, labour standards and environmental quality, especially in developing countries. In this case, the media are used to inform interested and concerned individuals about the offences committed by specific corporations and they are encouraged to contact the company or boycott its products. Corporations have responded by developing codes of conduct and 'corporate social responsibility' programmes. Both campaigns and corporate responses are premised on the idea of effecting political change through markets, by shifting individual consumer preferences from one product to another, and thereby affecting corporate revenues and profits through an aggregated impact. However, there is no effort, in any of this, to implement or enforce domestic or international regulations addressing the problems of concern.

### 'Stop the MAI!' (Multilateral Agreement on Investment)

The MAI was originally negotiated by the 25 or so industrialised and developing countries belonging to the Paris-based Organisation for Economic Cooperation and Development (OECD). It was meant to establish uniform rules governing both domestic and foreign investment in the OECD's industrialised countries, as well as in its two developing ones. But, working largely through the internet, a coalition of non-governmental organisations and social movements was able to convince the French and Canadian governments that the MAI would be disadvantageous and unfair to developing countries. As a result of the ability of activists to influence key states, the agreement was withdrawn from consideration. In this instance, groups working collectively lobbied governments and convinced them that, ethically speaking, the MAI would violate principles widely-held within their societies.

In each of these cases, global communications media are the means through which some actors in civil society affect the beliefs, ethics and practices of other actors, whether intentionally or not. In each case, the goal of the communication project can be seen as a laudable, although not necessarily the desired, one. But there are at least two important distinctions between the four 'effects'. First, the scale of political action differs among them. That is, in the case of the *CNN Effect* and *Save the Children!*, the target of the communicated information is the individual and the response is transmitted by way of aggregated individual decisions (total numbers of communications or donations). In the case of *Get Nike!* and *Stop the MAI!*, the target of the communication is the group, conceived either in terms of aggregated consumer preferences implemented against a named corporation or brand, or as groups of activists mobilising around specific ethical and political objectives.

Second, there is a difference in terms of normative outcomes. Both *Save the Children!* and *Get Nike!* appeal to individual norms and morals and try to convince their targets that action is virtuous. But they also recognise that, in a liberal capitalist society, not everyone will contribute or boycott. Some people will simply reject any responsibility for starving people while others will have little concern for the conditions under which consumer products are manufactured. There is no attempt here to change political terms of reference through an ethical stance that could be codified in enforceable laws and regulations. The *CNN Effect* generates a broad public demand that political institutions (the state) change its ethical stance and practices with respect to the problem of concern (e.g., overcome inhibitions on humanitarian intervention). The resulting policy is, however, a result completely unintended by the broadcaster.[1] Only *Stop the MAI!* can be said to alter the ethical basis on which decisions are made and actions are taken: it is political in the fullest sense of the word, in that it seeks to instantiate a new ethic that is different from or contrary to the old one (e.g., human rights trump open markets).

Why do these distinctions matter? They help us to understand better a critical point about global communication media: they are tools through which information and knowledge can be transmitted but, as Langdon Winner (1986) once pointed out, it is how they are used and what kind of information and knowledge are transmitted that is important in terms of politics. Moreover, as he wrote, 'If we examine social patterns that characterise the environments of technical systems, we find certain devices and systems almost invariably linked to specific ways of organising power and authority.' Without delving too deeply into the forms of power and authority that characterise global communication media, we do see here that some version of Arendt's (1958) 'space of appearance', in which 'face-to-face' politics are possible, is the only way in which those 'specific ways' can be challenged.

## GLOBAL CIVIL SOCIETY AND GLOBAL GOVERNMENTALITY

I have written extensively about the growing functional authority that has been transferred from the state to local groups and organisations in 'global civil society' (Lipschutz 1996), and GCS has become the focus of a rich, extensive and disparate literature (see, e.g., Walzer 1995; Keck and Sikkink 1998; Anhier, Glasius and Kaldor 2001). Here, I wish to problematise GCS as an element in an expanding liberal regime of power, expressed through particular forms of global governmentality, which is fostered by global communication media. Governmentality, as Michel Foucault put it, 'has as its purpose not the action of government itself, but the welfare of the population, the improvement of its condition, the increase of its wealth, longevity, health, etc.' (1991:100; see also Dean 1999: Ch. 1). It is, in other words, about *management*, about ensuring and maintaining the 'right disposition of things' of that which is being governed or ruled. Anything which challenges this disposition is to be absorbed; anything which disrupts it is to be eliminated.

Foucault's notion of governmentality is associated with the practice of *biopolitics* which, according to Mitchell Dean, 'is concerned with matters of life and death, with birth and propagation, with health and illness, both physical and mental, and with the processes that sustain or retard the optimisation of the life of a population' (1999:99).

Bio-politics must then also concern the social, cultural, environmental, economic and geographic conditions under which humans live, procreate, become ill, maintain health or become healthy, and die. From this perspective bio-politics is concerned with the family, with housing, living and working conditions, with what we call 'lifestyle', with public health issues, patterns of migration, levels of economic growth and the standards of living. It is concerned with the bio-sphere in which humans dwell. (Dean 1999:99)

The biopolitical management of human populations and their environments is the job of the myriad of governmental and international agencies, public and private associations, and even non-governmental organisations and corporations, each of which has its own instrumental function as well as normative objectives. This is not to say that all of these actors are in coherence with one another in either their activities or objectives. They are, however, engaged increasingly in what Kanishka Jayasuriya (2001) and others (Gill 1995) have described as the instantiation of a global 'economic constitutionalism', associated with neo-liberal globalisation. As Jayasuriya puts it; 'Economic constitutionalism refers to the attempt to treat the market as a constitutional order with its own rules, procedures, and institutions that operate to protect the market order from political interference' (2001:452). The market-oriented part of GCS, which includes corporate communication media, is deeply engaged in this project.

Foucault's concepts of governmentality and bio-politics help to highlight a critical point here. Civil society today is almost fully internalised within the system of governmentality that constitutes and subjectifies it, the very system that many GCS groups and organisations presume to contest, regulate and modify. Quite evidently, the arrangement of rules, regulations and practices characteristic of contemporary bureaucratic capitalist states does not and cannot address more than a fraction of the 'welfare of the population'. Much of the remainder of this function is provided, increasingly, through civil society. That is to say, the activities of civil society associations and organisations help to stabilise and normalise conditions that are seen as threats or disturbances to the welfare of human populations, *but not to alter the structural conditions responsible for those threats and disturbances.* The precise methods of accomplishing these ends are often highly contested, but the overall objective is the same. In this sense, much of what appears to be opposition – by civil society as well as many activist social movements – is better understood as integral to governmentality and the reproduction of neo-liberal globalisation.

To return, then, to the earlier discussions of the bifurcation of global civil society and its relationship to governmentality, it is clear that global communications media play a central role in govern-mentality. (Indeed, private media such as CNN are part of global civil society, too, while the internet is something of a mixed medium, so to speak.) Media such as television, cable, newspapers and journals provide, for the most part, a carefully modulated one-way flow of information, which is presented as 'balanced' and 'true'. Certain events are presented as deviations from the norm, to be con-demned, stopped or remedied by the appropriate authorities through approved means. Consumer viewers are merely expected to ratify judgments and decisions already made. Of course, things sometimes do get out of hand: revolutions are televised and, as Alex Colas has written, 'the political success of a given social movement ... clearly impact upon the formation of movements elsewhere without there being any formal links between groups' (2002:58).

Even those groups and organisation engaged in anti-corporate campaigns are, by and large, not engaged in politics. By this, I mean that most of them attempt, through an elucidation of 'real' interests, to leverage both consumer and corporate behaviours as a means of improving labour conditions in factories, reducing environmental externalities from industry and boycotting or managing inter-national trade in various kinds of goods, such as clothing and coffee (Lipschutz 2002, 2004). Many of these campaigns have been suc-cessful in terms of their instrumental goals, but they also suffer from serious *political* limitations. These limitations become very evident in apparel industry campaigns. For example, there are at least a dozen activist campaigns aimed at the Nike Corporation (Conner 2001; Lipschutz 2002). All focus on distributive strategies designed to improve health and safety conditions, and to provide minimum wages to workers in Nike's 600 or so subcontractors' plants scattered around the world. These campaigns have generated considerable public attention (although it is not clear that they have affected the company's financial performance) and Nike has responded ener-getically, concerned about its market share, its competitiveness and its image.

The company has adopted codes of conduct, contracted out audits of its subcontractors' factories and permitted independent monitors to either accompany auditors or conduct their own inspections. It has joined the Fair Labour Association and co-established the

Workers' and Communities' Association, as well as taken a number of other steps to improve both conditions of production and its own reputation. And, while there apparently remain significant problems in many, if not all, of its subcontractors' operations, there has been a not inconsiderable amount of ratcheting upwards of conditions within the Nike subsystem of global apparel production (Lipschutz 2002). But what have been the *constitutive* effects of these campaigns? How have these campaigns altered either corporation or capitalism in *discursive* terms? Nike offers improved conditions and higher wages to the workers in its subcontractors' factories, but both workers and consumers remain fully integrated into the regime of consumption that constitutes contemporary globalisation and objectifies both workers and consumers. Workers still have no power to make political decisions, and there are no changes either in the position of waged labour or in the structures of capitalism.

But, as the bifurcation of civil society suggests, not everyone is involved in neo-liberal governmentalism. Some social movements operate outside the institutionalised framework and discipline of governmentality and, indeed, frequently contest it, even violently. However, such movements do not operate through the 'normal' channels of communication or try to effect political change by influencing consumer preferences. Rather, they seek to engage politically with states and thereby to instantiate ethical principles that can counter the dominance of the market. Before such an instantiation can happen, civil society, or at least major segments of it, must be convinced to support and believe in the ethical project. What is critical here is not that *everyone* comes to support it, something which is, in any event, highly unlikely. Rather, it is sufficient that such a movement be regarded as an alternative to the dominant ethic. This begins to happen when groups in other places and countries take on particular projects and adopt the ethic that underpins it.

We can take as an example of this phenomenon the global justice movement (often called the 'anti-globalisation movement'). While the movement, as such, is not a coherent one, composed as it is of many disparate groups and tendencies around the world, it is nonetheless motivated by a shared ethical principle: that globalised neo-liberal capitalism is a source and cause of pervasive injustice and oppression. What is to be done is less clear, but this principle is clearly opposed to the dominant ethic underlying neo-liberalism: that 'free markets' are a source of prosperity, happiness and, ultimately, distributive justice. The movement's activities have been substantially organised through two-way media and communicated to a broad global public through one-way media. And even though activists could not number more than a few million in a world of six billion, the defenders of neo-liberal globalisation clearly viewed it as a political threat to their project, and sought systematically to denigrate and delegitimise it.[2]

## CONCLUSION

It is only through the efforts of such social movements, which attempt to change the ethical bases of action, that global civil society becomes truly political. The ethical principles that stand as society's rules for the good and virtuous life are also, within that society, authoritative and binding. These principles are immanent, in the sense that they come from the society. (By contrast, morality is transcendent, originating from some external source and not open to contestation.) Consequently, different societies subscribe to different ethical principles. Politics is about struggles to change these ethical principles and to ensure that they are taken seriously. These struggles are collective ones, for they require people to work together and not just change their individual preferences.

Global communications media – especially the two-way kind – play a role in these struggles, and not simply because they provide channels for the rapid transmission of information and narratives. Rather, these connections allow activist groups scattered all over the world to learn what others are doing, to observe and validate each other's actions and to disseminate the ethical bases for those actions. These ethical principles become integral to a globalised episteme, a political network that spans societies and cultures. In this way, global civil society becomes integral to the instantiation of a political ethos that might, at some time in the future, become the basis for a politics other than global governmentality.

## NOTES

1   This does raise questions about the nature of deliberate efforts to rouse public opinion in support of a position advocated by the medium, such as Rupert Murdoch's demands for an attack on Iraq.
2   The events of 11 September 2001 and the subsequent 'War on Terrorism' appear to have undermined the global justice movement to a considerable

degree; see Lipschutz (2002) for a discussion of changes in global govern-mentality as a result of the Bush Administration's 'reach for Empire'.

## BIBLIOGRAPHY

Adamson, W. L. (1987/88) 'Gramsci and the politics of civil society', *Praxis International* 7, 3/4, Oct. and Jan
—— (1980) *Hegemony and Revolution*, Berkeley: University of California Press
Anheier, H., Glasius, M. and Kaldor, M. (eds) (2001) *Global Civil Society 2001*, Oxford: Oxford University Press
Arendt, H. (1958) *The Human Condition*, Chicago: University of Chicago Press, 2nd edition
Avineri, S. (1972) *Hegel's Theory of the Modern State*, London: Cambridge University Press
Colas, A. (2002) *International Civil Society*, Cambridge: Polity
Connor, T. (2001) *Still Waiting for Nike to Do It*, San Francisco: Global Exchange, <http://www.globalexchange.org/economy/corporations/nike/NikeReport.pdf> [Accessed 5 May 2001]
Dean, M. (1999) *Governmentality – Power and Rule in Modern Society*, London: Sage
Ferguson, A. (1767/1995) *An Essay on the History of Civil Society*, New York: Cambridge University Press; edited by Fania Oz-Salzberger
Foucault, M. (1991) 'Governmentality', in G. Burchell, C. Gordon and P. Miller (eds) *The Foucault Effect: Studies in Governmentality*, Chicago: University of Chicago Press: 87–104
Gill, S. (1995) 'The global panopticon? The neoliberal state, economic life, and democratic surveillance', *Alternatives* 2, 1: 1–50
Gramsci, A. (1970) 'State and civil society', in A. Gramsci, *Selections from the Prison Notebooks*, New York: International Publishers; translated and edited by Q. Hoare and G. N. Smith: 206–78
Hegel, G. W. F. (1821/1952) *Philosophy of Right*, Oxford: Clarendon Press, translated, by T. M. Knox. Also at <http://marxists.anu.edu.au/reference/archive/hegel/> [Accessed 5 October 2001]
Huntington, S. P. (1981) *American Politics: The Promise of Disharmony*, Cambridge, Mass.: Belknap Press
Jayasuriya, K. ( 2001) 'Globalization, Sovereignty, and the Rule of Law: From Political to Economic Constitutionalism?', *Constellations* 8, 4: 442–60
Keck, M. and K. Sikkink (1998) *Activists Beyond Borders – Advocacy Networks in International Politics*, Ithaca, N.Y.: Cornell University Press
Lipschutz, R. (2003) *Regulation for the Rest of Us? Globalization, Governmentality, and Global Politics*, available at <www2.ucsc.edu/egirs/publications/wp/wp2003-1.pdf>
—— (2004) 'Sweating it out: NGO campaigns and trade union empower-ment', *Development in Practice*, February
—— (2002) 'Doing well by doing good? Transnational regulatory campaigns, social activism, and impacts on state sovereignty', in J. Montgomery and N. Glazer (eds) *Challenges to Sovereignty: How Governments Respond*, New Brunswick, NJ: Transaction

Lipschutz, R. and J. Mayer (1996) *Global Civil Society and Global Environmental Governance – The Politics of Nature from Place to Planet*, Albany, NY: State University of New York Press

Marx, K. and F. Engels (1932/1970) *The German Ideology*, New York: International Publishers, edited by C. J. Arthur

Nielsen, K. (1995) 'Reconceptualising civil society for now: some somewhat Gramscian turnings', in M. Walzer (ed.) *Toward a Global Civil Society*, Providence, R.I.: Berghahn Books: 41–67

Olson, M. (1966) *The Logic of Collective Action*, Cambridge, Mass.: Harvard University Press

Putnam, R. (2000) *Bowling Alone – The Collapse and Revival of American Community*, New York: Touchstone

Smith, A. (1776/1982) *The Wealth of Nations*, Harmondsworth: Penguin

de Tocqueville, A. (1835/1966) *Democracy in America*, New York: Harper & Row, edited by J. P. Mayer and M. Lerner; translated by George Lawrence

Walzer, M. (ed.) (1995) *Toward a Global Civil Society*, Providence, R.I.: Berghan

Wapner, P. (1996) *Environmental Activism and World Civic Politics*, Albany, NY: SUNY Press

Winner, L. (1986) *The Whale and the Reactor: A Search for Limits in an Age of High Technology*, Chicago: University of Chicago Press

# 2
# Media and the Global Public Sphere: An Evaluative Approach

*Colin Sparks*

This chapter discusses whether or not we can accurately use the category of the 'public sphere' to discuss the role of the mass media in contemporary international events and processes. The chapter first discusses the concept of the public sphere and considers its relationship to the mass media. It then considers what evidence there is that existing media, and the internet, help to constitute a global public sphere. Finally, given that the evidence does not support such a conclusion, it examines what might validly be said about these media.

The reasons for undertaking this task are obvious. Everyday events demonstrate conclusively that we cannot adequately conceptualise social processes within the boundaries of single states. Decisions that will have an immediate effect upon the lives and prospects of individuals, or even whole nations, are taken in institutions located thousands of miles away in other countries.

Neither can we consider traditional media systems in purely national terms. With the possible exception of the US, and a few small surviving communist regimes, media systems around the world are very open to foreign influences. Foreign satellites beam TV signals to viewers irrespective of political geography. Television programmes made around the world, but notably in the US, appear on the screens of every country, every night of the week. *Time* and *USA Today* are to be found in economy class departure lounges from Birmingham to Beijing and *The Economist* is a fixture in business class.

The internet adds to these flows. The fact that, online, geography no longer determines what media are available means that it is possible to read the *New York Times, The Times* (of London) and *The Times of India* from anywhere. One example of how this empowers people was during the 2003 invasion and occupation of Iraq, when many US citizens wanted an alternative to the uncritical patriotism of their own media. Some sought out the Guardian Unlimited website because it provided reporting and analysis that they could not find at home (Larsen and Malkani 2003).

## THE PUBLIC SPHERE

Most recent critical discussions of the political role of the mass media have employed the term 'public sphere'. This concept has a long history in the German-speaking academy, but it has only become current in the Anglo-Saxon world since the translations of the work of Jürgen Habermas (Kleinstueber 2001). The category has been much debated and much criticised, not least by Habermas himself, who has revised important aspects of his early formulations (Habermas 1992). Nevertheless, it retains a central place since it focuses attention on a number of key areas of the media that seem essential to any theory of democratic politics. A good starting point for any discussion is Habermas's classic early formulation:

> By the 'public sphere' we mean first of all a realm of our social life in which something approaching public opinion can be formed. Access is guaranteed to all citizens. A portion of the public sphere comes into being in every conversation in which private individuals assemble to form a public body. They then behave neither like business or professional people transacting private affairs, not like members of a constitutional order subject to the legal constraints of a state bureaucracy. Citizens behave as a public body when they confer in an unrestricted fashion – that is, with the guarantee of freedom of assembly and association and the freedom to express and publish their opinions – about matters of general interest. In a large public body this kind of communication requires specific means for transmitting information and influencing those who receive it. Today, newspapers and magazines, radio and television are the media of the public sphere. (Habermas 1964/ 1974:49–50)

This account puts an emphasis on the open and active dimension of the public sphere. The public sphere grants everyone equal rights of access and participation. The public sphere debates freely without any censorship or fear of reprisals. Above all, the concept is centred on the activity of citizens. It is through a process of discussion and exchange that citizens come to hold opinions on public matters. It is thus associated with theories of participatory democracy.

Habermas located the historical site of the public sphere in enlightenment Europe, in the gatherings of merchants in places like coffee houses, and in the early newspaper press. As critics have pointed out, the historical reality departed dramatically from Habermas' portrayal and, far from being inclusive, public life in eighteenth-century Europe was based upon exclusions, not only of propertyless free men but also of women and the millions of Africans enslaved by enlightenment Europe. The evolution of the modern media, which Habermas saw as leading to the decline of the public sphere, is defended by many authors as an extension of public life. It is not possible to defend the concept of the public sphere from an historical point of view. Why retain the concept at all? The answer is that as a normative category, against which we can measure the democratic claims of existing media systems, it retains a powerful appeal. We can ask of any mass media system just how far it contributes to the constitution of a public sphere. How open to diverse opinion is it? How free is it of censorship, either political or economic? How far are all citizens treated discursively as possessing equal rights and privileges?

The public sphere has always been closely bound up with the state system. In order to permit the resolution of differences through the operation of reason, there must be some fundamental agreement on aims and values. As Habermas put it in *The Theory of Communicative Action*:

> acting communicatively always come to an understanding in the horizon of a lifeworld. Their lifeworld is formed from more less diffuse, always unproblematic, background convictions. This lifeworld background serves as a source of situation definitions that are presupposed by participants as unproblematic. In their interpretative accomplishments the members of a communication community demarcate the one objective world and their inter-subjectively shared social world from the subjective worlds of individuals and (other) collectives. The world-concepts and the corresponding validity claims provide the formal scaffolding with which those acting communicatively order problematic contexts of situations, that is, those requiring agreement, in their lifeworld, which is presupposed as unproblematic. (Habermas 1984, I:70)

One of the major sources of such understandings is the nation state. It is precisely the formation of this set of 'unproblematic background convictions' that the modern state has seen as central to its historical mission. To that end it has emphasised a common linguistic register, a common education system, a common set of rules and laws, a common set of holidays and festivals and a common culture. Without these shared 'background convictions' it is difficult to see how reason alone could act as the arbiter between conflicting particular interests and allow the emergence of a consensual concept of the common good.

Historically, it is also clearly the case that many media institutions have seen the construction of a unified nation, and national culture, as central to their functions. The names of European public broadcasters – British Broadcasting Corporation, Radio Telefís Éireann, Arbeitsgemeinschaft der öffentlich-rechtlichen Rundfunkanstalten Der Bundesrepublik Deutschland and Zweites Deutsches Fernsehen, Radiotelevisione Italiana, and so on – bear witness to the national aspirations of broadcasters. Even the wholly commercial US broadcasters have names (National Broadcasting Corporation, American Broadcasting Corporation, Columbia Broadcasting Corporation) that testify to a national ambition. The printed press has been less obviously 'national' in its organisational structure, but as one of the best-known theories of the modern nation reminds us, it was 'print capitalism' that made it imaginable in the first place.

The contemporary world is not determined by the boundaries of the political state. Economic and political forces operate on a wider scale. As public affairs, broadly interpreted, have outgrown the boundaries of the state, so the need for a new, supranational, public sphere is ever more urgent:

> ... the development of an increasingly integrated global market and centers of private economic power with global reach are steadily undermining the nation-state, and it is within the political structure of the nation-state that the question of citizenship and of the relationship between communication and politics has traditionally been posed. We are thus being forced to rethink this relationship and the nature of citizenship in the modern world. What new political institutions and new public sphere might be necessary for the democratic control of a global economy and polity? (Garnham 1992:361–2)

The public availability and diffusion of information, and the possibility of public discussion of alternative policies, are certainly not in themselves sufficient for a global democratic order, but they are essential steps along that path.

A global democratic order is difficult to achieve, because the bulk of the media in the world are organised along the lines of states, they are produced by people who are denizens of particular states, they are articulated in the languages spoken in particular states, their business depends upon markets defined by particular states and they are subject to the regulatory regimes of particular states. Most of the press and broadcasting are national in scope and consequently they report and debate global issues from the narrow perspectives of the national interests with which they identify. The idea of a global public sphere coming is contrary to their entire practice.

## GLOBAL MEDIA?

Not all media fall into this pattern. Some have taken the opportunities presented by technology to spread over a much wider area. Some newspapers and magazines have used remote printing for international editions. Satellite broadcasters have a potential audience determined by their footprint, not political history. The internet means that media from around the world are available anywhere. It is tempting to claim that these developments represent at least the foundations of a global public sphere.

Satellite television is often thought to facilitate a global public sphere because it is free of national restrictions. Appadurai, for example, alleges that 'electronic mediation transforms pre-existing worlds of communication and conduct' and 'neither images nor viewers fit into circuits or audiences that are easily bound within local, national or regional spaces' (Appadurai 1996:3–4).

All signals need to be up-linked from somewhere, and there is nowhere that is unregulated. The nature of regulation differs from country to country, but it is inescapable. States determine who can broadcast and what they can broadcast. An example of the problems that arise was MED-TV. This was a Kurdish language channel, broadcasting to the 35 million or so Kurds living in the Middle East. When it flourished there was very little television in Kurdish. The majority of its programming originated in Belgium, Germany and Scandinavia, and its headquarters were in London. It broadcast under a licence from the British regulator for commercial broadcasting, the Independent Television Commission (ITC). This sounds very much like an emergent 'global' broadcaster fitting Appadurai's claims. This was not the case. MED-TV was closely linked to the Kurdish struggle for a national state (the Kurds are the world's largest stateless nation) and the reason it provided the only tele-vision in Kurdish from bases so far away from its audience was that the states within which most Kurds live (notably Turkey, Syria and Iran) did not permit such broadcasting except under very severe restrictions. In the case of Turkey, any broadcasting in Kurdish was for long completely illegal. In the view of many people, genuinely independent Kurdish television could only be produced and broad-cast outside the areas in which Kurds have lived historically. During the 1990s, the Kurdish PKK (Kurdistan Workers' Party) was at war with the Turkish state, which alleged that MED-TV supported the struggle. The Turkish government complained to the ITC and on 23 April 1999 it withdrew MED-TV's licence and forced it off the air, on the grounds that it was not displaying the impartiality called for in its licence (MED-TV 1999). MED-TV was unable to continue in its original form and the aim of Kurdish statehood was abandoned. The fate of satellite broadcasters lies with governments as much as does that of terrestrial broadcasters and 'the knots that bind the state to territory cannot be untied by communication technologies' (Hasanpour 2003:87). The idea that satellite television operates free of political restriction is wrong (Sakr 2001:61–3).[1]

Political constraint is matched by economic constraint. A satellite broadcaster needs landing rights and states try to control these, for example by insisting on easily policed Satellite Master Antenna TV systems. Advertising sales need offices, sales staff, bank accounts and numerous other things that are subject to the control of the state that houses the target audience. Subscriptions need a subscription management system, with a means of distributing and servicing decoders, of collecting revenues and of acquiring and maintaining subscribers, all of which are subject to the control of the state that houses the target audience. In order to make money out of broad-casting, a commercial satellite broadcaster is obliged to come to terms with the states into which it is broadcasting.[2]

The dependence of satellite broadcasters upon the states is illus-trated by Rupert Murdoch's attempts to enter the Chinese market. His current joint venture in China is called Phoenix TV, and it has managed to gain agreement from the Beijing government to allow it landing rights in elite hotels and, recently, cable systems in the south of the country. In exchange, Murdoch has made a number of compromises with the Chinese Communist Party. The most notable was dropping the BBC's world news from his Star TV because its reporting of China was judged too critical by Beijing (Page and

Crawley 2001:86). Another was the refusal of Random House, owned by News Corporation, to honour its contract with the last British governor of Hong Kong, Christopher Patten, because his projected volume was too critical of the Chinese leadership (Gleick 1998). Liu Chang Le, the main shareholder, Chairman and CEO of Phoenix TV, expanded these tactical concessions into a strategic principle:

> Foreign media companies need to develop a dialogue with the bureaucratic agencies that regulate the media and entertainment market. The purpose of this dialogue is on the one hand to enable the foreign company to understand the Chinese environment more clearly, and at the same time convince the Chinese side that foreign media organizations are not seeking to destabilise China, sow the seeds of social or political trouble, or weaken China's sense of cultural identity. (Liu 2002:4)

Neither politically nor commercially are satellite broadcasters magically free of the constraints that are experienced by their terrestrial cousins.

Claims that media help constitute a global public sphere are most frequently heard with respect to satellite broadcasters, in particular CNN. This is the most successful of the international news channels, and its founder, Ted Turner, was undoubtedly motivated by some sense of global citizenship. He saw the groundbreaking World Report as countering western news domination by providing 'the first chance to remedy it, where we allow everybody to speak their own words' (cited in Flournoy 1992:9). The success the channel enjoys has led to the judgement that CNN is 'a global entity, not just an American company with linkages abroad' (Flournoy and Stewart 1997:13). More substantially, one commentator asserts that 'global political communication (as launched by CNNI) results in the constitution of a *global public sphere*' (Volkmer 1999:4; original emphasis).

The evidence contradicts this. The aim of producing a global news agenda and coverage is not realised in practice. Most international news operations have been based on allowing 'differential domestication' in which stories are reformulated by journalists in national news organisations in line with national orientations (Cohen, Levy, Roeh and Gurevitch 1995:142). According to observers, CNN 'is simply too US-oriented, it provides pictures of too much coverage of made-for-the-media events in Washington or sensational, but essentially American stories' (Cohen, Levy, Roeh and

Gurevitch 1995:149). As the international situation has shifted, CNN itself has been forced explicitly to confront this reality. In the aftermath of 11 September 2001, the network found itself under heavy criticism internationally for carrying too much US domestic coverage and responded by separating its US news agenda from that of its international broadcasts. This recognition that the audiences in the US and the rest of the world have different interests and perceptions, and require different news with a different interpretative emphasis, has continued, particularly in the period around the 2003 invasion and occupation of Iraq. It is difficult to see how one can claim that a global public sphere is emerging in the work of a broadcaster that is consciously differentiating the material it broadcasts in the largest and most important state from that it provides to the rest of the world. As one American writer, agonised by the atrocities and  the aftermath of 11 September 2001, put it: 'Humanity is the subject of the global public sphere, not the United States' (Buck-Morss 2001:16).

The size and composition of the CNN audience also casts doubt on claims that it embodies a global public sphere. The potential audience for CNN and CNNI is given in Table 2.1. 242 million households sounds impressive, until one realises that one single medium-sized country like the UK has around 25 million households. Distribution is not the same thing as audience size, since it measures the number of homes able to receive the signal, not the number of homes in which the channel is being watched. According to William Hachten, the audience in the US was a tiny fraction of the number of people potentially able to watch. He gives figures of 572,000 homes viewing in 1995, falling to 372,000 in 1996 and 274,000 in 1997 (Hachten 1998:34). In Europe, the channel has a

*Table 2.1* Distribution of CNN International and CNN in the US 2001

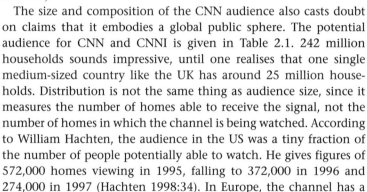

| | Europe, Middle East and Africa | Asia | Latin America | CNN En Espanol | CNN (USA) |
|---|---|---|---|---|---|
| Fulltime households | 91,203,000 | 18,193,467 | 8,459,645 | 11,280,838 | 84,319,000 |
| Hotel rooms | 1,555,955 | 643,482 | 183,687 | 234,826 | N/a |
| Part time households | 28,541,000 | 540,000 | | | |
| Total | 121,299,955 | 19,376,949 | 8,643,332 | 11,515,664 | 84,319,000 |

*Source:* <http://www.cnnmedia.com/cnncorp?pagetarget = KF1.jsp>

monthly reach, which is a measure of the total number of people who have seen it during a given four-week period, of either 12.7 or 3.9 million people, depending on which survey one believes (CNN International 2003: they provide both without stating a preference). To put this into perspective, the daily reach of BBC1 in the UK alone is around 29 million people (BARB (Broadcaster Audience Research Board Ltd) 2003a).

BBC1 is a general channel with both news and entertainment, while CNN is a pure news channel, so the figures are not directly comparable. A fairer comparison would be with the BBC's own news channel, BBC News 24. In May 2003, BBC News 24 had an audience share of 0.5 per cent in those (multi-channel) homes where it is available (BARB 2003b). The survey does not give any data for CNN, and presumably the audience must be so small as to be part of the aggregated 'Other non-terrestrial' category.[3] The only real conclusion that we can draw with certainty is a relative one: CNN is very much less popular than UK based general television, which includes a substantial amount of 'public sphere oriented' news and current affairs and much less popular than UK based news television. It is extremely probable that the audience for CNN in the UK is tiny, and unlikely that it is much larger in most other countries. The news preferences of most people in most countries are for news produced by organisations that are rooted in the same country.

The CNN audience might be few in number, but it has distinctive attributes. The audience for CNN in Europe, the Middle East and Africa is 75 per cent male and 80 per cent earn more than €40,000 (approximately US$46,000) per annum, while 26 per cent earn more than €80,000 (approximately US$92,000). 33 per cent have degrees (CNN 2003). It is, in other words, a predominantly male, well-educated and well-off group of people. To the extent that CNN is providing news and commentary, it is doing so not to 'all citizens' but to an elite minority.

A very similar, although more extreme, picture can be painted of the audience for 'international' printed publications. In addition to the fact that research shows that the audience for papers like the *Wall Street Journal* and the *Financial Times* or *The Economist* is few in number and wealthy. Printed publications highlight the linguistic barriers involved in discussing a global public sphere whose main vehicle is English. While it is possibly true that the global elite all have the developed knowledge of English needed to read papers like these, it is certainly not the case that this skill is evenly distributed throughout the population of the globe. Estimates for the number of people able to speak English vary, but even the more generous estimates tend to be in the order of 1,500 million (British Council 2003). This is a huge number of people, but it is still only one quarter of the world's population.

Unless by the category 'public sphere' we mean the dialogue of a tiny number of wealthy and highly-educated individuals, disproportionately located in the richest regions of the world, then it is impossible to claim that these television stations and newspapers are anything approaching an embodiment of a new global agora.

## WHAT ABOUT THE INTERNET?

The conventional media are trapped in a technology of central production and mass distribution which limits their ability to allow citizens to 'confer in an unrestricted fashion'. The internet is a technology designed for dialogic communication. The internet is global in design. The whole point of the internet is that any computer, anywhere, can connect with any other computer, anywhere else, provided both have access to a telecommunications link and the appropriate software. It is no wonder that a great deal of enthusiasm is often expressed about the ways in which this technology can help deliver a global public sphere:

> From this globalized angle, the world-wide Web with its new cybercasting facilities represents a new public sphere, in which 'the public' and its opinion is no longer a substantial element of the political system of one society ... but has transformed into a somewhat autonomous global public sphere, which can be described not as a common or collective space between the 'public' and the state but between the state and an extrasocietal, global community. (Volkmer nd.)

Once again, of course, the key issue is: what evidence is there to support such a positive conclusion?

The answer is so obvious that it hardly requires labouring: the claim reflects the narrow vision of the developed world even more crassly than does the argument about the traditional media. There are very large numbers of people in the world who do not have electricity:

> More than a quarter of the world's population [i.e. more than 1.25 billion people] has no access to electricity, and two-fifths still rely mainly on

traditional biomass for their basic energy needs. Although the number of people without power supplies will fall in the coming decades, a projected 1.4 billion people will still be without electricity in 2030. (World Energy Outlook 2002)

Without electricity, none of the other technical prerequisites for internet connectivity can possibly be employed. Without electricity, the idea of participating in a global public sphere via the internet is an unrealisable dream.

Even among those who do have access to electricity, access to the internet is less evenly distributed than are the old media, which are of course mostly available in the developed world (UNESCO 1999). In 2000, of the 173 countries listed in the United Nations Human Development Programme's Human Development Report 2002, only 35 were recorded as having more than ten internet hosts (defined as computers connected to the internet) per 1,000 of population. Only twelve of the 100 countries with the lowest human development index had more that one host per 1,000 people. Of that 100, more than 50 were reported as having no hosts, or were unable to supply an accurate figure. None of the top 25 countries on this index had fewer than ten hosts per 1,000 of the population, and five had more than 100 (UNDP 2003). In general, GDP per capita is a good predictor of the density of internet in a country (Sparks 2000).

The stark facts of global inequality are as evident with access to the internet as they are in any other area of human life. In the advanced world, and in pockets of wealth in the developing world, the internet is an integral part of the life of millions of people. But for millions of others outside these charmed regions it is simply absent. Talk of a global public sphere is meaningless in such circumstances.

What is more, even amongst those who have the technology, the time and the social competence to use the internet for information about the world, the evidence suggests that this usage is generally patterned on the states within which people happen to live. Table 2.2 gives figures for Unique Visitors to UK online news sites. As is evident, the BBC is by far the most dominant site and the other leading sites are also based in the UK. CNN does figure, but it has fewer visitors than do the sites of even very elite newspapers like the *Financial Times* and the *Daily Telegraph*. Even where the technology is global in potential, the social patterns of usage are primarily marked by geopolitical boundaries.

*Table 2.2* Visitors to main internet news sites, April 2002

| Site | Thousands of Unique Visitors |
|------|------------------------------|
| bbc.co.uk | 3,192.0 |
| Guardianunlimited.com | 719.6 |
| Channel4.com | 510.6 |
| Sky.com | 470.0 |
| Skysports.com | 467.9 |
| itv.com | 390.8 |
| Upmystreet.com | 351.4 |
| ft.com | 265.1 |
| Telegraph.co.uk | 261.8 |
| Cnn.com | 255.4 |

Source: Hargreaves and Thomas 2002:44 (From NetValue April 2002)

## ELITE COMMUNICATION

The global dimensions of both the old and the new media are predominantly means of elite communication. That does not mean that they are bad things. The roar of communication around the globe contains a rich mixture of messages. The vast majority of these messages are produced and consumed within the boundaries of the state system and the vast majority of them are commercial messages that have little direct relevance for theories of the public sphere. Some of messages, however, are concerned with public life, and some do circulate internationally. It is on this slender evidence of a minority of the communicative activity of a minority of the world's population that those who want to proclaim the reality of a global public sphere rest their case.

The point of deconstructing these claims is to confront soberly the realities of the contemporary world, in which states remain the dominant forces, and in which inequalities of wealth and power are the central features. The bulk of the media, old and new, reflect those realities. Most 'global' communication also reflects those inequalities quite uncritically, and the much-proclaimed political effects mostly concern changes to elite behaviour rather than any new form of empowerment for the majority.

Facing the realities of the contemporary world allows one to confront much more interesting questions. If it is true that the problems of the world increasingly demand an international solution, and if it is true that the current state of global information and debate is immeasurably far removed from anything that we might genuinely term a global public sphere, then what are the forces that might lead us closer to that desirable objective? Framing the question in this way, we can look again at some of the evidence.

Despite its subordination to concentrations of political and economic power, there is no doubt that under some circumstances satellite broadcasting has been able to expand the range of news and discussion quite considerably. The two best-known examples of this happening are in India and the Arab world. When Indian broadcasting was the exclusive privilege of the state-owned, terrestrial Doordarshan, it was centralised, extremely conservative and dominated by the governing parties. The introduction of Star TV and Zee TV, in the 1990s, meant that much more 'professional' and more 'objective' news became the norm (Page and Crawley 2001:35–61). While the audience for satellite channels remains predominantly the urban middle class, the newcomers also forced change on Doordarshan, which does reach the rural masses as well as the city dwellers. Broadcasting in India has not been transformed into a perfect embodiment of the public sphere, but news and discussions are today available that were not present 20 years ago.

Even more dramatic has been the change in the Arab world. For decades, all of the media in the Arab world have had to contend with state interventions of one kind or another. The coming of satellite television did not in itself end all of this: even when located in Rome or London, the new broadcasters were subject to political and economic imperatives originating in the Arab states (Sakr 2001:27–65). The one exception to the tendency to reproduce the official news agenda is Al Jazeera television, based in Qatar. This has, famously, introduced 'objective' news to the Arab world and has allowed debate and dissent a hearing that was never previously possible. The broadcaster has enraged the rulers of numerous Arab states, as the harassment of its journalists in Jordan, Egypt, Kuwait, Saudi Arabia and, most recently, the dying Saddam regime in Iraq, demonstrates. At the same time, Arab audiences across the region have been riveted by debates between a huge variety of positions, by uncensored, detailed and up to date news coverage of the great issues facing the world, and by challenging interviews with everyone from fundamentalist Muslim clerics to Ariel Sharon (Sakr 2001:119–24). This is not, of course, a global public sphere, but a strong case can be made out for it representing a big step towards an Arab public sphere (Miladi 2002).[4]

In the case of the internet, it is once again obvious that there are many ways in which it has been used to increase and extend the reach of information and debate. Access remains the preserve of the globally privileged, and those who make most use of it do so in the interests of the states and corporations who employ them, but there are thousands of examples of alternative usages. The technology may be beyond the reach of billions of the world's population, but organisations that represent the interests of the 'global South' can often scrape together the resources to have at least some presence online. As a supplement to, or extension of, the traditional means of informing and organising, the internet has been taken up by activist organisations and individuals with considerable enthusiasm. There are cases in which it has been the sole tool of organisation for new groups that would otherwise have been prevented, or at least severely hindered, by geography, politics, or some other impediment, from working through other mechanisms (O'Donnell 2001). These represent a genuine extension of the possibilities of the global exchange of information and opinion and some of the efforts undoubtedly contribute to global dialogue.

In neither case, however, is there some magical force called 'globalisation' that is pushing these developments forward. There is no teleology of either the state or of capital that drives towards extending the public sphere, either within the bounds of particular political entities or on a global scale. The highly desirable aim of all citizens being able to contribute to the formation of public opinion remains the object of aspiration and struggle at the level of the state. It is little more than a distant dream at the global level.

### NOTES

1  Sakr argues: 'when Middle Eastern interest groups both inside and outside the region decided to take advantage of this technology, their choice could be explained more clearly in terms of locally grounded politics than in terms of a concept taken from the lexicon of globalization theorists, such as deterritorialization' (Sakr 2001:207).

2  These economic tools were used by the British government to drive the broadcasters of pornographic channels, up-linked from more liberal European countries and aimed at the UK market, out of business. Declaring them 'proscribed satellite services' under the various Broadcasting Acts made all of the commercial activities specified above illegal and they could not raise revenue (ITC n.d.).

3   The most thorough recent study of the TV news audience categorises
    CNN along with Al Jazeera and other specialist 'diasporic' channels
    (Hargreaves and Thomas 2002:52).
4   The existence of Al Jazeera and its freedom to broadcast, does not contra-
    dict the dependence of satellite broadcasters on the state system.
    Al Jazeera broadcasts from Qatar. It was set up in 1996 on the initiative of
    the Qatari ruler. It was and is funded by the Qatari government. A mem-
    ber of the ruling family is the Chairman of the Channel. It is the Qatari
    government (the same one that provided the base for the US command
    in the 2003 invasion of Iraq) that supports this broadcaster (Sakr 2001:
    55–60).

## BIBLIOGRAPHY

Appadurai, A. (1996) *Modernity at Large: Cultural Dimensions of Globalization*,
    Minneapolis, Min: University of Minnesota Press
BARB   (2003a)  Weekly  Viewing  Summary,  <http://www.barb.co.uk/
    viewing summary/weekreports.cfm?report = total.> [Accessed 3 July 2003]
BARB   (2003b)  Monthly  Viewing  Summary,  <http://www.barb.co.uk/
    viewingsummary/monthreports.cfm?report = monthgmulti.>  [Accessed
    6 July 2003]
British Council (2003) Frequently Asked Questions: The English Language,
    <http://www.britishcouncil.org/english.engfaqs.htm#howmany.>
    [Accessed 8 July 2003]
Buck-Morss, S. ( 2001) A Global Public Sphere?, <http://www.nottingham.
    ac.uk/~ajxsm1/issue1/buck-morss.pdf.> [Accessed 8 July 2003]
CNN    (2003)   Audience   Overview,   <http://www.cnnmedia.com/
    cnncorp? pagetarget = audiencesOverview.jsp.> [Accessed 5 July 2003]
CNN   International  (2003)  Key  Facts,  <http://www.cnnmedia.com/
    cnncorp? pagetarget = keyFacts.jsp.> [Accessed 2 July 2003]
Cohen, A., M. Levy, I. Roeh and G. Gurevitch (1995) *Global Newsrooms, Local
    Audiences: A Study of the Eurovision News Exchange*, London: John Libbey
Flournoy, D. (1992) *CNN World Report: Ted Turner's International News Coup*,
    London: John Libbey
Flournoy, D. and R. Stewart (1997) *CNN: Making News in the Global Market*,
    Luton: University of Luton Press
Garnham, N. (1992) 'The Media and the public sphere', in C. Calhoun (ed.)
    *Habermas and the Public Sphere*, Cambridge, Mass.: MIT Press: 359–76.
Gleick, E. (1998) 'The Murdoch chill factor', *Time*, 9 March 1998, vol. 151,
    no. 10. Available at: <http://www.time.com/time/magazine/1998/int/
    980309/business.the_murdoch_chi9.html.> [Accessed 11 July 2003]
Habermas, J. (1992) 'Further reflections on the public sphere', in C. Calhoun
    (ed.) *Habermas and the Public Sphere*, Cambridge, Mass.: MIT Press: 421–61
——. (1984) *The Theory of Communicative Action 1. Reason and the
    Rationalization of Society*, Boston: Beacon Press
——. (1964/1974) 'The public sphere: an encyclopaedia article', *New German
    Critique* 3, 1:14–21
Hachten, W. (1998) *The Troubles of Journalism: A Critical Look at What's Right
    and Wrong with the Press*, Mahwah, NJ: Lawrence Erlbaum

Hargreaves, I. and J. Thomas (2002) *New News, Old News*, an ITC and BSC Research Publication, London: ITC

Hasanpour, A. (2003) 'Diaspora, homeland and communication technologies', in K. Karim (ed.) *The Media of Diaspora*, London: Routledge: 76–88

ITC. n.d. (but probably c. 1999) ITC Notes: 'Adult' Services, <http://www.itc. org.uk/itc_publications/itc_notes/view_note.asp?itc_note_id = 49.> [Accessed 11 July 2003]

Kleinstueber, H. (2001) 'Habermas and the public sphere', *Javnost/The Public* 8, 2:95–108

Larsen, P. and G. Malkani (2003) 'The Guardian looks to US', *Financial Times: Companies and Markets*, Tuesday 8 July 2003

Liu, C. ( 2002) 'The call of the Chinese market' Speech to the CAASBA Convention 2002. Delivered 4 December 2002. Available, Keynote at: <http://www.casbaa.com/doc/Speech_Liu%20Changle.pdf.> [Accessed 6 April 2003]

MED-TV (1999) MED-TV Kurdish Satellite Television, < http://www.ib.be/ med/.> [Accessed 8 July 2003]

Miladi, N. (2002) 'Is Al-Jazeera transforming the face of Arab broadcasting for ever?', Paper presented at the *23rd Conference and General Assembly of the International Association for Media and Communication Research*, Barcelona (Spain) 21–26 July 2003

O'Donnell, S. (2001) 'Internet and the public sphere', *Javnost/The Public* 8, 1:3–57.

Page, D. and W. Crawley (2001) *Satellites over South Asia: Broadcasting Culture and the Public Interest*, New Delhi: Sage

Sakr, N. (2001) *Satellite Realms: Transnational Television, Globalization and the Middle East*, London: I.B. Tauris

Sparks, C. (2000 ) 'The Distribution of online resources and the democratic potential of the Internet', in J. van Cuilenburg and R. van der Wurff (eds) *Media and Open Societies*, Amsterdam: Het Spinhuis: 229–56

UNDP (2003) Human Development Report 2003, <http://hdr.undp.org/ reports/global/2002/en/indicator/indicator.cfm?File = indic_380_1_1. html.> [Accessed 7 July 2003]

Unesco (1999) 1999 Statistical Yearbook, <http://portal.unesco.org/uis/ TEMPLATE/html/CultAndCom/TableIVS3.html.> [Accessed 6 July 2003]

Volkmer, I. (1999) *CNN: New in the Global Sphere. A Study of CNN and its Impact on Global Communication*, Luton: University of Luton Press

——. n.d. (but probably c. 1996) 'Universalism and particularism: the problem of global programme flow', <http://www.ksg.harvard.edu/iip/ GIIconf/volkmer.html.> [Accessed 8 July 2003]

World Energy Outlook (2002) World Energy Outlook 2002: Executive Summary, <http://www.worldenergyoutlook.org/weo/pubs/weo2002/ WEO20021sum.pdf.> [Accessed 8 July 2003]

# 3
# Social Movements and Global Activism[1]

## Neil Stammers and Catherine Eschle

The first two chapters of this volume examined 'global civil society' and the 'international public sphere' as spaces within which it is claimed that global activism takes place. In this chapter we look at some of the collective actors and forms of activism said to operate within such spaces, focusing particularly on transnational or global social movements. This is a difficult task because of the wide ranging and often competing claims that have been made about the nature and efficacy of social movements and because of the wide spectrum of activity attributed to them.

Below we look at four specific issues. In each we identify problems with existing literatures and then offer an alternative, reconstructive, analysis. The four issues are:

- the relation of social movements to organisations and networks;
- the relationship between 'the global' and 'the local';
- the relation between instrumental and expressive dimensions of movement activism;
- the oligarchical and democratising dynamics of movement activism.

Much of the existing literature has been concerned with activism believed to have the potential to foster 'progressive' social change. We replicate this pattern, partly in order to offer an immanent critique but also because we share the normative commitment to exploring such potentials. That said, significant elements of our analysis are relevant to the study of social movements in general.

### MOVEMENTS, ORGANISATIONS AND NETWORKS

We need to begin by noting the wide variety of ways in which movements, organisations and networks are described in existing literatures. While some have used the terms 'transnational' or 'global' social movements, others invoke compatible, competing or overlapping concepts such as 'networks of global civil society', 'the multitude' and 'social forces'. Furthermore, whereas social movement scholars use the terms Social Movement Organisations (SMOs) and Transnational Social Movement Organisations (TSMOs) authors from other disciplines have talked of 'interest groups', 'pressure groups', 'transnational activist groups' and – most importantly – non-governmental organisations (NGOs) or international non-governmental organisations (INGOs) (for details see Eschle and Stammers 2004). In recent years there has been a convergence in terminology towards NGOs and INGOs from a wide variety of positions.

Despite all these terminological differences and difficulties, there are clear patterns in the way in which the relationships between transnational movements, organisations and networks have been understood. Many of these understandings are, in our view, deeply flawed.

### Movements conflated with organisations

The first problem is that movements are frequently conflated with, or subordinated to, the organisations associated with them. In other words, TSMOs (such as Greenpeace or Amnesty International) are very often the exclusive focus of study to the neglect of any other dimensions of movement activism or indeed to the consideration of movements themselves. For example, Keck and Sikkink focus on the integration of NGOs, state agencies and international institutions in 'transnational advocacy networks' (TANs). The NGOs examined are clearly TSMOs linked to social movements and Keck and Sikkink claim that examining the role of NGOs in TANs 'helps both to distinguish NGOs from, and to see their connections with, social movements' (Keck and Sikkink 1998:6). Yet, despite its many other strengths, their study makes no attempt to explore this relationship at all. Even in work with a claimed explicit focus on social movements we typically find an overwhelming focus on TSMOs and their relation to other formally structured organisations. Figure 3.1 comes from a volume entitled *Transnational Social Movements* (Smith et al 1997) and is representative both of that particular volume and the general tendency we are criticising. TSMOs are only located with respect to other organisations. Quite literally, social movements have dropped out of the picture!

A rather different version of the same problem assumes that the world of NGOs is entirely populated by institutionalised,

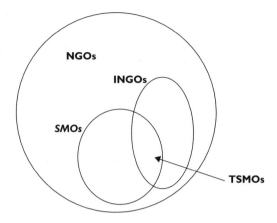

*Figure 3.1*   Distinctions between non-governmental organisations (no scale implied)
*Source:* Smith et al *Transnational Social Movements*, p. 13

professionalised and co-opted associations that, wittingly or otherwise, only serve to reproduce existing relations and structures of power. Here TSMOs are conflated into the categories of NGOs or INGOs and no analytic weight is given to links between social movements and TSMOs. As Craig Murphy puts it:

> Our own period is also characterized by non-governmental organizations (NGOs) playing a further essential role in international governance. Increasingly, as a consequence of neo-liberal marketization, the services once provided by public inter-governmental organizations are now contracted to private, non-governmental, often 'social movement'-style, organizations ... [This] has allowed donor aid budgets to remain stagnant or even fall throughout the post-Cold war era. (2000:795–6)

While offering an important reminder of the contribution of many NGOs to the diffusion of neo-liberal norms and practices, Murphy does so by refusing any distinction between NGOs and '"social movement"-style organizations'. He is clearly sceptical about the possibility of transnational organisations retaining any significant or radical grassroots movement connections.

### Organisations conflated with movements

A second substantive problem inverts the above relation. Here the organisational characteristics of INGOs and TSMOs are neglected and conflated with assumptions about the nature of 'progressive' global movements. Typically it is scholars who have drawn inspiration from theories of new social movements who fall into this trap. For example, an early influential article by Falk surveys a wide range of movements and organisations ranging from Greenpeace to the Sanctuary movement. Falk concludes that such groups are converging on a 'new politics', involving:

> repudiation of war and technologies of violence as inevitable instruments of social conflict; adoption of identity patterns and affinities that arise from shared commitments; ... coalitions and support activities in transnational arenas and networks; a refusal to regard access to state power as the prime stake of political activity ...; an emergent awareness that the decisive political battleground for the remainder of this century is associated with an activation of cultural energies. (Falk 1987:191)

Both formally organised and informal movement activism are depicted as sharing the same kinds of ideological commitments, strategic orientations and organisational proclivities. Now, while some TSMOs and INGOs may be structured according to the non-hierarchical principles supposedly characteristic of new social movements, these are exceptions rather than the rule. Further, as pointed out in Figure 3.1 above, many NGOs and INGOs are entirely unconnected to social movements. Boli and Thomas point out that *most* INGOs are economic or technical in character and do not attempt to challenge dominant cultural values in the ways suggested by new social movement theory (Boli and Thomas 1999:34–46).

### The concept of social movement: a network definition

It is clear that the concept of social movement is either absent or used in impressionistic and ungrounded ways in much of the relevant literature. Even when commentators do offer definitions they often do so in narrow and limited ways. To be fair, even within the specialist field of social movements studies, there is little consensus about what social movements actually are. That said, we feel that Diani (2000) has developed a synthetic concept of social movement that sheds some light on the problems dogging its global application. Diani defines a social movement as:

> ... a network of informal interactions between a plurality of individuals, groups and/or organisations, engaged in a political or cultural conflict, on the basis of a shared collective identity. (2000:165)

He also insists that 'social movements are not organisations, not even of a peculiar kind' (2000:166). It follows that we need to maintain a clear analytical distinction between organisations and the network of informal interactions that constitute a social movement. We should also note that even if an organisation has an internal network structure, that does not make it a social movement. Organisations may well be *part* of a movement (again think of Greenpeace and Amnesty International) but Diani argues that a social movement need not give rise to any formal organisations at all. We think this is an important corrective to accounts that see movements as largely created by and dependent upon formal organisations.

More problematically, Diani's definition also implies that a social movement could comprise a network of interactions linking *only* formal organisations. In our view, a social movement necessarily encompasses informal and non-institutional activism. Although the significance of this may vary, we believe that if informal grassroots activism and non-institutional articulations of collective identity entirely disappear then a social movement no longer exists. A network linking formal organisations is much more closely aligned to Keck and Sikkink's notion of a transnational advocacy network.

Some precision is clearly necessary in the way in which the term 'network' is deployed in much of the literature and we come back to this point later. Here we are distinguishing between:

- the flattening of hierarchies within an organisation that nonetheless remains formally constituted (a network organisation);
- a network of informal interactions linking formal organisations (an advocacy network);
- a network of informal interactions that ties together informal groups and individuals, and sometimes formal organisations, in struggles for social change on the basis of a shared identity (a social movement).

### Social movements as global networks

If network relations link informal activism and may also connect associated organisations, can such network relations exist transnationally or globally? While the network conception of social movement does not imply any necessary distinction in organisational *form* spatially, there may be a question of organisational *reach* – the extent to which networks can 'stretch' transnationally or globally.

For example, Tarrow has insisted that such networks are very difficult to transnationalise, arguing that social movements depend upon interpersonal social networks embedded in everyday life and 'domestic' (i.e., national) societies in order to generate collective identities (Tarrow 1998:184–9). In contrast, Keck and Sikkink claim that INGOs operating within transnational advocacy networks are frequently underpinned by diffuse interpersonal connections (Keck and Sikkink 1998:219–21). So for them, networks of informal interaction can at least stretch across state borders.

We see no particular reason why transnational networks should be so much more difficult to forge than national networks. Tarrow's claim relies on an *a priori* assumption of pre-existing national cultural cohesion but even national networks cannot rely on face-to-face relationships but must, to use Anderson's phrase, be 'imagined'. While such questions remain open to dispute it is clear is that the study of transnational social movements and TSMOs needs to pay much closer attention to the nature and dynamics of networks linking activists together.

## THE RELATIONSHIP BETWEEN 'THE GLOBAL' AND 'THE LOCAL': REDUCTIONIST UNDERSTANDINGS OF GLOBALISATION

This brings us to the second issue we want to examine: how understandings of globalisation impact on the comprehension of the relationship between global and local activism.

Much of the relevant literature assumes globalisation to be primarily economic and/or technological, with political shifts occurring as a consequence. The growing integration and liberalisation of worldwide market relations receives particular emphasis, along with the development of communications and transport technologies and the rapid growth of global governance institutions above and beyond the state. The latter two dimensions are often stressed by social movement theorists in their explanations of the new enabling conditions and sources of grievance that underpin the transnationalisation of activism (e.g., Smith et al 1997; Guidry et al 2000). In contrast, Marxist and neo-marxist critics tend to see technological and institutional developments as reflective of a shift in the more fundamental structures of capitalism but disagree over the question of whether resistance is thus newly enabled or more constrained (e.g., Gorg and Hirsch 1998; Colas 2002:149; Hardt and Negri 2000).

Whatever the emphasis, these approaches share a tendency to characterise globalisation as centripetal and homogenising, sucking economic and political forms 'upward'. This means that globalisation is perceived as eradicating local or national cultural difference although there is extensive disagreement over the extent to which this is occurring.

## A hierarchy of levels

One result is a strong tendency to assume that the informal, socially-embedded aspects of movements must be local or national in character and that only formally structured TSMOs can be active in global politics. There are very different readings of the implications of this. Most pessimistically, economic globalisation is characterised as overwhelmingly totalising and destructive and that, while resistance can be instantiated locally, it is ultimately futile. At the global level, as noted above, NGOs/INGOs are interpreted as supporting and reproducing existing structures of global power.

Other readings privilege the global level as the source of progressive change but consequently reinforce the tendency to focus on INGOs/TSMOs rather than local and less formal, more socially embedded, aspects of movements.

There are strands of literature that offer a broader understanding of what constitutes a transnational or global movement, one more inclusive of localised, grassroots activism. Thiele, for example, argues that networks embedded in everyday life and specific localities should be considered as an aspect of global struggles and that such activism can have a global impact. He points to the potential of social movements to induce long-term changes in 'the worldviews and life-styles of the general public as much as influencing policymakers ... the political significance of this social osmosis should not be ignored' (Thiele 1993:281). Turner makes a similar argument when he defines global civil society in terms of small-scale movement activity that is oriented 'toward general transformation of public consciousness, which in turn affects the parameters of legitimacy within which traditional institutions must operate' (Turner 1998:29–30).

While avoiding separating out the global and local, accounts such as these often depict movements and TSMOs as pursuing a settled 'progressive' global agenda. Some accounts even go as far as presenting diverse groups as constituting a *single*, unified movement (e.g., Nerfin 1986). Here, the uncritical application of new social movement theory is compounded by an accompanying interpretation of globalisation as homogenising. In effect, such accounts carve out a global role for the informal and local aspects of movement activism only by making the contentious assumption that the claimed characteristics of new social movements, particularly their supposed cultural orientation, are now applicable to movements and TSMOs worldwide.

### Complex globalisation and global/local activism

We believe the problems discussed above can be resolved through a perspective that can grasp the complexities of globalisation. Multidimensional, multicausal and 'intersectional' accounts of globalisation (e.g., Held et al 1999; Marchand and Runyan 2000) insist on the intertwining of economic, political, technological and cultural relations of power on a global scale. These multiple processes intersect with each other in crucial but uneven and unpredictable ways. Thus there is neither a single underlying 'driver' nor a pre-determined direction to globalisation. Rather, attention is focused on the rising density and stretching of social relations, the reshaping of space and time, and the role of consciousness, reflexivity and agency.

One important implication of such a perspective is the need for sensitivity to the tension between homogenising and fragmenting tendencies within globalising processes and the potential emergence of diverse, innovative and hybrid cultural, political and even economic forms. Most importantly here, this understanding of globalisation implies an equally complex and open-ended relationship between localised activism and global processes. Whilst very much aware of the vast asymmetries of power in the world, we are seeking an analytic formulation of the relationship between the global and local that does not make an *a priori* assumption about the totality and impact of such power. Two ideas seem particularly significant here.

The first is that the local and the global are mutually constitutive, with localities playing an active role in shaping the impact and reception of global processes as well as being shaped by them. This idea is most often elaborated in anthropological and feminist accounts (Robertson 1995; Sassen 1996; Freeman 2001). The long-standing slogan, 'think global, act local' goes some way to capturing the nature of the involvement of these kinds of movements in global politics, but only by separating abstract consciousness of the global from concrete action that remains locally expressed.

The approach to globalisation advocated here implies that locally-situated actors may not only think global but *act* global, because global processes are manifested in local spaces and can be, at least partially, shaped and redirected there (see also Guidry et al 2000:7–16). It should be added that a global consciousness is very likely to be accompanied by efforts to forge relationships with activists elsewhere, so that apparently localised movements may actually be connected to broader, transnational movement networks.

The second idea derives from an extrapolation of Gidden's understanding of the disembedding and re-embedding of social relations, bringing previously separated traditions and activities into new proximity. It is not sufficient to assume that networks only stretch across neighbouring state boundaries, or follow in the wake of the physical movement of people, as Keck and Sikkink imply. There may be sharp spatial discontinuity apparent as networks re-emerge in disparate locations, bringing physically distant people into new relations of affinity.

Little detailed study has as yet been paid to such discontinuous networks but there is suggestive evidence from the emergent 'global justice and solidarity movement' (Waterman 2002b).[2] The key role of large gatherings and protests held in diverse geographical locations indicate that such events provide the space and place for otherwise disparate activists to recognise and construct commonalities around identities and goals, taking them back to localities when they return home. Such commonalities may also be reinforced when large gatherings are held simultaneously in several locations throughout the world, in designated days of global protest. Some recent commentary on the movement has criticised the emphasis on large-scale protests as functioning to privilege young, white, rootless, middle-class activists, arguing instead for the need to recognise and strengthen plural and socially embedded identities in terms of links between diverse local community struggles. Either way, there does appear to be socially embedded movement networks underpinning this movement, even though they are clearly complex, contested and territorially discontinuous.

## INSTRUMENTAL AND EXPRESSIVE DIMENSIONS OF MOVEMENT ACTIVISM

The third issue we want to examine concerns the relations between instrumental and expressive dimensions of movement activism.

By the instrumental dimension of movement activism we mean the articulation of concrete strategies and demands, frequently aimed at powerful institutions and intended to produce specific material effects upon social relations. By the expressive dimension we mean activism oriented towards the construction and reconstruction of norms, values, identities and lifestyles both inside a movement and in the wider social and cultural milieu.

### Privileging the instrumental

The strong tendency to focus on TSMOs both feeds off and reinforces an emphasis on the instrumental dimension of movement activism. In so far as TSMOs are primarily engaged in pressure group type activity – campaigning, lobbying, negotiating and so on – they will be pursuing concrete demands through inter-state organisations. Reductionist understandings of globalisation outlined above also impede recognition of the implications of expressive movement activism. Tarrow's work is, again, illustrative. His definition of a transnational social movement involves 'sustained contentious interaction with power holders in which at least one state is either a target or a participant' (Tarrow undated). Unsurprisingly, Marxist and neo-marxist writers also have a strong inclination to privilege the instrumental dimensions of activism.

This is not to say that all those who privilege the instrumental dimension of activism completely ignore the expressive dimension. The Commission on Global Governance (1995:41–75) saw NGOs in global civil society as helping to disseminate a new 'civic ethic' encompassing universal values meant to encourage a more co-operative mode of politics. Smith et al go as far as saying that the 'deep politics of shaping individual thinking and action ... clearly occupies much, if not most, social movement energies' (1997:70–3). It's curious, therefore, that they focus instead on TSMOs.

### Privileging the expressive dimension

Some authors claim a sharp divide between what they depict as the technocratic values and culture of international political and economic institutions on the one hand and the 'progressive' or emancipatory values and cultures assumed to be articulated within and through global civil society. Thus authors such as Falk, Thiele and Turner, cited earlier, privilege the expressive dimension of movement activism. But in so doing they downplay the significance of cultural differences between and within movements worldwide as well as the instrumental dimension of movement activism (including instrumental dimensions of the so-called new social movements). The instrumental and technocratic orientation of many INGOs/ TSMOs tends to disappear from view.

### The 'dual faces' of social movements

In our view, both the instrumental and expressive dimensions of activism and the interactions between them need to be properly acknowledged and examined. Adapting the work of Cohen and Arato (1992) we suggest that movements typically have 'dual faces' and adopt 'dualistic strategies'. Cohen and Arato elaborate this model with regards to western feminism and they stress the complexity of the relationship. They argue that activists cross the 'organisational divide' in both directions. 'Nor has learning on the part of activists entailed a one-directional shift from expressive to instrumental rationality ... learning has occurred on both sides and in both directions' (1992:558).

This can be mapped on to the network conception of social movements set out above. We distinguished between the informal grassroots groups intrinsic to any movement and the TSMOs that are often associated with them. TSMOs typically 'face' national and/or international institutional structures and tend to pursue instrumental strategies. Informal grassroots groups, whilst they can have global dimensions, are nevertheless embedded locally in everyday social relationships. Informal activism thus 'faces' this everyday world. That said, we would expect to find instrumental and expressive dimensions of activism in both 'branches' of movement activism. Continuity and feedback between these dimensions exists through the communicative, interpersonal and informational linkages of the social movement as a whole.

Further, it seems likely that the instrumental demands of informal groupings are potentially strengthened by the activities of 'their' TSMOs, in the sense that the TSMOs are likely to have a more direct and effective impact upon international institutions. Conversely, the expressive dimensions of TSMO activism are potentially strengthened by their articulation through informal, grassroots, activism in the everyday world, connecting to and stimulating more diffuse, long-term shifts in social processes. We try to depict such processes diagrammatically in Figure 3.2.

While admittedly abstract as presented here, we feel this perspective potentially offers an important analytic corrective to the limited

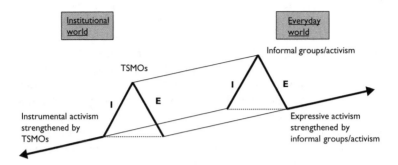

Key: I = instrumental dimension of movement activism
   E = expressive dimension of movement activism

*Figure 3.2*  Instrumental and expressive dimensions of movement activism in the institutional and everyday worlds

ways in which instrumental and expressive dimensions of activism are usually portrayed. It links TSMOs back to 'their' social movements and enables a more complex understanding of the importance of grassroots, expressive activism. There is clearly a need for thorough-going research of the complex network relations linking these dimensions of transnational social movements and the strategic uses of both instrumental and expressive strategies throughout a movement.

## OLIGARCHIC AND DEMOCRATISING DYNAMICS

The fourth and final area we wish to consider concerns the dynamics of oligarchic threats and democratic possibilities in movement organisation and activism. The lack of analytical attention given to this issue is a startling omission given that key strands of the existing literature strongly emphasise the democratic character and democratising potential of social movement activism and TSMOs and INGOs. Particularly important here is the extent to which TSMOs and INGOs necessarily encounter problems of oligarchy and bureaucratisation. Initially identified by Weber and Michels, these are widely recognised as common organisational trajectories, if not exactly iron cages or laws. Trends in this direction find confirmation in parallel claims about movements being 'NGO-ised', and

TSMOs becoming professionalised and institutionalised (Alvarez 1999:181–209; Meyer and Tarrow 1998:20). It has also been pointed out that an oligopoly of INGOs is currently emerging: a handful of 'operational' INGOs becoming 'market leaders', dominating interactions with the UN and functioning to stifle diversity as other NGOs are forced to adopt similar practices and management styles if they are to survive (Donini 1996:88–92). In sum, there are strong dynamics likely to push INGOs and TSMOs to become increasingly integrated into elite structures of power over time, detached from both the control of their memberships and from potentially broader social movement constituencies.

Thus we are very doubtful about the efficacy of demands restricted to arguing for an enhanced role for INGOs/NGOs in the UN and in the international financial institutions.While it is claimed that increased NGO/INGO involvement would make these institutions more democratic, such arguments are often rooted in assumptions that elite rule (and thus oligarchy) is inevitable and that liberal democratic political structures are the pinnacle of democracy. Yet liberal democracy has long been criticised for its limited, procedural character and the extent to which formal political equality obscures asymmetries of power in the wider social context.

One potential challenge to our argument about the pervasiveness of oligarchic tendencies can be made by reference to the proliferation of networks. Many authors claim or assume that both social movements *and* INGOs/TSMOs are increasingly taking a network form. Assumptions from new social movement theory are at play again here, together with more general claims about the ascendancy of the network form as a key organisational feature of globalisation in the contemporary era. The network form is claimed to involve a flattening of hierarchies so that authority and legitimacy flows more horizontally and interactively. Networks are seen as 'lighter', less bureaucratic and more flexible than traditional organisational forms. There are also strong hints that the network form is necessarily more egalitarian and democratic. Yet there is nothing inherently democratic about networks. As Waterman points out, 'networking is both the oldest and the most common form of human social relationship' and can include 'vertical' as well as 'horizontal' relationships, among 'unequals and unalikes'. Networks can also 'have different architectures, such as the star, the wheel and the web ... implying differential influence and control' (Waterman 2002a:143–4). There is little detail or evidence in the literature of the type of network form that INGOs/TSMOs are supposedly adopting and thus it is far too soon to conclude that the oligarchical tendencies identified above are disappearing. All of that said, we also reject the blanket assumption referred to earlier, that any INGO/TSMO that attempts to engage with institutional structures of power can only serve to sustain and reproduce that power.

Perhaps the most important lacuna in the literature is the lack of attention to the nature and role of networks that link TSMOs and informal dimensions of movement activism. Gorg and Hirsch argue that 'the democratic significance of NGOs depends on the existence and development of social movements' seen as necessary to prevent them 'from evolving into elitist-bureaucratic and quasi-state formations' (Gorg and Hirsch 1998:607). They do not say how that might work but we suggest below that conscious work on democratising such networks might begin to offer a solution.

### Implications of network relationships and pointers to democratisation

We think the character and dynamics of network relationships *within* social movements may be crucial for considering the potential of movements to contribute to a shift towards a more democratic world order. Earlier we suggested that TSMO instrumental strategies are likely to contribute most effectively to such a shift when they remain connected informal, grassroots activism. However, we have also argued that TSMOs remain subject to pressures toward bureaucratisation, oligarchy and co-option. There clearly needs to be attention paid to the internal constitution of TSMOs but it could also be essential to construct and maintain democratic relationships between the different dimensions of movement activism if TSMOs are to be 'inoculated' against the dangers of oligarchy. In other words, there needs to be a reconceptualisation of the kinds of democracy possible within and between TSMOs and informal movement activism involved in transnational social movements.

We can only provide some pointers here but there seems to be an urgent need for a systematic recovery of participatory, informal, group-based modes of democracy and a more systematic attempt to apply them to social movements active in global politics. As well as a diverse body of work in political theory that could be useful, there is important literature generated by movement activists themselves.

Current mobilisations by the global justice and solidarity movement offer examples, with a strong normative emphasis on the need for enriching and globalising democracy. This extends to claims that the movement itself must be structured on a devolved and consensual basis, involving the construction and democratisation of modes of self-organisation (e.g., World Social Forum 2002).

Lessons from second-wave, western feminism could also be instructive here. Just as western feminism strategically combined instrumental and expressive strategies, so ways were sought to integrate representative and participatory modes of democracy. Feminist debates have also been extended to global movement relationships. Commentators have emphasised the emergence of a distinctively non-hierarchical network form of feminist TSMO and there is a growing feminist literature on the notion of 'transversal politics' – a version of coalition-building based on the recognition that all participants speak from a specific material location giving them a distinct but always partial perspective. A notable example of this strategy can be found in the efforts of feminist peace activists to build strategic solidarities between women on different sides of ethnic conflicts (Yuval-Davis 1997). It seems to us that such ongoing efforts point to both an emergent model of democracy emphasising the importance of open and participatory dialogue alongside efforts to counter the multiple forms of coercive and hierarchical power.

This model provides instructive lessons for the ways in which TSMOs and transnational movement networks of a wide range of orientations could be constructed on a more democratic basis. Further, it offers an important – if as yet underdeveloped – alternative to the dominance of liberal models of representative democracy in arguments about global governance.

## CONCLUSION

In each of the four areas examined in this chapter we have identified common weaknesses in existing analyses and made proposals for analytic reconstruction. Taken together, these reconstructive proposals point towards quite different and innovative ways of assessing the potential and limits of social movement activism as global activism. Much research still needs to be done in trying to identify the extent to which social movements can contribute to progressive processes of global change and we believe that further analytic insight would be gained from the study of the fertile ground of movement praxis. But our approach also raises important issues for activists about appropriate strategy and organisation. In particular we have identified the need for the construction of democratic relationships between the formal and informal dimensions of social movement activism. Whether transnational social movements can help to change the world for the better is one that, ultimately, only the praxis of the movements themselves will answer. Hopefully, though, our proposals for analytic reconstruction can provide a more fruitful way of conceptualising the potential transformative agency of the global activism of social movements.

## NOTES

1  This chapter is a much-shortened and revised version of an article published in *Alternatives* (Eschle and Stammers 2004). Here we only provide sparse referencing. For an extensive analysis of patterns in the existing literature and for full citations and commentary please refer to the longer article.

2  Also called the 'anti-capitalist' or 'anti-globalisation' movement. Many activists reject the latter label, arguing that the movement involves the construction of globalisation 'from below': one that is based on more humane, just and democratic interconnections between people on a worldwide scale.

## BIBLIOGRAPHY

Alvarez, S. (1999) 'Advocating feminism: the Latin American feminist NGO "Boom"', *International Feminist Journal of Politics* 1, 2: 181–209

Boli, J. and G. Thomas (1999) *Constructing World Culture: International Nongovernmental Organizations Since 1875*, Stanford, CA: Stanford University Press

Cohen, J. and A. Arato (1992) *Civil Society and Political Theory*, Cambridge Mass: MIT Press

Colas, A. (2002) *International Civil Society: Social Movements in World Politics*, Cambridge: Polity Press

Commission on Global Governance (1995) *Our Global Neighbourhood*, Oxford: Oxford University Press

Diani, M. (2000) 'The concept of social movement', in K. Nash (ed.) *Readings in Contemporary Political Sociology*, Oxford: Basil Blackwell

Donini, A. (1996) 'The bureaucracy and the free spirits: stagnation and innovation in the relationship between the UN and NGOs', in T.G. Weiss and L. Gordenker (eds) *NGOs, The UN and Global Governance*, Boulder Co.: Lynne Reiner

Eschle, C. and N. Stammers (2004) 'Taking part: social movements, INGOs and global change', *Alternatives: Global, Local, Political* 29, 3: 333–72.

Falk, R. (1987) 'The global promise of social movements: explorations at the edge of time', *Alternatives* 12: 173–96

Freeman, C. (2001) 'Is local:global as feminine:masculine? Rethinking the gender of globalization', *Signs* 26, 4: 1007–37

Gorg, C. and J. Hirsch (1998) 'Is international democracy possible?', *Review of International Political Economy* 5, 3: 585–615

Guidry, J. A., M. D. Kennedy and M. N. Zald (eds) (2000) *Globalizations and Social Movements: Culture, Power and the Transnational Public Sphere*, Ann Arbor: University of Michigan Press

Hardt, M. and A. Negri (2000) *Empire*, Cambridge Mass.: Harvard University Press

Held, D., K. McGrew, D. Goldblatt and J. Perraton, (1999) *Global Transformations*, Cambridge: Polity Press

Keck, M. and K. Sikkink (1998) *Activists Beyond Borders: Advocacy Networks in International Politics*, Ithaca, NY: Cornell University Press

Marchand, M. and A. S. Runyan (2000) *Gender and Global Restructuring: Sightings, Sites and Resistances*, London: Routledge

Meyer, D. and S. Tarrow (1998) 'A movement society: contentious politics for a new century' in D. Meyer and S. Tarrow (eds) *The Social Movement Society: Contentious Politics for a New Century*, Lanham MA: Rowman and Littlefield

Moghadam, V. (1995) 'Transnational feminist networks: collective action in an era of globalization', *International Sociology* 15, 1: 57–85

Murphy, C. (2000) 'Global governance: poorly done and poorly understood', *International Affairs* 76, 4: 789–803

Nerfin, M. (1986) 'Neither Prince nor Merchant; Citizen – An Introduction to the Third System', *IFDA Dossier* 56: 14

Robertson, R. (1995) 'Globalization: time-space and homogeneity/heterogeneity', in M. Featherstone, S. Lash and R. Robertson (eds) *Global Modernities*, London: Sage

Sassen, S. (1996) 'Toward a feminist analytics of the global economy', *Indiana Journal of Global Legal Studies* 4, 1: 7–41

Smith, J. and H. Johnston (eds) (2002) *Globalisation and Resistance: Transnational Dimensions of Social Movements*, Lanham: Rowman and Littlefield

Smith, J., C. Chatfield and R. Pagnucco (eds) (1997) *Transnational Social Movements and Global Politics: Solidarity Beyond the State,* Syracuse, NY: Syracuse University Press

Tarrow, S. (1998) *Power in Movement: Social Movements and Contentious Politics,* 2nd edition, Cambridge: Cambridge University Press

Tarrow, S. (undated) 'Beyond Globalisation', available at the Global Solidarity website: <http://www.antenna.nl/~waterman/tarrow.html>

Thiele, L. P. (1993) 'Making democracy safe for the world: social movements and global politics', *Alternatives* 8, 3: 273–305

Turner, S. (1998) 'Global civil society, anarchy and governance: assessing an emerging paradigm', *Journal of Peace*, Research 35, 1: 29–30

Waterman, P. (2002a) 'Social movements, local places and globalized spaces: Implications for "Globalisation from Below"', in B. K. Gills (ed.) *Globalization and the Politics of Resistance*, Basingstoke: Palgrave

Waterman, P. (2002b) 'The Global Justice and Solidarity Movement: a bibliography', at <http://www.tni.org/tat/docs/bibliography.pdf>

World Social Forum (2002) 'World Social Forum Charter of Principles', <http://www.forumsocialmundial.org.br/main.asp?id_menu=4&cd_language=2>

Yuval-Davis, N. (1997) *Gender and Nation*, London: Sage

# 4

# Between a Political-Institutional Past and a Communicational-Networked Future? Reflections on the Third World Social Forum, 2003

*Peter Waterman*

If the First World Social Forum (WSF) in Porto Alegre, 2001, was mostly marked by protest against the World Economic Forum taking place at the same time, and the Second, in 2002, by attempts to specify the meaning of 'Another World is Possible!', the Third, in January 2003, was marked by a questioning of the extent to which the Forum – now an increasingly globalised phenomenon – itself embodies what it is preaching to others. This chapter therefore considers WSF3 in terms of: (a) the danger of going forward to the past of social movements and internationalism; (b) the problematic relationship with the 'old' trade unions; (c) the uneven age, gender, ethnic, etc., composition of the Forum; (d) the uncertain future of a proposed global social movement network; (e) the necessity of a communications/media/cultural internationalism.

## THE FUTURE OF THE MOVEMENTS AND INTERNATIONALISM: FORWARD TO THE PAST?

At the centre of initiative and decision-making within the World Social Forum has been the Brazilian National Organising Committee (OC) and the International Council it created (IC). These are not subject to the principles of participatory or even representative democracy. The historical justification for the existence of both has been the quite remarkable vessel they have launched – an international and internationalist encounter, outside the immediate spheres of capital and state, targeted against neo-liberalism and capitalist globalisation, increasingly concerned with proposing radical-democratic alternatives to such. And this all on the understanding that the place, space and form is the guarantee for the necessary democratic dialogue of countries and cultures, of ideologies, of political levels, collective subjects and movements/organisations. In so far as *re*-presentation is today as important, or even more important, than *representation* (a problematic quality within both liberal democracies and, for example, labour movements), the forms and contents of a new counter-hegemony have been at least sketched out by the committees of the Forum and on a global scale.[1]

This space has never been, however, a neutral or innocent one, or as far beyond the old politics or parties and parliaments as it might like to claim. The OC consists of a number of representatives of social-movements and non-governmental organisations (NGOs) – which may address social movements and civil society but are answerable only to themselves. (It consists of two Brazilian movement organisations and six NGOs; of seven men, and only one woman.) These bodies have been oriented towards, or circulate around, the Partido dos Trabalhadores (PT, Workers' Party), and/or its recently successful presidential candidate, Lula da Silva. Just as the Porto Alegre Forums have been places where this (and other Brazilian parties) could influence events and publicise themselves, so was the European Social Forum, Florence, November 2002, in which the Rifondazione Communista (and other Italian political parties) did the same. Such parties, and far-less-sophisticated and interesting others, have often hidden their political lights behind NGO bushels. The WSF has been a site to which various interstate agencies, such as those of the United Nations, have access to or upon which they exercise influence. State-dependent funding agencies, national and international, and the massive private-capitalist US foundations, have supported the Forum itself, or various, selected, inter/national NGOs influential within it.

The IC was created top-down by invitation of the OC (of 90–100 members, mostly NGOs and inter/national unions, only eight to ten are women's networks). This gargantuan assembly has no clear mandate or power, therefore acting for the OC largely as a sounding board and international legitimator. The nature and representativity of the members, and the extent to which they are answerable to any but themselves, remains obscure. Many of them do little other work in the IC than turning up and then fighting for their corner. The IC does not operate behind closed doors, but its proceedings are barely reported by its members even to the interested public. There has, recently, been formal discussion about the role and rules of the IC, consequent on an intended shift of weight from the Brazilian national to the international committee. But whilst part of this discussion, actually more like an interesting experiment in online *consultation*, for which see <http://www.delibera.info/fsm2003ci/ GB>, is posted on a publicly accessible website, the latter's existence is known to few. Moreover, only a tiny fraction of IC members have taken part in this consultation, again suggesting that their motivation for membership has more to do with a search for recognition and influence than with the advance of this – admittedly novel and complex – project as a whole. The Committee, however, is not a monolith. On the contrary, it is itself in movement, under its own momentum, as indicated by post-Forum web updates <http://www. forumsocialmundial.org.br/home.asp>. At the very least, however, it has signally failed to *communicate itself* even to an interested public.

The Porto Alegre Forum is an agora in which there are a few large, well-publicised and well-placed circus tents, surrounded by a myriad of differently-sized others (now around 1,700–3,400 events per *day*), proposed by social movements, international agencies, political organisations, academic institutions and even individuals. The suburban/peripheral events compete for visibility, for sites, for translators/equipment, often overlap with or even *reproduce* each other, and – whilst certainly adding to the pluralism of the Forum – have an inevitably minor impact. Whilst, again, the decision that the Forum is not a policy-forming body allows for pluralism and creativity, the result is, inevitably, domination by the official programme – one which has been conceived without notable discussion beyond the governing committees. The concentration of power at the Centre is reinforced by the presence of our very own celebrities, who themselves may have to choose between appearing in a hall seating thousands, or in a classroom seating 25. Indeed, even the major Central Themes (sets of panels on specific problem areas) were somewhat marginalised, either by being placed away from the central university site, or simply by the attention focused on the celebrity events, the rallies and demonstrations.

This formula is out of control in different ways. WSF3, 2003, with maybe 70,000 Brazilian and 30,000 foreign participants, was too big for the hosts to handle: a number of experienced local organisers had apparently been lured away to Brasilia by the new government, and the original PT local-government sponsors had lost influence in both the city and the state. Unlike the previous year, the programme was never published completely in either English or Portuguese. A well-organised North American left, internationalist and pro-feminist group, *invited* to run a five-day programme on 'Life after Capitalism', found itself without publicity, and then geographically marginalised in a country club unmarked on the Forum maps, unknown to the information booths and a taxi-ride away from the main site <www.zmag.org/lac.htm>. The Brazilian feminist tent, a major focus of attention at WSF2, had been moved to some anonymous site elsewhere in the city. Other radical groups likewise complained of marginalisation (check websites cited at end of bibliography).

The Forum is also out of control in the sense that it is moving beyond the reach of the Centre, with regional, national, local and problem-specific forums mushrooming worldwide. Here the OC/IC can give guidance and blessing (and even hypothetically withhold such) but little more. The Forum may slip out of the hands of the original inter/national NGO elite (I use this term loosely) as it is challenged by those who are demanding that its decision-making bodies consist of *regional/national* representatives (or elites?). The Forum is in danger of losing its *social* profile, as major politicians and governments recognise the importance of this agora, and turn up invited (President Lula da Silva) or uninvited (President Hugo Chavez). There was no way that the Forum could fail to invite Lula, or even to wish him well on his way to Davos (the location in Switzerland of the IMF meeting). But well-wishers might have been alarmed by such newspaper headlines as 'Lula is Applauded in Davos and Starts the Dialogue between Porto Alegre and Davos', and 'IMF Approves Financial Discipline of Lula Government'. This is not to speak of Lula's conciliatory Davos speech itself. The Forum's place as a focus for the 'new global solidarity' is being put in question by those who seek to give it not only a national but also a national*ist* character. This is evidenced in the Indian case. Here a declaration of the Asian Social Forum (ASF), dominated by a major Indian Communist Party, attacked *imperialist* wars in Asia but forgot about the *nationalist* Indo-Pakistani conflict – in which nuclear threats are issued by two opposed chauvinist regimes, both enjoying US imperial military cooperation! An informative report on the ASF, in India's left-leaning *Economic and Political Weekly* (Jain 2003), proposed that strong nation states, and alliances of such, were the necessary answer to globalisation, this traditional – not to say archaic – notion being reinforced by an editorial sub-head that turned the writer's proposal into an ASF-WSF *conclusion*!

Given all these problems, there is a danger that the Forum will be overwhelmed by the past of social movements and internationalism, in which such movements were dominated by the institutions they spawned, by political parties that instrumentalised them, in which the movements were state-oriented and/or state-identified, and in which internationalism was literally that – a relationship between nations, nationals, nationalisms, nationalists. Proletarian solidarity turned into military aid to approved regimes. West–Rest solidarity came to be dominated by one-way state-funded 'development cooperation' (in areas, on problems, with funding, and to 'partners' determined by the north-western one). And Rest–Rest solidarity could be reduced, for example, to slogans of solidarity with the revolution in El Salvador, in a tribal village of India, where any sign of solidarity with other tribes, or tribes in the neighbouring Indian state, were absent.

### THE UNION–FORUM RELATIONSHIP: MOVABLE OBJECTS AND RESISTIBLE FORCES

WSF3 saw a growth and deepening of the relationship between the Traditional International Union Institutions (TIUIs) and the Forum. There are already about a dozen inter/national unions on the IC, most of which are anti-neoliberal but not anti-capitalist, and many of which are, due to globalisation, in considerable crisis. There is no evidence that they have tried to act as a bloc. With one or two exceptions, they may have been primarily concerned with finding out what kind of exotic animal this is.

The increasing interest of this major traditional movement in the Forum was demonstrated by the presence, for the first time, of the General Secretary of the International Confederation of Free Trade Unions (ICFTU). But top officers of Global Union Federations (GUFs, formerly International Trade Secretariats) were also present, either prominently on platforms or quietly testing the water. Present, further, were inter/national union organisations/networks from beyond the ICFTU 'family' (now formalised as Global Unions). Noticeable also was an increasing openness amongst even the most traditional of TIUIs. Whilst the first big union event was a formal panel with only gestures in the direction of discussion, another major panel saw the platform shared between the Global Unions, independent left unions and articulate leaders of social movements or NGOs identified with the Forum process. The unions, moreover, seem increasingly prepared to recognise that they *are* institutions and that it is *they* that need to come to terms with a place and process that, whilst lacking in formal representativity and often inchoate, nevertheless has the appeal, dynamism, public reach and mobilising capacity that they themselves lack. The question, however, remains of what kind of relationship is developing here. From the first big union event, patronised by the charismatic Director of the International Labour Organisation, veteran Chilean socialist, Juan Somavia, it seemed that what was shaping up was some kind of understanding or alliance between (a) the unions, (b) the Social Forum and (c) progressive states/men (evidently represented by the unconditionally-praised PT Government and President Lula). Somavia made explicit comparison between the ILO's new programme/slogan of 'Decent Work' and Lula's election slogan 'For a Decent Brazil'. In so far as the TIUIs appear to have adopted 'Decent Work' what is here surely suggested is a global neo-keynesianism, in which the unions and their ILO/WSF friends would recreate the post-1945 Social Partnership model (or ideology), but now on a global scale – and with the aid of friendly governments! The model is problematic in numerous ways: principally whether the role of the WSF, or the more general Global Justice and Solidarity Movement, is going to be limited to supporting a project aimed at making capitalist globalisation 'decent', or whether the movement should have a project for labour that might be simultaneously more utopian (post-capitalist) and, under present conditions, more realistic (making work-for-capital an ethical issue, treating 'non-workers' as equals of wage-earners, addressing the closely inter-related civil-social issues such as useful production, sustainable consumption). There surely needs to be discussion about the political, theoretical and ethical bases of the two labour utopianisms, one within and the other beyond the parameters of capitalism.

## COMBINED AND UNEVEN DEVELOPMENT: GENDER, ETHNICITY, CLASS AND AGE

At WSF3 I was somewhat alarmed by the number of people who looked like me: white, male, middle-aged and, evidently, middle class. I suspect the bias applies to the decision-making committees. This does not, of course, mean that women, Africans, Indians, indigenous peoples, workers or the under-30s are excluded. But the youth were under canvas in the Youth Camp or in private 'solidarity accommodation', the Argentinean *piqueteros* (protesters) were in the streets (sleeping who knows where?) and the women were less visible than they had been at WSF2 (though this may have been an effect of the decentralisation and dispersal at WSF3).

Amilcar Cabral, assassinated leader of anti-Portuguese struggle in Africa, once suggested that after independence there would (or should) occur the 'suicide of the petty-bourgeoisie'. As the more sceptical Frantz Fanon argued at the same time, however, the post-colonial elites would do everything they could to increase their privileges. There are striking power/wealth differences between Forum participants, particularly visible, predictably, in the case of the south. In two or three Latin American cases known to me, the poorer participants travelled by bus – this sometimes meaning a four or five day journey, with entry obstacles at various border-crossings. There is no reason to assume that the existent Forum elites are suicidal (even I was not going to abandon a hotel with hot and cold running internet). In so far, on the other hand, as the WSF has declared certain principles relating to liberty, equality, solidarity, horizontality and pluralism, it might be possible to confront them (us) with the necessity of re-balancing the power equation. The elites could then put their efforts, in their home states/constituencies, into facilitating rather than dominating or controlling the Forum process.

## A POSSIBLE SOLUTION TO ABSENCES AND UNDER REPRESENTATION

The experience of women and feminists within the Forum might point here in different directions. I have no figures for 2003, but at both previous events, women were almost 50 per cent of the participants. There are powerful feminists and feminist networks on the panels and in at least the IC, quite capable here of making the Forum a feminist issue. Feminists at the Forum are confronted, however, with devising a strategy that combines working within decision-making bodies, making their presence felt within the Forum itself and addressing a feminist and general public beyond the Forums. Whereas leading figures might declare good intentions with respect to women and feminism, the step from talking to walking has still to be taken here also. The power/presence imbalances within the Forum might be corrected by two measures. One would be quotas for under-represented categories. The other would be a Forum pro-gramme structured according to collective subjects as well as major problems. Thus one could have major panels/programmes on labour, women, youth, indigenous peoples – even the aged. At present, for example, labour may be represented in a series of union-sponsored or union-approved events, some within and some beyond the core programme. But this implies a dispersal of attention and impact where there should, surely, be concentration.[2] Alternatively, or additionally, imbalances can, could and should be corrected by autonomous forums.

## A SOCIAL MOVEMENT NETWORK: DE/CENTRALISED?

Two previous Forums have issued a 'Call of Social Movements'. The initiative for this has come from members of the OC and IC, some of them recognisable social movement organisations, others recognisable NGOs. Both Calls have been publicly presented and then signed by 50–100 other organisations and networks. This year, the notion of a 'Social Movements World Network' (SMWN) was widely circulated on the web and subject to a two-session public discussion within the Forum. This eventually produced a declaration, proposing a continuation of discussion about the nature of such a network, with further meetings to take place during major movement events this year (Social Movements World Network 2003). However the call – like other Forum bodies and initiatives – is surrounded by a certain amount of mystery. There is a serious lack of communication, which implies a concentration of crucial information amongst a limited circle. The creation of such a network is favourable, because none such exists internationally and because it could provide information and ideas on a continuing basis – and to those people/places otherwise excluded from the periodic Forums. In so far as this will have an existence in 'real virtuality' (Manuel Castells), it may go beyond a WSF that remains largely earth-bound and institutional. However other questions remain. Is the network going to be primarily political/institutional or primarily communicational? In the first case, communication is likely to be made functional to the political/ institutional. In the second case, we may be into a different ballgame – or ballpark. In the first case, there is likely to operate a 'banking' model of communication, in which information is collected, sorted and classified, to be then dealt out to customers/ clients in terms of power, influence or profit, as determined by the information-bank managers. In the second case, there can operate the principle of the potlatch, or gift economy, in which individual generosity is taken to benefit the community.

Even in the best of all possible cyberworlds, however, there remain questions of appropriate *modes* (information, ideas, dialogue), of *form* (printed word at one end, multimedia at the other) and *control* (handling cybernuts and our own home-grown fundamentalists). There do exist various relevant models of international social movement, civil society, anti-globalisation networks – earth-bound or cyberspatial. Indy Media Centre (IMC) (see also Chapter 11) is the most important here, and needs to be publicly reflected upon both for what it does well and what it doesn't. Finally, any Social Movements World Network is going to have to go beyond network-babble and recognise that even networks do not exist on one, emancipatory, model. In discussing the issue, Arturo Escobar (2003) has said that:

> It is possible to distinguish between two general types: more or less rigid hierarchies, and flexible, non-hierarchical, decentralised and self-organising meshworks ... Hierarchies entail a degree of centralised control, ranks, overt planning, homogenisation, and particular goals and rules of behaviour conducive to these goals. Meshworks ... are based on decentralised decision making ... self-organisation, and heterogeneity and diversity. Since they are non-hierarchical, they have no overt goals. It can be said they follow the dynamics of life, developing through their encounter with their environments.

In the end, however, it does not matter too much in which place/ space, or on which model the SMWN takes shape. The existence of the web, combining low cost of entry, wide reach and high speed, provides the assurance that such a network will be supplemented or challenged by others.

## FROM ORGANISATION TO COMMUNICATION IN THE GLOBAL JUSTICE AND SOLIDARITY MOVEMENT

I am here moving from cyberspace to communication, and from the World Social Forum to the Global Justice and Solidarity Movement. Whereas the movement-in-general has shown, at its best, an almost instinctive feel for the logic of the computer (Klein 2001), and has expressed itself in the most creative and provocative ways, this is not the case for the WSF. It uses the media, culture and cyberspace but it does not think of itself in cultural/communicational terms, nor does it live fully within this increasingly central and infinitely expanding universe.[3] The WSF website remains problematic – promoting year-old ideas (chosen by whom?) in its meagre library.

The only WSF daily is *Terra Viva*, an admirable effort by the customarily unaccountable NGO, but with space-limitations, delays and superficialities a heavier bias toward the Forum establishment. The commercial, professional, substantial regional paper in Rio Grande do Sul, *Zero Hora*, gave wide coverage but, unsurprisingly, in Portuguese. For background information and orientation one was this year dependent on free handouts of *La Vie/Le Monde* (inspired by French social Catholicism), and *Ode*, a glossy, multilingual, New Age magazine from Rotterdam, with impressively relevant coverage (which I have used in this chapter). Other alternative, non-Forum sites provide better information and/or discussion than the Forum itself (www.choike.org/links/about/index.html, www.nadir.org/nadir/initiativ/agp/free/wsf/).

The FSM is something of a shrine to the written and spoken word. At the core of the Forum is The Panel, in which five to ten selected panellists do their thing in front of an audience of anything from five to 5,000. At the other end of the Forum's narrow spectrum of modes there is The Demonstration. Here euphoria is order of the day: how can it not be when surrounded by so many beautiful people, of all ages, genders and sexual options, of nationality and ethnicity, convinced that 'another world is possible'? But here we must note the distinction made 30 years ago, between mobilisation and mobility, as related to the old organisation and the new media:

> The open secret of the electronic media, the decisive political factor, which has been waiting, suppressed or crippled, for its moment to come, is their mobilizing power. When I say *mobilize* I mean *mobilize* ... namely to make [people] more mobile than they are. As free as dancers, as aware as football players, as surprising as guerrillas. Anyone who thinks of the masses only as the object of politics, cannot mobilize them. He wants to push them around. A parcel is not mobile; it can only be pushed to and fro. Marches, columns, parades, immobilize people ... The new media are egalitarian in structure. Anyone can take part in them by a simple switching process ... The new media are orientated towards action, not contemplation; towards the present, not tradition ... It is wrong to regard media equipment as mere means of consumption. It is always, in principle, also means of production ... In the socialist movements the dialectic of discipline and spontaneity, centralism and decentralization, authoritarian leadership and anti-authoritarian disintegration has long ago reached deadlock. Network-like communication models built on the principle of reversibility of circuits might give indications of how to overcome this situation. (Enzensberger 1976:21–53)

The paucity of cultural expression at WSF3 is surprising. The WSF3 song, which has an attractive but complex lilt, is sung only in Portuguese, and did not seem to be available in written or CD form, even in this language. It was, in fact, the WSF2 song. As in 2002 the T-shirts were still not going to win any design prizes. And the most popular icon remains Che. I suspect there might be a market for Subcomandante Marcos, for Rigoberta Menchú, for Chico Mendes, for La Naomi, for El Noam, for Arundhati, and even for Frida and Diego, or a Beatle Giving Peace a Chance, but I may be wrong.

## CONCLUSION: THE SECRET OF FIRE

I am concerned but not worried about the future of the Forum process. Pandora has opened her box, the genie is out of the lamp, the secret of fire for emancipatory movements is now an open one. This secret is: keep moving. In other words: a moment of stasis within a movement (institutionalisation, incorporation, bureau-cratisation, collapse, regression) requires of activists that they make ready to move to its periphery, or to move beyond it, or to create a new movement to advance, again, the potential represented by the old movement during its emancipatory moment. Already in Florence, young libertarians were grumbling, and mumbling 'another Forum is possible'. This possibility is not only a matter of information and communication technology. It may be the combi-nation, precisely, of this with youth – given that at least urban kids are growing up with cellular phones, playing arcade computer games, and therefore with an affinity for other computer technology (and a healthy disregard for attempts to coral such).

For the rest, I am inspired by energetic and innovative social protest, and original analyses of the local–national–global dialectic in Argentina; by the belated appearance in Peru of a network, Raiz (Root), which clearly has some feeling that the WSF is more than an NGO jamboree; by the Kidz in the Kamp who were discussing under a tree, and with informal translation, how to ensure that the emancipatory and critical forces have more impact on the Forum process; by the struggle, against all odds, of the US Znet people to mount 'Life after Capitalism', an event of post-capitalist *propuesta* within the Forum; by the massive global anti-war demonstrations of 15–16 February 2003 – something that puzzled even radical special-ists on the new social movements; by the increasing number of compañeras (action groups), of various ages, identities, movements and sexual orientations, who believe that, in the construction of a meaningfully civil global society, transparency is not only the best policy but the only one.[4]

## POSTSCRIPT: JULY 2004 BY MARIANNE MAECKELBERG

There have been several significant developments in the World Social Forum (WSF) since the meetings and events of January 2003. These developments have occurred within two intertwined processes, first in the organising process (meetings and committees and councils) and then, second, in the WSF process itself (the five days of meetings, events and encounters). Waterman's description of the WSF 2003 focuses primarily on the organising process. Within this domain, the most significant change has been the expansion of the Indian Organising Committee (OC) to include 57 organisations, and the creation of the Indian General Council which consists of over 250 organisations. This increased 'openness' has trickled over to the Brazilian WSF, which now has an OC of 24 organisations, a four-fold increase.

When India opened up the OC to allow more organisations to affiliate, the result was a more diverse committee with considerably better gender statistics. Perhaps due to this change, one of the four main WSF 2004 events was entitled 'War against women, women against war' and the OC adopted the principle that all official panels should have gender parity (a task that was obviously easier in principle than in practice).

This slightly more diverse OC was then forced to create a much cheaper and less luxurious WSF due to the government in India being unwilling to provide money, space or other resources. The Indian context also required a different relationship to foreign funding bodies. India has a tradition of strong opposition to foreign funding and consequently 2004 saw the first WSF without funding from the Ford Foundation.

These two differences collided with several other factors to create a WSF whose legacy has been strong enough to eclipse any problems within the organising process (at least in the collective mythologising of the WSF). The Indian WSF shifted the space for politics from the conference halls to the streets, not by organising the traditional opening and closing demonstrations, but by having an ongoing spirit of festival and political self-expression all over the UNESCO grounds. The important spaces of the WSF were no longer the official programme spaces, but rather the self-created spaces of 'cultural' and political expression. Perhaps more importantly, this change was largely due to the presence of the Dalit movements and Adivasi groups, as well as movements that have been historically marginalised by the left, including people with disabilities, AIDS, sex trade workers and sexual minorities (Conway 2004). It appeared as if the movements understood Enzensberger's difference between mobility and mobilisation.

And it was this spirit that was remembered most clearly at a recent organising meeting in Porto Alegre, where the discussion focused around making the WSF 2005 more self-organised. The halls of the posh old university in Porto Alegre are being abandoned for tents; a consultation process has been added to the top-down system of determining the programme (via the website) and at the IC meeting in Italy in April there was discussion of using the internet to start a self-merging procedure for the seminars and workshops.

However, these changes to the WSF process itself will not provide solutions to the problems within the organising process. The organising process is still a space controlled largely by political parties (in India various communist and socialist parties) and many of the other concerns Waterman has outlined are still unresolved. There is no visible progress for the Social Movement World Network. The relationship of the trade unions to the WSF remains unclear, with the notion of a 'decent' globalisation squarely on their agenda. There is still a strong nationalist character within the organising process and, perhaps most importantly, there is still a very strong middle and upper class bias in the organising meetings of the WSF processes (for an excellent critique of the Indian organising process see Sen 2004).

Nevertheless, while the organising process of the Indian WSF was problematic and requires deep examination and critique, the image branded on the collective memory of the WSF 2004 participants is not one of a power struggle between political parties, but one of powerfully positive transformation. And this image, accurate or not, is setting the standards for WSFs to come, as the messy race towards utopia continues.

### NOTES

1   Since this piece was first drafted, Boaventura de Sousa Santos (2003b, in Sen et al. 2004) has produced the most original analysis and theorisation of the Forum that has yet appeared. He gives considerable importance to

the 'self-democratisation' of the Forum – the aspect on which this chapter concentrates.

2 Fisher and Ponniah 2002 has but two contributions on the union movement as such, and the single one on feminism does not address the international/global at all!

3 For more on this new and challenging area, see Cardon and Granjon (2003) and the Cyberspace panel within Life after Capitalism <http://www.zmag.org/lacsite.htm.>

4 In an effort to ensure that this should be the case, I am co-editing, with Jai Sen, and others, a collection of committed but critical texts on the Forum. See Sen et al. (2004).

## BIBLIOGRAPHY

Anheier, H., M. Glasius and M. Kaldor (eds) (2001) *Global Civil Society Yearbook 2001*, Oxford: Oxford University Press

Cardon, D. and F. Granjon (2003) 'The Alter-Globalisation movement and the Internet' (Jane Holister, Coorditrad volunteer translator), *Sand in the Wheels – ATTAC Weekly Newsletter*, 19 February 2003

Castells, Manuel (2002) *The Internet Galaxy: Reflections on the Internet, Business and Society*, Oxford: Oxford University Press

Conway, J. (2004) 'India's challenge to Brazil at the World Social Forum', available at: <http://www.radiofeminista.net/ene04/notas/india.htm>

Enzensberger, H. M. (1976) 'Constituents of a theory of the media', in *Raids and Reconstructions: Essays in Politics, Crime and Culture*, London: Pluto, 20–53

Eschle, C. (2002) 'Engendering global democracy', *International Feminist Journal of Politics*, 4:3; 315–41

Escobar, A. (2003) 'Other Worlds Are (already) Possible: Cyber-Internationalism and Post-Capitalist Cultures'. Draft Notes for the Cyberspace Panel, Life after Capitalism Programme, World Social Forum, Porto Alegre, 23–28 January, <www.zmag.org/lac.htm.>

Fisher, W. and T. Ponniah (eds) (2002) *Another World is Possible: Popular Alternatives to Globalsation at the World Social Forum*, London/New York/Nova Scotia/Capetown: Zed/Fernwood/Sird/David Philip

Glasius, M., M. Kaldor and H. Anheier (eds) (2002) *Global Civil Society 2002*, Oxford: Oxford University Press

Jain, D. (2003) 'The empire strikes back: a report on the Asian Social Forum', *Economic and Political Weekly*, 11 January: 99–100

Klein, N. (2001) 'A fete for the end of the end of history', *The Nation*: New York, 19 March

Munck, R. (2002) 'Debating: Globalisation and its Discontents', Liverpool: Department of Sociology

Sen, J. (2004) 'The long march to another world' in Sen et al. (2004).

Sen, J., A. Anand, A. Escobar and P. Waterman (eds) (2004), *The World Social Forum: Challenging Empires*, New Delhi: Viveka Foundation

Social Movements World Network. (2003) <http://www.movsoc.org/htm/socialmovementsmeetings.htm>

Sousa Santos, Boaventura de (2003a) 'The Popular University of Social Movements: To Educate Activists and Leaders of Social Movements, as web as Social Scientists/Scholars Concerned with the Study of Social Change. Proposal for Discussion', Email, 12 January, <bsantos@sonata.fe.uc.pt>, <bsantos@facstaff.wisc.edu>

—— (2003b) 'The World Social Forum: Toward a Counter-Hegemonic Globalisation'. First Draft, presented to the International Congress of the Latin American Studies Association, Dallas, March 2003, <http://www.ces.fe.uc.pt/bss/fsm.php>

Waterman, P. (2003) 'Place, space and the reinvention of social emancipation on a global scale: second thoughts on the third World Social Forum', *Working Paper Series*, No. 378, Institute of Social Studies: The Hague

Zibechi, R. (2003) 'Los movimientos sociales latinoamericanos: Tendencias y desafios', *Observatorio Social de Am'erica Latina*, 9 January: 185–8

## Audio-Visuals

Cotidiano Mujer/CFMEA (2003) *Tu boca fundamental contra los fundamentalismos.* (Your Mouth is Fundamental against Fundamentalism). Flash Programme. Articulación Feminista Marcosur <http:// www.cotidianomujer. org.uy>

OSAL/CLACSO (2002) *Am'erica Latina en Movimiento*. Video. Spanish. 14 mins. PAL Buenos Aires: Observatorio Social de Am'erica Latina. <http://www.osal.clacso.org.>

Social Watch (2003) *The Citizens' Report on the Quality of Life in the World*. CD-Rom. Multi-media. Montevideo: Social Watch. socwatch@social-watch.org. <http:www.socialwatch.org>

Vision Machine (2002) *The Globalisation Tapes*. Video. English. 71 mins. PAL. London: Vision Machine/International Union of Food and Agricultural Workers/Independent Plantation Workers' Union of Sumatra (Indonesia). visionmachine@unreal.at

Walger, Eduardo (2002) *El pensamiento critico a comienzos del siglo XXI: Un documental de Eduardo Walger*. Buenos Aires: Coop. De Trab. Videola Ltda. <http://www.conlamismared.com.ar. NTSC, Eng/Spa

## Websites

Call of Social Movements, <http://www.movsoc.org/htm/social_movements_meetings.htm>

Choike, <http://www.choike.org/links/about/index.html>

Ciranda News Service, <http://www.ciranda.net/>

CLACSO, <http://www.clacso.org/wwwclacso/espanol/html/fprincipal. html>

Focus on the Global South, focus-on-trade@yahoogroups.com

Global Civil Society Yearbook, <http://www.lse.ac.uk/Depts/global/Yearbook/>

Hub/Inventati List, <http://www.inventati.org/mailman/listinfo/hub>

Life after Capitalism, Zmag/Znet, <www.zmag.org/lac.htm>

Network Institute for Global Democratization, <http://www.nigd.org/>

Next GENDERation, <http://www.nextgenderation.let.uu.nl/>

North American Congress on Latin America, <http://www.nacla.org/>

OSAL, <http://osal.clacso.org/>

Peoples' Global Action, <http:www.nadir.org/nadir/initiativ/agp/ free/wsf/>
Radio Fire, <www.fire.or.cr>
Raiz, Peru, <http://www.iespana.es/movimiento-raiz, http:www.tni.org.tat>
Reinventing Social Emancipation, <http://www.ces.fe.uc.pt/emancipa/en/ index.html>
The Commoner, <http://www.commoner.org.uk/>
Voice of the Turtle, <http://www.voiceoftheturtle.org/>
Web Community of Social Movements/Comunidad Web de Movimientos Sociales, <http://movimientos.org/>
WSF International Committee Consultation, <http://www.delibera.info/ fsm2003ci/GB/>
WSF, <http://www.forumsocialmundial.org.br/home.asp>
WSFitself, WSFitself@yahoogrupos.com.br

For more information see:
On women and feminism in the WSF 2004: <http://www.awid.org/go. php?stid = 846>
On trade unions in the WSF/WEF: <http://www.icftu.org/displaydocument. asp?Index = 991218883&Language =EN>
<http://www.global-unions.org/special.asp?LN = E&page = wsf2004>
On the organisational structure and the new consultation process: <www.formsocialmundial.org>
On the Ford Foundation funding: <http://www.opendemocracy.net/ debates/article-6–91–1678.jsp>
<http://varnam.org/blog/archives/000316.html>
On the self-merging process and the IC: <http://www.nigd.org/wsf/ 1081098950/wsf.html>
On the Social Movement World Network: <http://www.movsoc.org/htm/ call_2004_english.htm>

# 5

# From Aldermaston Marcher to Internet Activist

*Sarah Berger*

Alone with my computer I campaign late at night. Not for me the meetings in smoke-filled rooms, meals interrupted by phone calls and sessions with duplicators of the past. Forty-five years after my first experience of activism within the Campaign for Nuclear Disarmament (CND), I am now a trade justice activist and debt campaigner. I have participated in international protests at world summits including the World Bank/International Monetary Fund (IMF) summit in Prague in 2000, the G8 summit in Genoa in 2001 and the European Social Forum in Florence.

In this chapter I will map my life as an activist and comment on the seismic shift in ways of organising and using the media during this period. I will trace the common threads in campaigning techniques over the last four decades. I started young. A teacher observed that I seemed to want to 'paint the school red'. I cut my teeth on the 'Ban the Bomb' Aldermaston march in 1958 at age 14 when I organised a group of school friends to join the four day event. Battersea and Clapham Youth CND then became the centre of my teenage social and political life.

## VIRTUAL CAMPAIGNING

Now, virtual campaigning means I send and receive dozens of emails a week. These deal with plans for local campaigns, bulletins from hotspots such as Palestine or online petitions from around the world. I also visit Indymedia websites for up-to-the-minute reports of international struggles. Connecting to a global movement in this way inspires me. An email from an activist friend direct from the occupied territories in Palestine can have an enormous impact. The email will describe the latest outrage, appeal for worldwide protests about detentions, shootings and call for immediate action. It is not difficult to respond by writing to MPs, government or the media and so much easier than calling a meeting. Results can be

*Photo 1*   Sarah Berger at G8 Summit in Genoa, July 2001

quick too; for example an email protest about an African debt campaigner who had been arrested resulted in his release within a few days after an outcry from around the world. Another instance of the power of an email campaign was the crash of an Italian Government computer system following a 24-hour global Drop the Debt campaign targeting the Italian Finance Ministry in the run-up to the Okinawa G8 summit in 2000.

But, as in corporate and personal life, there is a danger of email overload and compassion fatigue. I become desensitised easily. Dozens of emails, arriving into my home late at night, begging for help, can be horribly intrusive however worthy the cause. Yet the simple solution of deletion or unsubscribing to the e-list feels a difficult step to me. Either way, the guilt produced is considerable.

I can't remember if the pressure to act was as great in my earlier campaigning days of marching, meetings and newsletters.

## LOBBYING VERSUS DIRECT ACTION

Despite the fact that activism now involves so much time working solo via the internet and email, the classic methods of marching, meeting and lobbying still remain central. Familiar divisions within progressive movements still rage just as they have over the last 45 years. One of the most fundamental splits concerns the question as to which is ultimately the most effective – parliamentary lobbying, public meetings and marches or direct action? During the 1950s the struggle in Youth CND was between the hot-headed young Communists and Trotskyites, and the reformists. The revolutionaries wanted to confront state power by 'picking a fight with the fuzz', or scaling a wall to enter a government building, while the reformist 'peaceful protesters' wanted to cooperate with the police in order to gain positive media coverage and win over majority public opinion. This was as much an issue on the Aldermaston marches as it is at world summit protests now. A splinter group would typically break away at the end of the annual four day Aldermaston march to make a dash for Downing Street, only to be blocked by police. The resulting violence would hit the news headlines.

## THREAT OF VIOLENCE NECESSARY?

Four decades later I witnessed this tension between revolutionaries and reformists at the G8 Summit in Genoa in 2001. Travelling to Genoa meant overcoming daunting obstacles including a cancelled coach and train followed by heavy police surveillance at the border. Dressed as conventional middle aged tourists, my age and that of my companion acted in our favour. We dodged the police blockades and reached the city centre. Walking into Genoa was like entering a war zone. Helicopters circled above burnt-out cars and smashed shop windows. Smoke and tear gas hung in the air and puerile graffiti despoiled beautiful Italian buildings. It struck me as systematic and mindless thuggery. I was appalled to find myself associated with a political event that could include such behaviour. The 'Black Block', infiltrated of course by Italian agents provocateurs, had been on the rampage. Later, the 'Black Block' confronted tanks and responded to high-pressure hoses, tear gas and batons by throwing cobblestones at the 'globocops'. Meanwhile the 'fluffies' in pink tutus accompanied by giant puppets used humour, ridicule and street theatre to convey their opposition to the failures of the G8 and to reject the domination of multinationals in enforcing international trade rules which put profit before people.

At that event I was part of 30,000 peaceful demonstrators. We felt the 'Black Block', who numbered less than 300, had overtaken us. The violence, including the death of Carlo Giuliani (one of the protesters) at the hands of the Italian police, attracted enormous media attention around the world. Scenes of rioting and mayhem dominated the television screens, yet the coverage was not all sensationalist and hostile. It included extensive analysis of neo-liberalism and the underlying causes of debt amongst the world's poorest countries. Although I was traumatised by my experiences in Genoa, I have reluctantly concluded that it seems necessary to have both the threat and reality of violence and property destruction and even possible loss of life, in order to force our agenda for a fairer world onto the international stage.

## INNUMERABLE MEETINGS STILL THE BEDROCK

Certain elements of campaigning never change because the bedrock of activism is organising in groups. At its most basic this means innumerable meetings plus sharing ideas via the written word. That in turn requires endless reading. Whether it is a multinational or a small protest group, good organisational skills are needed. This includes the ability to coordinate people, share tasks and delegate, handle resources over time.

## FROM WHITEWASH TO TEXT AND SHORT WAVE RADIO

Despite these common elements, campaign communications have clearly changed dramatically over the last 45 years. One of my earliest memories in Youth CND was creeping out late at night to whitewash 'Ban the Bomb' on street walls. Although one of the attractions as a teenager was certainly the thrill of the illicit, nevertheless it was an effective way to get a message over. It still has its place, though a minor one. Now, along with email and the internet, electronic campaigning tools include text messaging and short band radio. By registering in advance for the Trade Justice Movement's (TJM) mass lobby of Parliament in both 2002 and 2003, I was able to receive regular updates. A text gave me instructions about when to do the Mexican Wave, a fun way of coordinating thousands of protesters encircling the Houses of Parliament. A short wave radio station set up for the event enabled us to hear a commentary on what was happening at the other end of the demonstration. It provided reports on which MPs had already been lobbied and broadcast interviews with celebrity supporters. However, the technology was not quite up to the task as it was difficult to get a reasonable reception. Even at the 2003 TJM event, campaigning via text produced hiccups. Hundreds of simultaneous events were being held across the UK and were intended to climax at noon. I received a text message that campaigners on Snowdon were poised for action. The text instructed our group to prepare for our simultaneous photo opportunity and told us there were only three minutes to go to noon. However this arrived two minutes *after* our Trade Justice event at Brighton beach stunt had taken place (40 people dressed in white lying in the shape of Giant Scales of Justice plus television crew). Despite these glitches, which will undoubtedly get ironed out, we felt excited and empowered to hear, in real time, about simultaneous actions taking place all over the country.

### WHO'S GOT THE BANNER?

Text messaging and calling from the ubiquitous mobile phone are now routine at demonstrations. I can't think how I ever met friends at demos before. How did we marry up the person bringing the banner with the person with the poles? Interestingly, the failure rate of mobiles during demonstrations has led to widespread rumours about mobile networks being deliberately jammed.

The instant nature of new technology means we can organise quickly and effectively. I was at a public meeting in Brighton organised at a few days' notice just after the bombing started in the Afghanistan War in 2002. Two or three individuals had called it with no existing campaign group behind it. At a critical juncture in a fluid and almost chaotic meeting attended by 90 people, it was possible to establish the rudimentary elements of a campaign there and then. During the meeting a call by mobile phone was made to arrange to use an existing local activist website <www.not4profit. org.uk> as the information point. The website address was then announced to the meeting so that participants with ideas for campaign actions could send in details. Over the following few days activities proposed on the website included a daily vigil, press interviews, stalls and plans for direct action. The moderator of the website agreed to do daily updates. What in earlier years would have necessitated several further meetings and endless dialogue was accomplished during the initial gathering itself.

## ACTION EXCHANGE WEBSITE

A linked website was used during the run-up to the 2003 TJM activities mentioned above. The TJM campaign was organised by a coalition of over 40 national NGOs, church groups, unions and campaign groups. The aim was to lobby every MP in the UK over a period of 24 hours. Local groups were urged to plan stunts and photo opportunities in order to gain maximum local and national media coverage. Any individual or local group with an idea for an event was encouraged to put the details onto the 'Action Exchange' web page of their own national organisation, in my case the World Development Movement (WDM). So, by going to the 'Action Exchange' web page of Christian Aid, Friends of the Earth, WDM or Oxfam, it was possible to see the same entries for groups all over the UK, outlining plans for events as they developed. In our case it enabled local members of Oxfam, Christian Aid and CAFOD to find out about WDM's events in Brighton and join the lobby of MPs and the 'Scale up for Trade Justice' beach stunt.

## MOBILISING FOR WORLD SUMMITS VIA THE INTERNET

In this discussion I have described the impact of a range of electronic campaigning tools. However, the occasions when power of internet campaigning really struck home for me was in the lead up to my participation at the World Bank/IMF summit in Prague in 2000, the G8 summit in Genoa in 2001 and the European Social Forum in Florence in 2002. Before setting off I was able to log on to get daily updates and warnings about how to overcome border controls and police harassment from activists already there. The websites appealed for help with specialist skills such as legal observers, translators and photographers and also gave details about developments as they unfolded. They provided legal briefings and accommodation addresses and other practical advice, all updated daily and translated into many different languages. Logging on before and after the summits was heady stuff. It reinforced my sense of international solidarity and my belief in the potential power of what seems to be a growing global social movement.

## MARGINALISING OFFLINE ACTIVISTS

However, while many older activists are wedded to the computer, some are not. We have found the digital divide is a real barrier to the continued involvement of non-computerised members of our local WDM group. Email contact is now our main method of communication with newsletters being posted to members only a few times a year. I think the ease and low cost of email makes this process irreversible. The challenge for us is how we avoid marginalising offline activists.

## TRADING ON MY ROLE AS GRANDMOTHER TO GET MEDIA INTEREST

I am much more attuned to the media implications of campaign actions than I was in the 1960s and 1970s. This reflects a widespread recognition by activists that successful use of the media is essential in order to be effective. I sometimes trade on my role as grandmother to get media interest. I produced press releases as a member of the local WDM group, before, during and after participating in international mass action such as at Prague and Genoa. In Prague, I took my mobile phone for live interviews with local radio stations or local press. I sent bulletins and updates by email to the local newspaper, the *Brighton and Hove Argus*, from an internet café there. A live telephone interview with Independent Radio News (IRN) was conducted from a call box in Prague, surrounded by thousands of very volatile demonstrators, one of whom climbed on the top of the call box to rock it. With helicopters droning above and chanting almost obliterating my voice, this was action-reporting indeed. Describing myself as 'grandmother and peaceful protester', I was trying to counteract the global media portrayal of all protesters as violent anarchists or mindless 'grungies'.

## SAILING TO GENOA IN A DINGHY

Another example of an ambitious attempt to attract media interest involved a boat stunt before the Genoa Summit. Media preoccupation with possible violence at the G8 Summit in 2001 and the Italian government's attempt to stop protesters from entering Italy provided the peg for a successful action leading to national and local television and radio coverage including *Newsnight* on BBC2. As our bookings for travel to Genoa by train and coach had been cancelled following intimidation of transport companies by the Italian government, Brighton and Hove WDM issued a press release stating that we would set off for Genoa from Brighton beach in an inflatable dinghy! Although organised by our group, the stunt had the support of a group called the Brighton Collective, which included people involved with Globalise Resistance and individuals with anarchist leanings. The combination of a humorous stunt by the seaside with the opportunity to interview people who might talk on camera about the case for forceful protest in Genoa clearly attracted the media. Although the coverage of the stunt in most media was brief, on *Newsnight* it formed part of a balanced and informative in-depth feature on the economic and social policies of the G8.

## AGEING ACTIVISTS HAVE ENERGY AND CONFIDENCE

So, I am part of a significant cohort of ageing activists. Although understandably, many older people prefer to lobby, write letters and attend local meetings rather than demonstrate, an increasing number of participants at world summit protests are older people. Some are veteran campaigners, others are from church groups. I have also met significant numbers of older people relatively new to political activism. These are people who, on ending full time work or child rearing, re-evaluate their lives and develop a passion to try to leave the world a better place. They throw themselves into a flurry of activity, chairing meetings, note taking, coordinating lobbies or responding to email petitions. With families behind us, we have the energy, confidence and experience to make a big contribution to the new global social movement plus the time and often the money to travel to international mass actions.

# Part II

# Global Activism and Mainstream Media

# 6
# Dying for Diamonds: The Mainstream Media and the NGOs – A Case Study of ActionAid

*Ivor Gaber and Alice Wynne Willson*

In this chapter we address the issue of how national and international non-governmental organisations – campaign groups, aid organisations, etc. – can influence the international media and hence the international debate. It is in two sections: the first puts the current international media system within an historical context and looks at the key debates which have surrounded the north/south divide as they relate to the activities of NGOs; the second section moves from the broadly theoretical into how one particular international NGO has sought to use this understanding of the global media system to intervene better in debates in the international arena.

Our starting point is the notion that there is such a phenomenon as an international 'public sphere'. Whatever its merits as a descriptor in a national context, at the international level it clearly has major shortcomings. The most obvious is that the gross inequalities between nations makes the notion of equality of access – one of Habermas's key definers – risible. The voice of the United States dominates the international media with the voices of the other elite nations of the north also being heard, though at a far lower volume. But the voices of the remaining countries of the world – the vast majority – are, to all intents and purposes, silent.

Nonetheless, in formulating what we perceive to be 'international public opinion', no matter how deformed, the Habermasian characterisation is a helpful way of theorising the nature of the space within which this international conversation takes place. Moreover, it is into this space that the NGO that wishes to make its voice heard must operate. But any discussion about the international public sphere cannot take place without placing it in the context of the earlier debates about the New World Information and Communication Order (NWICO) that dominated, and almost destroyed, the United Nations Educational, Scientific and Cultural Organisation (UNESCO) in the 1970s and 1980s. For it was this debate that first defined the problem outlined above and groped towards solutions that might, on the face of it, have appeared attractive to those seeking to influence the international public sphere.

To understand the debate one has to go back to the 1960s to a time when the initial optimistic assumptions about the benefits of decolonisation had begun to wane and politicians, academics and others began to ponder the causes of continuing underdevelopment. The initial focus of the debate was on the structure of international capitalism and the existing trading relations between the north and the south. This led to the United Nations and its agencies conceiving the notion of a 'New World International Economic Order', as a way of grappling with the gross distortions in the world's economic structures and trade relations that seemed to be perpetuating the imbalances between the rich north and the poor south. Out of this analysis grew a linked critique about similar distortions in the world's international news and information resources. In summary, advocates of the NWICO claimed that the world's media was dominated by news organisations, and specifically the then big four international news agencies – Associated Press (AP), United Press International (UPI) based in the United States, Britain's Reuters and Agence France Presse. The advocates argued that these organisations routinely ignored news from the south unless it concerned wars, famines or other natural or man-made disasters. Hence, the world's media created and reproduced negative stereotypes of the south which were transmitted not just to audiences in the north but also to those in the south as well.

Out of this analysis, which most scholars would accept as unexceptional, grew NWICO's somewhat more controversial 'solutions', central to which was the notion that sovereign states had the right to control the flow of information moving in and out their borders. In effect this would have given approval to governments, not all of whom could claim an undying commitment to democratic values, to control what news and information reached their citizens from the outside world and would also have enabled them to control what the outside world learnt about events inside their own borders. This argument was packaged under the label of 'developmental journalism' – the idea being that the media should be contributing to the process of development as much as any other part of society. This was a seductive notion but behind it lay the inescapable fact that the concept provided governments with the justification to censor the flow of both incoming and outgoing news and to ban journalists and news organisations that it did not believe were contributing to its 'developmental process'. Such restrictions would have made it virtually impossible for NGOs working in the international public sphere to undertake any meaningful media activities without the full-hearted approval of their host governments. If they were seen to be providing information that suggested criticism of a host government, they would have found it extremely difficult to continue national or international campaigning activity in that particular country.

The NWICO debate, principally within UNESCO, began in 1970 and raged through the organisation culminating in the withdrawal from the agency of the United States and then the United Kingdom and Singapore in the mid-1980s. International media organisations argued strongly against the NWICO proposals, both from the perspective of protecting their own commercial interests, but also in defence of broader issues of freedom of expression. However, the lead in the campaign against NWICO was taken by a US-based right-wing think-tank, the Heritage Foundation, partly funded by the Australian media magnate Rupert Murdoch – although it has to be said that the governments of President Reagan and Margaret Thatcher did not need a great deal of persuading to convince them of the value of leaving UNESCO – striking a significant blow against the whole concept of 'collectivism' upon which the United Nations system is based.

So what of the situation today? Whilst the concept of 'developmental journalism' might now be discredited, the analysis at the heart of NWICO remains not just intact but if anything even more relevant. The imbalances in international news flows have intensified as a result of the collapse of the Soviet Union, massive technological development in the media and the impacts of globalisation and media concentration. Today, even more so than at the time of the NWICO debates, the single most important medium for distributing news to audiences both in the north and the south is television. The changes in the international distribution of television news over the last 30 years have been dramatic. Perhaps the single most important change is that in 1970 there was no such thing as all-news television channels – now the world (or at least its hotels, airports and newsrooms) would sound unnaturally quiet without the constant murmur of CNN and other international newscasts, humming away in the background.

CNN, which is part of the world's largest media conglomerate – AOL Time Warner – now operates in Spanish, Turkish, German and Japanese and claims a potential audience of 1 billion in some 200 countries. Its daily audience is many times smaller but undoubtedly it does reach international opinion formers on a daily basis and when the world's attention is gripped by a major news event, then millions do switch to CNN. But there are other international 24-hour television news providers. Fox News (part of Rupert Murdoch's News Corporation) and the BBC's World Channel provide 24-hour news coverage to global audiences from an American and British perspective. In Europe 24-hour news channels available include Sky News (also part of News Corporation), ITV News (operated by ITN on behalf of UK commercial broadcasters), Deutsche Welle (operated by the German public broadcaster ARD) and EuroNews, operated by the major broadcasters of the European Union (excluding the British).

In the Middle East Al Jazeera, based in Qatar, has established itself as an important source of news and now faces competition from a second Arabic station, Al Arabia, based in Bahrain. In Asia, News Corporation broadcasts 24-hour news on its Star News Channel and this competes with the Indian-owned Zee News, part of the Zee network. All news TV channels are also operated by the state-owned China Central Television and by CNA (Cable News Asia) which is backed by the government of Singapore. In Latin America Brazil's TV Globo operates the Globo News 24-hour news channel. In addition to these general news services the American-owned Bloomberg TV and CNBC offer 24-hour news channels focusing on financial news to a worldwide audience. Inside the United States CNN competes for the 24-hour news audience, not just with Fox but also with NBC's own all-news station – MSNBC – which it operates jointly with Microsoft.

In terms of international television news these are the 'retail' news outlets; equally as important are the world's major international news 'inputters'. These include the domestic television networks of the North (the BBC, CBS, etc.) and the world's news 'wholesalers', the news agencies – which have an inter-dependent relationship with the broadcasters. The two major television news agencies are Reuters TV and Associated Press TV (APTV) which are also the world's leading international news agencies (and bore the brunt of much of the NWICO attack 30 years ago). Reuters TV claims that its daily news feeds have a potential reach of 1.5 billion whilst APTV, through its 500 client stations, claims a potential reach of over 1 billion. Reuters TV and APTV are both based in London and work closely with the home broadcasters, the BBC and ITN, and with the American networks – CBS, NBC and ABC – whose international headquarters are also in London.

Within this Anglo-Saxon nexus crucial decisions are made, on an hour-by-hour basis, about what are the 'big stories of the day' are and how they should be interpreted. The news agencies have clients in virtually every country of the globe but overwhelmingly their most important clients are in the north, and specifically in the US and UK, and they are not only the most important clients but are also key suppliers, making available to the agencies foreign coverage of their own. CNN, which also has its international base in London, acts as both a customer and supplier to the agencies and in addition supplies material direct to broadcasters as well as direct to consumers.

In other words, a large percentage of the world's international television news is generated as a result of decisions taken in London and New York and is distributed by news organisations that are largely owned by northern interests. This inevitably means that decisions about news priorities are being made on the basis of the priorities and judgements of the broadcasters of the north. This does not mean that these decisions and the criteria being used to make them are explicitly aimed at enhancing northern interests, but they are taken from this perspective and, to a large extent, with a largely domestic northern audience in mind. Inevitably, this means that story selection and approach is unlikely to be seen by audiences in the south as addressing their interests or relating to their lives.

All of these trends have made it harder, but also easier, for NGOs to make their voices heard in the international public sphere. Marshall McLuhan's well-worn aphorism about the existence of the global village conceals as much as it reveals. For whilst, on the one hand, the trends towards concentration and globalisation, in terms of the mass media, have given the phrase a revitalised currency, it is a currency that is not freely available to all. For if the NWICO debate highlighted the unequal flow of information between north and south, the intervening years have seen an intensification of that unevenness – a growth in the ubiquity of northern media which has led to greater access to the products of the north by audiences in the south, but also, concomitantly, the creation of more opportunities for NGOs to access these media and reach northern and southern audiences with their messages.

One approach that NGOs could take would be to reject the news values and news agendas of the north and seek to persuade the international media to adopt a more southern-focused approach. This might be an appropriate strategy for media reform campaigners but, for those who need to work with the international media – as it is now rather than how it might be at some indeterminate time in the future – it would be a strategy of impotence. The news values of the western media, for good or ill, are now ubiquitous – they infiltrate every society whether directly through outlets such as CNN or the BBC, indirectly via the news agencies, or, at one stage removed, through the output of the local media which largely follow the journalistic precepts of the north – because many journalists and editors working in the south have immersed themselves in these values either as a result of undergoing training by northern news organisations or by observing, absorbing and replicating the news cultures and values of these organisations.

NGOs have to recognise that in a world where governments and corporations devote vast resources to managing their images, the mainstream media is the international public sphere. Working with the media can help NGOs to intervene in negotiations, influence international conversations, to inspire action and change policies and practice. Media coverage offers NGOs a fast-track means of building public support and leveraging political will. The knowledge that media regularly give coverage to what a particular NGO says, or does, strengthens immeasurably the impact the organisation might have in closed-door meetings.

So while NGOs do produce their own websites and magazines and support the development of alternative media voices, in terms of audience, these activities tend to amount to little more than preaching to the converted. To influence decision-makers and achieve their campaigning goals, NGOs must – as part of their advocacy strategy – engage with international news outlets and agencies. How effective that engagement is depends to a great extent on their understanding of news values. With that understanding comes an inevitable pressure for campaigners to seek to maximise their creativity in conveying their messages; to use existing news values to move the debate on and challenge preconceptions. One example of this is the work of ActionAid, an international NGO, in campaigning against the use of diamonds to fund civil war and unrest in Africa.

## ACTIONAID'S CAMPAIGN: DYING FOR DIAMONDS

ActionAid is one of the UK's largest development charities. It works in partnership with poor communities in Africa, Asia, Latin America and the Caribbean to address the root causes of poverty as well as its devastating effects. This involves raising challenging questions around the HIV/AIDS epidemic, food insecurity, international trade rules, access to education and war and conflict. It involves finding creative local solutions but also highlighting problems, making global connections and showing where responsibility and power lies in order to change the situation. It involves ensuring voices from the developing world are heard in international debates, especially where the decisions made will affect their future. Working with the media is a crucial part of the ActionAid 'toolkit'.

In October 2002, ActionAid's 'Dying for Diamonds' campaign featured a small but original demonstration designed to influence key players in the international diamond arena. The protest caught the attention of diamond industry representatives as they arrived at a meeting; on a grey day in London, who could fail to notice 'Marilyn Monroe', dressed in pink satin singing 'Diamonds are a Girl's Best Friend'? And the fact that it generated extensive media

*Photo 2*   Dying for Diamonds Campaign: Marilyn (Nick Cobbing/ActionAid, 2002)

coverage, amplifying the campaign message, meant it could not be ignored.

Conflict diamonds are the rough diamonds that fund war and human rights abuses in Africa. They are portable, anonymous and easily smuggled. Over the last decade an estimated US$300–400 million worth of them have been bought and sold each year. ActionAid campaigners provided statistics to illustrate the human cost of the illicit trade. These included the estimates that wars funded by the trade in 'conflict diamonds' had:

- left 1.5 million homeless in Liberia;
- caused the deaths of 2.5 million killed in the Democratic Republic of the Congo;
- led to the abduction of 10,000 children in Sierra Leone; and
- resulted in 90,000 amputees in Angola.

These statistics were featured on diamond-shaped placards carried by the protesters surrounding 'Marilyn' and were repeated in campaign literature and media interviews. The death, poverty and suffering caused by wars fuelled, in part, by conflict diamonds is something ActionAid understands intimately through its rehabilitation, peace building and development work with communities in West Africa.

With the aim of ending the trade in conflict diamonds, governments, the diamond industry and NGOs, including ActionAid, in 2000 started a series of United Nations-backed negotiations called the Kimberley Process, named after the South African diamond-mining centre. Negotiators agreed to introduce a certification process for diamonds in January 2003. The system included provisions for tracking the international trade in rough stones. This was to be complemented by a self-regulatory scheme against conflict diamonds for the jewellery business.

During the last few months of 2002, as negotiations drew to an end, ActionAid's delegate to the Kimberley Process became increasingly concerned that the diamond industry was unprepared for the official start of the tracking scheme. The industry body – the World Diamond Council – had failed to produce any written guidelines and NGOs feared that the Kimberley Process would grind to a halt before tracking had even started. Having engaged in lobbying and related media work on conflict diamonds for two years, ActionAid felt it was time for a short, sharp, awareness-raising push that would get the diamond industry to take tracking seriously.

The key campaign targets were the World Diamond Council, the British Jewellers Association and the National Association of Goldsmiths. A secondary but influential target was the UK public.

The campaign objectives were to:

1. Shame the diamond industry into adopting, publishing and disseminating a strong self-regulation scheme. (For media purposes campaigners called this a 'code of conduct'.)
2. Raise retailer awareness that conflict diamonds are a problem that could hit them where it hurts (i.e., affect their sales) and that they should be ready for introduction of the code of conduct in January 2003.
3. Raise awareness that members of the public can and should ask their jewellers to confirm that any diamonds they are buying are conflict-free.

The World Diamond Congress represented an important influencing opportunity and potential media peg. This biennial meeting of industry leaders from around the world was due to be held in London in October 2002, followed by a meeting of the Kimberley Process a month later in Switzerland. At the World Diamond Congress meeting, key industry players – the International Diamond Manufacturers Association and the World Federation of Diamond Bourses – were to decide whether to adopt the code of conduct. Campaigners needed to ensure that delegates saw the trade in conflict diamonds as a problem and that a strong code of conduct would be part of the solution. An important tactic was to reach those parts of the media that delegates, and their industry colleagues, would be watching, listening to and reading. This meant in particular the international media that would be consumed by delegates ensconced in their hotel rooms in London and Switzerland.

The campaign push comprised two key elements, both with media potential. First, research was commissioned to test awareness levels amongst UK jewellery retailers of the Kimberley Process. Its findings were startling:

- no jeweller on the high street mentioned the Kimberley Process;
- few retailers were even aware of conflict diamonds;

- there was a tendency to misinform customers, with sales staff assuming that gemmological certificates guaranteed that stones were conflict free. (In fact a gemmological certificate provides proof of quality, not source.)

The research was published in the form of a glossy report. This was sent to media (and diamond industry representatives) with a press release highlighting the general lack of preparedness for the introduction of the Kimberley Process and the key findings of ActionAid's 'mystery shopper' who had asked UK jewellers what they knew about conflict diamonds. By releasing original research that linked conflict diamonds to high street shops and UK consumer rights, ActionAid provided a news angle for business editors and consumer affairs correspondents and a serious backdrop for the second, more populist element of the campaign. The report also helped to emphasise their spokesperson's credibility as a commentator on the issue.

With limited time and money campaigners planned a small, concept-led demonstration designed to grab attention and provide a focal point for photographers and camera crews. Campaigner Mark Lattimer, in the 'Campaigning Handbook', sums up the rationale for using this type of action:

> The influence of the mass media has radically altered the art of the demonstration. Small-scale, high impact stunts are now used to reach the huge audiences that a few column inches or broadcast seconds can bring. Highly visual, they pack at least as much media appeal as a mass demonstration, but at a fraction of the cost and effort.

The challenge for ActionAid campaigners was to make the action distinctive and ensure it had the right tone, look and feel. Imagery employed by conflict diamonds campaigners had thus far been shocking: pictures of women and babies with amputated limbs or stylishly clever twists on classic diamond jewellery advertising. ActionAid was seeking something bold and creative that had a sense of humour but would immediately engage members of the diamond industry and not enrage or alienate them.

One idea was to involve a famous diamond-wearer. It was felt 'celebrity' would bring that touch of glamour to the proceedings that the delegates themselves would applaud. It would also boost the media currency of the stunt and show the jewellery industry that customers (including their high-profile ones) cared.

A brainstorm of internationally recognisable diamond-wearing celebrities turned up a handful of names including rapper P Diddy, footballer David Beckham, actress Liz Taylor and model Iman (who at the time was the star of an advertising campaign for diamond giant De Beers). It was hard to imagine any one of them clearing their diaries to carry placards and hand out leaflets on a wet October morning, especially with less than a month's notice. And even if they could, which one of them would best complement the campaign action?

In fact there was no competition, the most appropriate celebrity was a dead one: Marilyn Monroe who in *Gentlemen Prefer Blondes* became the ultimate diamond-wearing icon. Who can forget the scene where she descends a magnificent staircase in a pink satin evening dress and matching gloves, set off by some of the most serious rocks in the business, singing 'Diamonds are a Girl's Best Friend' and attended by a small army of dancing men in top hat and tails?

So, Marilyn Monroe look-a-like Lorelie Lee joined ActionAid campaigners (who were clad in top hat and tails) to make a song and dance about conflict diamonds outside the World Diamond Congress. The all-singing all-dancing protesters held placards drawing attention to the abductions, mutilations and deaths that follow the trade in conflict diamonds, and lobbied delegates on the need for industry action.

When it came to media coverage, 'Marilyn' stole the show. Good footage can mean the difference between a good story being transmitted or not and with a picture opportunity like this, the news value of ActionAid's story shot up. Lorelie Lee was also a Monroe sing-a-like so the action had a distinctive audio component, giving radio reporters just as much material as photographers and camera crews. The final touch was to provide an 'expert' to give media interviews – someone with in-depth knowledge of the Kimberley process that could convey ActionAid's messages with authority in simple accessible terms, and hold her own in the face of tough questioning. In their highly experienced policy officer, Amboka Wameyo, ActionAid put their best foot forward. Amongst a largely white male and balding crop of media 'experts', Amboka, a striking Kenyan woman, was memorable as a strong positive voice from the developing world.

The broadcast results were impressive. The action and glossy diamonds report were covered on BBC Breakfast TV's business bulletins; CNN produced a news feature that was shown on their business programmes throughout the two days of the conference. BBC Radio stations 2, 4 and 5 all reported the story on their breakfast programmes, Radio 4's agenda-setting *Today* programme featured a debate between Amboka Wameyo and the head of the World Diamond Council. Coverage continued on BBC Wales and Scotland's lunchtime radio news programmes and local radio stations. International and business radio stations and websites picked up the story via newswire services including Bloomberg and Reuters.

The story was covered by the UK's national news agency – the Press Association – and was used by UK national papers, the *Guardian, Metro* and the *Financial Times*. A wide number of weekly and regional publications also covered the story. Particularly important was an article and an editorial comment piece in the December and January issues of RJ (Retail Jeweller magazine), the monthly trade publication for the UK's diamond industry. The editorial called on the jewellery trade to get its act together otherwise ActionAid would continue to put pressure on the industry.

Media coverage, together with campaign literature and direct lobbying by 'Marilyn' and the campaigners outside the World Diamond Congress, had a big impact on delegates. Many joined the ranks of the press 'snappers' and took photographs of 'Marilyn' and her pals, but more important was the realisation that they needed to take clear action on the issue of conflict diamonds. Feedback from delegates indicates that NGO efforts (specifically the protests outside the meeting) were crucial in getting the industry to pass the code of conduct and in influencing key speakers to make strong statements on the importance of preventing conflict diamond trading. For campaigners this represented an advocacy victory – an important step towards the goal of ending the trade in conflict diamonds.

Members of the British Jewellers Association told campaigners that the ActionAid report alerted them, for the first time, to the fact that manufacturers and retailers have a role to play in the implementation of the tracking system. Media coverage and public awareness of the issue provided extra impetus for them to take their role seriously by appealing not just to their conscience, but also their business sense. As one delegate remarked: 'Every time we switched on CNN there were the demonstrators with charity spokespeople talking about jewellers' complacency.' A survey undertaken for ActionAid showed that awareness of conflict diamonds had risen amongst the UK general public from 9 per cent in 2001 to 25 per cent at the beginning of 2003. Additionally, 70 per cent of the

jewellery-buying public stated that they would not want to purchase
diamonds that were not conflict free.

By the close of the final meeting of the Kimberley Process, a
month after the World Diamond Congress, the diamond industry
had endorsed the certificate scheme for rough diamonds that had
been produced and signed by governments. Industry representatives
also agreed to make public their system of self-regulation for cut
diamonds and jewellery and to produce a written code of conduct.

Operation Marilyn was well timed and perfectly pitched. It enabled
campaigners to intervene in the international public sphere by engaging the media and thus influencing diamond industry decision-
makers. Its success must be viewed against the backdrop of an
ActionAid campaign that had already spanned two years. ActionAid
itself was just one NGO in an international network of organisations
working on the issue. The joint efforts of all those involved in the
Kimberley process – the UN, governments, diamond industry, NGOs
and the journalists who have investigated and reported the problem –
had already succeeded in raising the profile of conflict diamonds.

The Monroe stunt worked because, held up to close scrutiny, it
had depth and credibility. It was informed by an understanding of
how the international public sphere, at least that part of the sphere
that was concerned with the global trade in diamonds, operated.
Campaigners were aware how the issue of conflict diamonds had
been addressed over time, the key players involved and the roles
that governments and institutions, traders and consumers needed to
play to make the Kimberley process effective. Through decades of
work with communities affected by conflict and poverty in Africa,
ActionAid also had first hand experience of how people were being
affected by diamond-fuelled wars.

While ActionAid had engaged in its own research and lobbying,
in-depth knowledge of the policy environment was only achieved
through collaboration with other organisations such as Global
Witness, a small but feisty NGO engaged in painstaking documentation of the trade in conflict diamonds, oil and timber. As part of a
campaigning network, ActionAid set specific short-term objectives
aimed at helping achieve the goal of ending the trade in conflict diamonds and the poverty and suffering it caused. Together with Global
Witness and Amnesty International, ActionAid identified target
audiences, sought out opportunities to influence them and established how each organisation could contribute to the campaign.

Towards the end of 2002 the immediate objective had been to ensure that the diamond industry adopted a code of conduct (self-regulation) and was prepared for the imminent introduction of a scheme tracking the international trade in rough diamonds. The key influencing opportunity was the World Diamond Congress, where representatives of the diamond industry from around the world would gather. The location – London – is an important hub for the diamond trade but also for the world's leading news agencies and broadcasters.

Whilst NGOs were able to deliver written information direct to delegates detailing their concerns and recommending action, to be really persuasive these messages needed to be repeated and amplified in order to make a powerful impact with delegates and reach out to potential customers as well as those engaged in the diamond trade. Media coverage was the key – achieving it in a highly competitive news environment required creativity, a good grasp of news values, well-timed delivery and a reasonable dose of luck. At the time of writing, an international tracking scheme for rough diamonds has been launched and the industry has adopted a system of self-regulation. The next challenge is to push the industry to introduce a scheme of regular impartial monitoring of all Kimberly Process member countries.

### CONCLUSION

ActionAid's Marilyn Monroe stunt was just one part of ongoing international advocacy work on conflict diamonds involving different processes, operating on differing time scales. One consideration that NGOs have to bear in mind, when conceptualising their engagement with the international public sphere, is that some of these processes do benefit from exposure in the international media while others, involving sensitive negotiations, can potentially be harmed by it.

When seeking media coverage, campaigners must rise to the creative challenge of turning an ongoing process into a potential news story. In 'activist media' (such as websites or newsletters produced by campaigners themselves) coverage can be guaranteed and messages perfectly controlled, but when it comes to influence and audience size, it simply cannot compete with mainstream media coverage. Success in providing stories or angles that both meet journalists' requirements and highlight their own campaigning agendas gives NGOs an opportunity to harness the power of mainstream media and amplify their voice in the international public sphere. Used well it can help campaigners to motivate large numbers of people, hold the few up to the public scrutiny of many and shame the powerful into change.

## FURTHER READING

Boyd-Barrett, O. and T. Rantanen (eds) (1999) *The Globalisation of News*, London: Sage

Boyd-Barrett, O. (1992) *Contra-Flow in Global News*, Paris: UNESCO.

—— (1980) *The International News Agencies*, London: Sage

Chapman, G., K. Kumar, C. Fraser and I. Gaber (1997) *Environmentalism and the Mass Media: The North South Divide*, London: Routledge

Curran, J. and M. Gurevitch (2000) *Mass Media and Society*, London: Arnold

McBride S. (1980) *Many Voices, One World: Communication and Society Today and Tomorrow*, Paris: UNESCO

McLuhan, Marshall (1989) *The Global Village: Transformations in World Life and Media in the 21st Century*, New York: OUP

Smith, J. (2000) *The Daily Globe: Environmental Change, the Public and the Media'*, London: Earthscan

Thussu, D. (2000) *International Communication – Continuity and Change*, London: Arnold

—— (ed.) (1998) *Electronic Empires – Global Media and Local Resistance*, London: Arnold

# 7

# The Power and Limits of Media-Based International Oppositional Politics – A Case Study: The Brent Spar Conflict

*Wilma de Jong*

In North America, Nike has been at the forefront of the burgeoning political movement taking aim at the power of multinationals, but in Britain, Germany and the Netherlands, that dubious honor has belonged to Royal Dutch/Shell.

(Klein 2000:379)

A new anti-corporatism is on the rise. After the demise of political action in the 1960s and 1970s against, for example, Nestle, Coca-Cola and Exxon, criticism and protest re-emerged in the wake of the 1980s' neo-liberal discourse and the economic policies of western governments, described by Schiller as the 'corporate-take over of public discourse'. The mid-1990s represented a moment in history when a cluster of events reached a climax. At the same time as the Brent Spar conflict was taking place, the McLibel case against another multinational, McDonald's, reached the front page and Shell, once again, was in the limelight being accused of human rights and environmental abuses in the Niger delta in Nigeria. In the second half of the 1990s anti-corporate protest, or what is now referred to as the anti-globalisation movement, took off, with protest events in Seattle, Prague, Genoa as well as at other international meetings of the WTO and the World Bank. Looking back from 2004 it is evident that the mid-1990s was a formative moment when, as in the 1960s, protest again found a voice and diverse activist groups emerged from civil society.

## A CORPORATE NIGHTMARE AND A PRESSURE GROUP'S DREAM

In 1995 a multinational was brought to its knees over a redundant oil storage buoy in the North Sea, the Brent Spar. After three years of

research, taking environmental, financial and safety factors into
account, Shell UK decided that deep-sea disposal was the best
solution. Greenpeace objected to Shell's plans, not only on environmental grounds, but also because the action could set a precedent
for hundreds of redundant oil rigs and installations to be 'dumped'
in the sea. Above all, Greenpeace felt that it was necessary to take a
moral stance to defend the future of our seas. As the drama unfolded,
groups in civil society in Germany, the Netherlands and the
Scandinavian countries protested to Shell and the UK government,
which was supporting the multinational on the grounds of the
legality and scientific credibility of the disposal plans and had
provided Shell with the necessary license. In April and May 1995
the first occupation of the Brent Spar by Greenpeace took place,
followed by legal actions by Shell, and then subsequent removal by
the Grampian police. Greenpeace then reoccupied the Brent Spar
by helicopter, and protest actions at petrol stations and Shell buildings took place in the Netherlands and Germany, which report-
edly included bomb threats directed at Shell buildings and petrol
stations. When Peter Duncan, Shell's German chief executive,
finally issued a press release announcing Shell's U-turn, he declared,
'It cannot go on like this' (press release 20 June) clearly illustrating
Shell's distress and sense of powerlessness.

How was it possible that a multinational could not exercise its
authority, even while being supported by a government? By contrast,
what had made Greenpeace so efficient in communicating its message to the mass media, a message which also spurred groups in civil
society and governments on the continent into action? As Jordan
puts it: 'The puzzle is why the Brent Spar example succeeded where
others failed' (1998:18).

This chapter will focus on the media strategies of Greenpeace and
Shell and on the roles that civil society and national cultures in the
countries involved have played in the articulation and framing of
what was, in the first instance, considered to be an environmental
conflict. I will make two arguments. First, that the perception of
multinationals in both the public and academic imagination as
omnipotent and monolithic appears to be a myth. This case also
seems to undermine the understanding that financial resources are
one of the dominant factors in having access to the media.

Second, that national cultures can enhance or undermine 'global'
or international activism due to the fact that media production is
shaped by national cultures.

Much of the research on the Brent Spar conflict (Bennie 1998; Hansen 2000; Jordan 2001) has been based only on the UK situation. In my view, however, this cannot explain why Greenpeace was successful, since as Jordan and Ridley (1998) and Bennie (1998) note, there was hardly any protest in the UK. Their research concludes that 'a myth of popular protest has grown up. ... A myth of the extent to which there was large-scale concern about the issue, a myth about the mechanics of change, and a myth of the role of the public' (Jordan and Ridley 1998:17). It is highly probable that the Brent Spar would have been dumped if Greenpeace had limited their protest to the UK. Its success remains a puzzle, then, if one limits analysis to the UK and excludes consideration of mass media involvement in the mobilisation of civil society and its role in informing public opinion in the Netherlands and Germany.

This chapter seeks to address this wider international context and is based on a comparative analysis of the press and broadcasting media of the Brent Spar conflict in Germany, the Netherlands and Britain.[1] Both Greenpeace and Shell in these countries have allowed me to use their archives of newspaper articles, broadcasts and press releases, as well as to interview people involved in the campaign. The following section will focus on Greenpeace and Shell as sources for the media and on the interpretative frameworks used by the British, Dutch and German press. This will be followed by a consideration of the effectiveness of media-based oppositional politics in the international public sphere.

## GREENPEACE AND SHELL AS SOURCES FOR THE MEDIA

Research on access of sources to news production (Anderson 1991; Hansen 1993; Deacon 1996; Manning 1998; Cottle 2000) all suggests that in the highly pressurised and ritualised world of news production a clear preference exists for bureaucratic, governmental and corporate sources. Hansen (1993) argues that environmental groups tend to be marginalised from the formal institutive news production process. This process creates a hierarchy of established sources, the government and main political parties guaranteed media attention, followed by corporate organisations and the big unions. Deacon (1996) argues that pressure groups have to work very hard to convince journalists of the legitimacy of their claims and to convince them that they not just 'pestiferous minorities'. He maintains that those organisations with professional press officers in contact with the relevant political arenas are the most successful. His argument neglects the fact, however, that pressure groups not only need sophisticated media strategies to overcome their structural weakness in the news production process but also to take advantage of one of the dominant characteristics of current news production: the hunt for visually attractive events, to gain access to news media. In the case of the Brent Spar conflict, Greenpeace, an experienced mass media communicator, embarked on a systematic strategy to target the media in different countries. Journalists were invited to climb on board its vessels or attend specific events. In addition, press releases, video and photographic material were sent to press agencies, news papers and broadcasters. All of these actions secured media coverage, not only because of their 'visual' appeal, but also because they coincided with the occurrence of important events in the political arena, such as the Esbjerg conference on the future of the North Sea (June 1995), where the governments involved would discuss the Brent Spar conflict.

In all three countries the press paid comparable attention to this conflict. The Dutch papers published 106 articles, the German 95 and the British 86 during the period studied. Although the UK published fewer articles, news broadcasts were more intensive and, in my sample, broadcast news was far more favourable towards Greenpeace than was the press. Considering the conservative nature of the press landscape in the UK this is not surprising. Moreover, a MORI (Market and Opinion Research Institute) survey at the time of the Brent Spar conflict reported that notwithstanding unfavourable press coverage, 63 per cent of the population agreed that Greenpeace 'had won the argument' and supported its case.

Although most of Greenpeace's actions tended to be reported, its arguments were used in a more limited and determining way. Both in the Netherlands and in Germany Greenpeace reiterated environmental arguments in its press releases. The Brent Spar was referred to as a 'toxic refuge dump' (press release Germany 19 April), or 'toxic waste mountain' (press release Germany 3 May). The media, however, had already decided these arguments were no longer valid. The environmental argument was further undermined when the media reported that Greenpeace's scientific research on the 'toxic' content of the Brent Spar was false; Greenpeace's subsequent admission undermined their credibility. It has been argued that environmental groups' alliance with science in particular enables them to achieve greater success than that of other groups (Greenberg 1985;

Eyerman and Jamison 1989; Hansen 1993). Greenpeace's alliance with science has been highly contested, and not only in this case. Anderson reports that even in 1991 nine out of twelve British journalists interviewed expressed doubts about Greenpeace. As a reporter from the *Independent*, who had decided not to read its literature any more, expressed it, 'It will be wrong in its science, its evidence or its balance' (Anderson 1991:471). In 1995, journalists in three countries collectively decided that this was again the case. One Dutch journalist fumed about their scientific arguments 'heavy metals and radioactive materials ... the chimeras of overheated activists' (*NRC* 15 June). Instead, media coverage emphasised different aspects of the range of arguments Greenpeace offered, such as the slogan 'the sea is not a garbage bin' and its fear that the dumping of the Brent Spar could be a precedent for the other 400 redundant oil platforms in the North Sea.

The occupation of the Brent Spar took Shell UK by surprise and it was an even bigger surprise for Shell Netherlands and Shell Germany. Within the organisational structure, Dutch or German branches are not involved in any of the research or decisions made in the UK and, therefore, the responsibility for media and public relations belonged to Shell UK. One of the Dutch public relations officers facing journalists described Shell NL, during a conference on crisis management in The Hague in January 1997, as 'an organisation in a crisis not caused by us and not managed by us'. As a consequence Shell NL used Shell UK's press releases and never published its own. Shell Germany only published two press releases. In short, Shell's media strategies were actually undermined by its own internal structure and lack of coordination between the companies in the different countries and this could explain why Shell was slow and reactive in its media approach.

A closer examination of Shell's press releases reveals further problems. First, press releases seemed to have been published after discussion had taken place in the newspapers, with the result that they tended to be outdated at the moment of release. For example, on 13 June the UK press discussed a leaked report of an offshore company, Smit Engineering, and the possibilities and costs of onshore disposal. Shell's press release addressing this issue was not released until 16 June, by which time the debate had moved on.

Second, almost all of 18 press releases of Shell UK related to the content of the Brent Spar and Shell's policies. In other words, Shell's press releases often seemed to emphasise its own, often highly technical, perspective and did not take into account the issues that were being debated in the public domain.

Third, Shell undermined its own media access by not releasing its press releases on a website and by relying largely on telephone or face-to-face contact. This did not always prove successful since, as Palmer notes, 'no comment' (Palmer 2001) appeared to be a regularly occurring answer. In contrast, Greenpeace offered daily updates and an ongoing diary on their highly acclaimed website, which has won numerous national and international prizes. Shell did not have a website.

In addition to these weaknesses, in Germany Shell was undermined by its own personnel and gave the public impression of being a divided organisation. Both Shell management and Shell *Betriebsrat* (Council of Employees) released public documents and it is important to pay attention to the *Betriebsrat* because from day one it expressed employees' doubts about the decisions of Shell UK. The *Betriebsrat* even wrote a letter to Greenpeace expressing its sympathy with the occupation of the Brent Spar, but explained that, within the organisational structure of the multinational, Shell Germany had no voting or discussion rights concerning matters arising in other countries. Its attitude subsequently hardened and it accused the media and Greenpeace of deliberately representing Shell as an 'abstract organisation' without 'real' human beings working there. The employees argued: 'Greenpeace as well as politicians and the evangelical church are thoughtlessly prepared to sacrifice the livelihood of many people' (16 June).

Finally, Shell's advertising strategy appeared to lack coherence and conviction. At the time of the Brent Spar conflict, Shell ran a commercial in Germany which emphasised their social responsibilities as a multinational. This commercial made it on to the main evening news broadcast of ZDF (Zweites Deutsches Fernsehen) (3 May) and was labelled as an 'advertising slogan'. Subsequently Shell withdrew the commercial from television. In the UK a national campaign ran on the theme of social responsibility, and this too was withdrawn. In the Netherlands Shell published an advertisement in all national newspapers in an attempt to give their argument more prominence. However, the advertisement deployed a technical drawing of the Brent Spar and the accompanying text explained in too technical terms why deep-sea disposal was defensible.

Again by contract Greenpeace published advertisements in all three countries, which supported their point of view and used very mediagenic slogans, 'Soon Shell is the only Shell in the North sea', or 'A better environment start with you and finishes with Shell'. In short, while Greenpeace embarked on a proactive and sophisticated action strategy to gain media coverage, Shell often failed to get its press releases out on time or escape from its own highly technical perspective. Shell's complaints about being misunderstood seem understandable in this light.

## THE MEDIA'S INTERPRETATIVE FRAMEWORKS

Media frames, largely unspoken and unacknowledged, organise the world both for journalists who report it, and in some important degree for us who rely on their reports. (Gitlin 1980:7)

The debate regarding media frameworks has a long history (Goffman 1974) and above all foregrounds that through a process of selection, emphasis, exclusion and/or elaboration an event comes into being and is integrated into existing discourses. As Dunwoody and Griffin put it, 'Frameworks are the mental maps journalists routinely deploy as interpretative filters. It is the central organising idea for news that supplies context and suggests what the real issue is' (1993:24).

The emphasis in this concept is on the role of the media, that is, the journalists. Recent changes in the perception of media frames as a process in which the media, and their stakeholders interact has proved to be essential for this research (Mc Nair 1994; Miller and Parnell Riechert 2000). The understanding of this concept does not avoid the question of power, but invites the scholar to consider how frameworks may change during the course of a conflict, as well as changes in the relationships between the different stakeholders. In addition, one should also consider, first, that media frames are, in the first instance, the product of national cultures, and second, that a strong tendency exists to create frames of 'us' and 'them' (Van Ginneken 1998). International news may be international in content and brought to the foreground by different sources but the framing of the event will take place within national (media) culture.

### Media frames in the German press

The German press, aligning itself with Greenpeace's stance, initially framed the Brent Spar affair as an environmental concern about the disposal of 'our toxic waste'. However, a moral framework displaced the environmental framework as the dominant means for interpreting events: 'One does not dump one's waste into the sea.' This view, a slogan created by Greenpeace, was expressed both by ordinary people and by politicians across the political spectrum and spread rapidly. Within two weeks, the German public and organisations in civil society were up in arms and, according to the press, politicians were queuing up to express publicly their support for Greenpeace.

In this situation, described by the papers as 'chaotic', an us/them dichotomy emerged. 'Us' was used to signify environmentally-aware people, while 'they' usually identified as 'the English', referred to those environmentally unaware. Shell and the UK merged into one category of the 'other'. As the *Bild Zeitung* put it: 'Those Greenpeace people are defending our sea against them for you' (9 June). Many examples appeared in the press which made it clear that these 'others' were not only an obstacle in the implementation of European environmental policies (*Frankfurter Algemeine Zeitung* (*FAZ*) 6 June), but were also making a 'mess' of their own country. The German press provided in-depth analyses of Britain's air pollution, asthma epidemic and transportation of livestock (*FAZ* 20 June) and argued that 'the Germans have a more developed environmental awareness'. 'The UK wants to use the military against environmentalists' *TAZ* (*Berliner Tages Zeitung*) cried out on 21 June. The British were considered the dirty men of Europe because of what is described by *FAZ* and *TAZ* as their 'island mentality' (6 June). All three papers emphasised the difference in environmental awareness between the UK and Germany and the poor environmental credentials of the UK government. The *FAZ* argued that UK environmentalism focused on animals (*FAZ* 20 June) and strongly emphasised the moral standards argument. One headline read 'The platform of morality is unsinkable' (*FAZ* 20 June 1995).

The strong reaction in civil society in Germany came not only from so-called 'leftwing' organisations, such as environmental groups and unions, but also from church leaders, celebrities, petrol station workers, students and people on the street. *Bild Zeitung*, especially, drew on quotations from an apparently wide range of citizens, all of whom expressed their moral dismay regarding Shell.

One Shell Press Manager described to me how the office in Hamburg had to be evacuated every time a bomb threat was issued. There was increased sickness among Shell employees, who were also challenged and sometimes even harassed in their private lives.

Similar unpleasant personal experiences were reported by Wolfgang Mantow, a Shell PR consultant (Palmer 2000:111). *FAZ* concluded on 21 June, 'A whole nation dances to Greenpeace's tune and the politicians have lost their mind.'

### Media frames in the Dutch press

Initially, Greenpeace's environmental framework was also successfully communicated in the Netherlands. For almost four weeks the Dutch newspapers analysed scientific papers and discussed the issue with various scientists, before concluding: 'Heavy metals, radioactive materials? Chimeras of overheated activists' (*NRC Handelsblad* 18 June). However they argued: 'Rationally, Shell may be right, but that does not mean they are going to get what they want' (*Volkskrant* and *NRC* 18 June). The framework subsequently shifted to a moral one. The seeds for this interpretation were sown by Greenpeace with its slogan, 'The sea is not a garbage bin', which was adopted by the media and subsequently by politicians and the public. All the newspapers drew on quotations from the public and Greenpeace, which centred on the contrast between the responsibility of Dutch citizens in disposing of waste and the lack of responsibility of the multinational: 'We [citizens] have to separate our waste and they [Shell] just dump it.' Similar arguments substantiated this discrepancy in treatment of waste by corporations and citizens: 'We cannot dump our old car wrecks in the IJ [Dutch river]'; 'We even have to pay to dump old cars' (*Telegraaf* 31 May). As the moral framework became more pronounced so did the criticisms of UK environmental attitudes. The *Volkskrant* and the *NRC* branded the UK 'Dirty Men of Europe' (1 June 1995) and the NRC added, 'It smells of oil interests in the British government' (10 June 1995).

The Dutch government, while it had not responded during the legally obligatory consultation process, now conducted several debates in parliament on how to stop deep-sea disposal. Groups in civil society raised their voices through large environmental organisations such as 'Nature and Environment', unions such as the police union and several youth organisations. Whereas Greenpeace gained third party endorsement, several offshore companies and banks undermined Shell's position. Offshore firms issued press releases, arguing that the estimated costs given by Shell for onshore disposal were too high (15 June). Moreover the large merchant bank, Mees and Pierson, argued that £45 million for onshore disposal is 'peanuts' for a company making an estimated profit of £4.6 billion

(*NRC* 15 June) and that the Brent Spar was a test case for the other 200 redundant oil installations in the Brent Spar field. Shell also undermined its own environmental credentials by protesting against a proposal from the Dutch government for an environmental tax on waste disposal in Rotterdam harbour. Shell argued: 'IR J. Slechte: the waste is not so harmful that we should pay 6 million guilders. If the tax goes ahead, we may have to consider closing down the factory' (*NRC* 2 June).

In short, as in Germany, Greenpeace received endorsements from third parties, whereas Shell was undermined by controversial voices in its own organisation and other offshore industries. The moral standards of the multinational operations and the lack of environmental credentials of the UK government, became the framework within which the Brent Spar conflict was debated.

### Media frames in the British press

Greenpeace tends to have a problematic relationship with the British press which was the reason it moved its head office to Amsterdam. This was also the case in the Brent Spar conflict. The *Guardian*, for instance, referred to Greenpeace as 'ecoguerillas' whose operations were 'strikingly efficient' (6 May) while Michel Heseltine argued in the *Sun* on 22 June, 'We must beat the militants of Greenpeace.'

Debate over the environmental effects had hardly developed before it was superseded by a new interpretative framework: the legal issue, put forward by the UK government and Shell. The Conservative government argued that deep-sea disposal was in accordance with national law and international treaties and that the occupation of the oil buoy was illegal. Moreover, the *Guardian* also used a legal framework, but from a different angle: it argued that the conflict was problematic because the UK lacked the proper legislation to deal with environmental issues (25 May). Thus, despite opposing political ideologies, papers drew upon a legal framework.

This framework set the stage for a shift to a third framework based around British perceptions of long-standing differences between Britain and other European countries. The primary actors in this affair, Greenpeace and Shell, receded more into the background as they became marginalised by these shifts in interpretative frameworks. The third framework partly drew on the legal framework, because one aspect of the differences represented was the belief that Europeans were more disrespectful of the law than were the British. The *Daily Mail*, for instance, declared: 'Europe is not

respecting international treaties: double standards rule the waves'
(11 July).

## MEDIA-BASED OPPOSITIONAL POLITICS IN AN
## INTERNATIONAL PUBLIC SPHERE

Anderson (1997) and Rootes (1999) advanced the argument that
'consumer power' had been the cause of the Shell's U-turn. But
would a decrease in turnover in Germany of just under 20 per cent
really panic one of the biggest multinationals in the world with an
estimated profit of £4.6 billion? As the bank, Mees and Hope, and
Shell itself argued, financial considerations were not of critical importance. We need to take other dimensions of this conflict into account
in order to fully understand its dynamics. The much disputed moral
argument, dismissed by Shell, is key here. Ulrich Beck takes the
moral argument to another dimension:

> Shell has done everything correctly and in line with rational criteria that
> seem to lead to 'organised irresponsibility'. The environmental crisis is not
> an environmental crisis but an imminent crisis of industrial and societal
> institutions, the basis on which these institutions operate and on which
> legitimisation takes place is in crisis. (*TAZ* 1 July 1995)

This echoes the underlying perceptions of the press on the continent
and Greenpeace itself. Even if deep-sea disposal was not environmentally harmful, why should we dump waste in the sea?

Bennie (1998) writes dismissively about Greenpeace's historical
attempts to address issues at different levels but in 'media friendly'
terms: 'The seizing of the moral high ground, and the use of
symbolic, emotionally charged moral messages has been a common
theme throughout Greenpeace's campaigning history' (Bennie
1998:90).

Pressure groups operate on the moral high ground; this must be
considered as one of the prominent aspects of their role in society.
The role of pressure groups in influencing and challenging existing
discourses and codes might even be of greater importance in the
long run than individual actions, an argument advanced by many
theorists (Melucci 1996; Castells 1997). Indeed this was an essential
feature of the Brent Spar conflict. Even after its U-turn, Dr Chris Fay,
Chairman and Chief Executive of Shell UK, dismissed the attitude
on the continent by saying, 'I don't go with the moral issue' (BBC

News 20 June) while Mr Cor Herkeströter, Chairman of the Committee of the Royal Dutch Shell Group, fully admitted that Shell was not in tune with social concerns. That corporate industry is showing signs of 'social disembeddedness' was noted by research executed by the Communication Group (1996) on pressure group activism in Europe. It concluded that 'people seem to be more and more disillusioned with industry and government' (1996:7), while emphasising the lack of engagement with civil society and the self-admitted fear of corporate industry of activist activities.

In the public and academic imagination, the present conception of multinationals as monolithic and omnipotent entities undermines progressive politics. Multinationals have serious problems with their corporate culture and admit to being scared of pressure group activities. This is not to deny or underplay the power of multinationals, and the author has no doubt that in an internationalised economy, corporate power is being strengthened at the expense of democratic governments. But Shell, notwithstanding its financial power and professionally operating press departments, was seriously restricted in its access to the media and therefore to society. Its cultural power and strategic ability in the public sphere appeared to be very limited. It is therefore incorrect to present the Brent Spar conflict as a 'symbol of the power that political protest can exert over the powerful interests of big business and big government' as Bennie suggests (1998:89). The point is that they are 'big' in certain respects but actually quite 'small' in other respects.

## INTERNATIONAL CIVIL SOCIETY AND THE PUBLIC SPHERE

The wide range of organisations and networks operating in the fields of human rights, environmentalism, peace, feminism and development have given form to an international civil society, described as 'global cultures of solidarity' (Waterman 1995), 'globalisation from below' (Falk 1994), 'deep democracy' (Appudurai 2002), or 'a solidarity in difference' (Sreberny-Mohammadi 1996). Sharing common concerns, like environmental concerns, has led to new forms of political action, described by Beck (1997) as 'subpolitics'; the reinvention of politics, which is seen to be producing a new reflective, rule-altering kind of politics, operating from a 'local' level, which sidesteps the national and reaches up to the global level. But it's actually in the national dimensions where serious risks can be found which might bite international actions in the tail. The international media public sphere is for obvious reasons limited to common concerns; in the case of the Brent Spar dispute common concerns such as environmentalism, and moral concerns about the criteria on which corporate industry based its decisions, triggered off a reaction in the countries under consideration where the wider debates and interpretations have taken place within national public spheres.

The concept of a 'global' public sphere might actually hide the strength and dominance of these national public spheres. Therefore, it might undermine its usefulness as an analytical tool. Braman's (1996) concept of interpenetrating public spheres better describes how these public spheres relate to each other. National public sphere have becomes part of each other, they overlap but are still distinctly separate entities.

Greenpeace would not have been as successful as it was if pre-existing discourses disparaging the environmental credentials of the 'British' had not been so prominent on the continent. Greenpeace lacked scientific credentials, but its cultural and symbolic power mobilised a variety of groups in civil society. In first instance, by tapping in to prevailing environmental concerns, and second by raising concerns about the ethical dimensions of multinational operations. However, the final leverage was provided by 'others'; the 'British' in its different disguises: Shell, the British government and British environmental awareness. Germany, although having no interests in the Brent Spar platform, was deliberately included in Greenpeace's actions. Essentially they played off one country against the other. One can not, then, refrain from asking what would have happened with the Brent Spar if the UK government and 'those others' who lacked environmental awareness had had an unblemished history in their environmental and social awareness and policies.

## NOTE

1  Three newspapers were selected from each country on the basis of circulation and political diversity: the *Guardian*, the *Daily Mail* and the *Sun* in the UK, *Volkskrant, Telegraaf* and the *NRC Handelsblad* in the Netherlands and the *Bild Zeitung*, the *Frankfurter Algemeine Zeitung* and the *Berliner Tages Zeitung* in Germany.

## FURTHER READING

Allan, S., B. Adam and C. Carther (2000) *Environmental Risks and the Media*, London: Routledge

Anderson, A. (1997) *Media, Culture and the Environment*, London: UCL Press
—— (1991) Source strategies and the communication of environmental affairs, *Media, Culture and Society* 13, 4: 459–76
Appudurai, A. (2002) 'Deep democracy: urban governmentality and the horizon of politics' *Public Culture* 14, 1: 21–47
Beck, U. (1997) *The Reinvention of Politics: Rethinking Modernity in the Global Social Order*, Cambridge: Polity
Bennie, L. (1998) 'Brent Spar, Atlantic Oil and Greenpeace', in F. Ridley and G. Jordan (eds) *Protest Politics: Cause and Campaigns*, Oxford, New York: Oxford University Press
Braman, S. (1996) 'Interpenetrated globalisation: scaling, power and the public sphere', in S. Braman and A. Screberny-Mohammadi (eds) *Globalization, Communication and Transnational Civil Society*, IAMCR, Creskill, NY: Hampton Press
Castells, Manuel (1997) *The Power of Identity*, Oxford: Blackwell
Communication Group (1996) *Putting the Pressure On; the Rise of Pressure Group Activism in Europe*, London: The Communication Group plc.
Cottle, S. ( 2000) 'Rethinking theories of news access', *Journalism Studies* 1, 3: 427–48
Deacon, D. (1996) 'The voluntary sector in a changing communication environment', *European Journal of Communication* 11, 2: 173–99
Dunwoody, S. and R. J. Griffin, (1993) 'Journalistic strategies for reporting long-term environmental issues: a case of three superfund sites' in Hansen, Anders (ed.) *The Mass Media and Environmental Issues*, Leicester: Leicester University Press
Eyerman, R. and A. Jamison (1989) 'Environmental knowledge as an organisational weapon; the case of Greenpeace', *Social Science Information* 28, 1: 99–119
Falk, R. (1994) 'The Making of Global Citizenship', in B. Van Steenbergen (ed.) *The Conditions of Citizenship*, London: Sage
Giddens, A. (1991) *The Consequences of Modernity*, Cambridge: Polity
Gitlin, T. (1980) *The Whole World is Watching: Mass Media and the Making and Unmaking of the New Left*, Berkeley: University of California Press
Goffman, E. (1974) *Frame Analysis: An Essay on the Organisation of Experience*, Cambridge, MA: Harvard University Press
Greenberg, D.W. (1985) *Staging Media Events to Achieve Legitimacy*, Leicester: Leicester University Press
Hansen, H. (2000) 'Claims making and framing in British newspapers of the 'Brent Spar' controversy', in S. Allan, B. Adam and C. Carther (eds) *Environmental Risks and the Media*, London: Routledge
—— (1993) *The Mass Media and Environmental Issues*, Leicester: Leicester University Press
Jordan. A.G. (2001) *Shell, Greenpeace and the Brent Spar*, Basingstoke: Palgrave
Jordan, G. and F. Ridley (1998) *Protest Politics: Cause Groups and Campaigns*, Oxford, New York: Oxford University Press
Klein, N. (2000) *No Logo, No Space, No Jobs; Taking Aim at the Brand Bullies*, London: HarperCollins
Linne, O. (1991) 'Journalistic practices and news coverage of environmental issues', *Nordicom Review of Nordic Communication Research* 1: 1–7

Miller, M. and B. Parnell Riechert (2000) 'Interest groups, strategies and journalistic norm', in S. Allen, B. Adam and C. Carter (eds) *Environmental Risks and the Media*, London: Routledge

Manning, P. (2001) *News and News Sources: A Critical Introduction*, London: Sage

Mc Nair, B. (1994) *News and Journalism in the UK*, London: Routledge

Melucci, A. (1996) *Challenging Codes; Collective Action in the Information Age*, Cambridge: Cambridge University Press

Palmer, J. (2001) *Spinning into Control*, London: Continuum International Publishing Group

Rootes, C. (1999) 'Acting globally, thinking locally? Prospects for a global environmental movement', in C. Rootes (ed.) *Environmental Movements: Local, National and Global*, London: Frank Cass: 290–310

Sreberny-Mohammadi, A. (1996) 'Feminist internationalism: imagining and building global civil society', in D. Kishan Thussu (ed.) *Electronic Empires*, London: Arnold

Schiller, Herbert (1989) *Cult. Inc.: The Corporate Take-over of Public Expression*, New York: OUP

Van Ginneken, J. (1998) *Understanding Global News; A Critical Introduction*, London: Sage

Waterman, P. (1995) 'Holding mirrors out of windows: a labour bulletin, a feminist agenda and the creation of global solidarity culture in the New South Africa', *Working Paper series No. 188*, Institute of Social Sciences: The Hague

# 8
# The World Development Movement: Access and Representation of Globalisation – Activism in the Mainstream Press

*Dave Timms*

Founded in 1970, the World Development Movement (WDM) is a UK-based democratic membership organisation, campaigning on issues of international development. It has approximately 15,000 supporters and about 100 local groups nationwide. In 2003 WDM had a turnover of approximately £1.2 million and employed just under 30 staff between its London and Edinburgh offices.

WDM's press coverage log for 2002, not untypical of recent years, records a total of 330 media 'hits'. Each hit is a single item of press coverage. These range from a listing of a WDM local group meeting in the *Swindon Evening Advertiser* to an interview with the organisation's director on BBC2's *Newsnight*. WDM is widely seen as punching above its weight for a small to medium sized campaigning organisation.

*Figure 8.1*   Polyp cartoon <www.newint.org/shop/uk/bigbadworld.htn>

The vast majority of WDM's access to the media is through print (69 per cent in 2002). The rest is divided between online (15 per cent), TV (5 per cent) and radio (11 per cent). WDM's radio coverage comes overwhelmingly through public service broadcasting (83 per cent). Almost half (42 per cent) of WDM's total print coverage appeared in local newspapers, giving the organisation a significant media footprint at a local level despite limited resources. This is only possible because a high priority is given to building policy knowledge at the grassroots and because local groups have the autonomy to decide on campaigning priorities, thus reducing their dependence on the central organisation.

WDM's local presswork is activism driven. Typically this consists of notices and subsequent reports of WDM-organised public meetings, media stunts, protests in town centres and reports of meetings with local politicians (lobbying a local MP, for example). More occasionally it might include comment and opinion articles written by local WDM campaigners. This contrasts with the national and international press strategy which is driven by policy and research. This is mainly built around the publication of reports providing evidence and analysis to formulate WDM's policy and back up campaigning demands.

Press coverage performs a number of, often overlapping, functions for WDM: retention of existing members and raising the value of those members (for example placing features in magazines read by WDM members during a fundraising drive), gaining new members, exerting direct political pressure on specific campaigns, raising the profile of WDM campaign within the activist community and political education of that community, and general awareness raising of global issues and the impact of corporate globalisation among the general public.

It is easy, for example, to see how a feature in *New Internationalist* on the damage caused by the International Monetary Fund (IMF) could help WDM gain and retain members, and build capacity within the activist community. However, it is unlikely to trouble directly the UK Government. A news item in the *Financial Times* on the same subject would achieve the reverse.

## ACCESS TO THE MEDIA: MEDIA STUNTS

In recent years, WDM has staged media stunts outside company AGMs, corporate headquarters and government departments.

The aim is to provide a visual metaphor for a campaigning message. For example, on budget day 2003, WDM and War on Want staged a demo in Whitehall drawing attention to the vast cost of the war in Iraq to the British taxpayer compared with the small amount committed by the Treasury to debt relief. The image of a coffin stuffed with dollar bills baring the message 'Drop Debt Not Bombs' made a quarter page picture in the *FT*.[1] However, also in 2003, WDM and the Jubilee debt campaign organised over 30 MPs to take part in a race against third world debt with Olympic athlete Steve Cram. The stunt took weeks to organise and several national photo agencies, two national newspapers and a BBC camera crew turned up, yet the event received no subsequent national media coverage.[2]

Media stunts are a high-risk strategy, they can soak up huge amounts of organisational time and funds for a very uncertain return. This makes them only ever an additional tool in WDM's national media strategy. They are often designed to be reproduced by local activists at little cost where they do, however, form a central part of WDM's local media work.

The ideological content of the images is also crucial. Highly uncomplimentary images of the business community as cigar chomping 'Fat Cats' or 'pigs in the trough' have been firmly established in the public consciousness as synonymous with big business. This must at least in part be attributed to the constant reinforcing of these messages through their repeated use of these images by NGOs and campaigners.

### ACCESS TO THE MEDIA: CELEBRITIES

The Jubilee 2000 campaign for cancellation of developing country debts attracted mass support from celebrities across the entertainment industries, for an NGO-led campaign with a radical and highly political message. This was very different from the earlier humanitarian relief of Band Aid and Comic Relief.

For NGOs with the resources, flying a celebrity around the world accompanied by an in-house film crew so that they can talk about their experiences in Bangladesh or Bolivia doesn't come cheap – the potential gains from working with celebrities are extensive: tabloid coverage, glossy lifestyle magazines, primetime TV documentaries (such as following the celebrity to Africa) and daytime TV, in addition to deeper coverage in broadsheets. The chances of success for an NGO media stunt are dramatically increased by the involvement of a celebrity. News agencies are more likely to send a photographer/ reporter/camera crew and the subsequent image is more likely to be used. The main concern for NGOs working with celebrities is that they go 'off message' or 'misbehave' in a way that overshadows the campaign.

There is some concern within NGOs that dependence on celebrities is contributing to a culture of lazy journalism (and indeed lazy campaigning), where it is not the story that counts but the way you present it. The depressing assumption is that the public will only read about the impact of trade rules on African farmers if there is a famous face attached. This is not restricted to tabloids and lifestyle publications – it is not unusual for broadsheets and public service broadcasters to show interest in a report, issue or campaign only if their is a celebrity interview on offer. The *Financial Times* carried a large interview with the band Radiohead exploring their support for the Trade Justice Movement's mass lobby of parliament. It is unlikely that the *FT*, not a paper known for its support for NGO campaigns, would have otherwise given the policies championed by Radiohead quite so much space.[3]

Alternatively it may also be argued that by taking international development issues into the pages of *OK* magazine or *Marie Clare*, NGOs are hijacking and subverting celebrity culture for a more constructive end than selling records or the latest Hollywood blockbuster. Celebrities can also assist in 'mainstreaming' an issue, moving what may have been regarded as a marginal position on peripheries of political life to being accepted – turning the previously radical into the everyday. Diana, Princess of Wales', visits to AIDS sufferers is perhaps the best example of this.

WDM uses celebrities less than many comparable organisations, though it has no principled objection. WDM's radical image, the complexity of the issues and the directly political nature of the campaigns makes working with celebrities more difficult.

### ACCESS TO THE MEDIA: REPRESENTATION OF THE SOUTH

The representation of the global south by northern NGOs in the media, and the relationship between southern civil society organisations and northern NGOs is complicated, sensitive and constantly evolving.

The central role for case studies and stories in any strategy has already been outlined. Those NGOs with the resources can make those stories even more telegenic by bringing the victims of corporate globalisation to the UK or by taking journalists to the scene of the crime – providing pictures and putting names, faces and voices to those on the receiving end of corporate exploitation or the policies of the World Bank, IMF and WTO. It is much harder for governments or companies to call into doubt the motives of campaigners or the authority of the evidence.

There is a danger though that the poor are only allowed to articulate their poverty, but it is important that the northern NGO put these personal stories in a policy context and formulate the demands. These may be less radical than the demands of civil society in the country concerned.

WDM has a different relationship with the south because it does not fund projects in developing countries and campaigns on a basis of solidarity with southern civil society. It tries to provide a platform for NGOs and social movements from the south who may have limited access to the international media.

Through its annual 'States of Unrest' report detailing resistance to IMF and World Bank policies in developing countries WDM tries to provide a platform for those in the south engaged in struggle.[4] This is partly in order to combat the image of communities in the south as passive victims of northern policies. It also gives greater legitimacy to the actions of the global social justice movement in the north, defending it from the charge made by former UK Secretary of State for International Development, Clare Short, that the critics of globalisation, especially those engaged in protest, are entirely drawn from the 'white, privileged and middle class'.[5]

## INTERNATIONAL SUMMITS: ACCESS AND INTERVENTION

WDM invests significant time and money in its intervention in major summits. In the period leading up to the WTO's Cancun ministerial meeting in September 2003, WDM released two policy reports, two media briefings, organised a media stunt outside the DTI and flew Martin Khor, Director of the Third World Network, to London to take part in a press briefing.

Access for NGOs to the press at summits is severely limited, if they are allowed to attend at all (there is no system of NGO accreditation to the G8, for example). They are usually banned from the press room, while government representatives have unlimited access. Regular press conferences are held by government spokespeople, civil servants or politicians in custom built rooms. These facilities are either not made available to NGOs at all or access is highly restricted. An official NGO centre is usually provided some distance from the summit and the press centre (at the Johannesburg Earth Summit in 2002 the NGO centre was a one-hour drive from the press centre and summit venue). Access to summits of NGOs or other organisations in civil society tend to be a much lower priority than access for the media.

## WDM IN THE 'RED ZONE'

Gaining access to the media centre to during the summit is crucial. It is not unusual for NGO press officers to be repeatedly thrown out of summit media centres for distributing press releases and briefing journalists. Improvised press conferences are often held in cafes and corridors.

In 1999 the World Trade Organisation's third ministerial meeting, held in Seattle, collapsed amid massive street protests. The media 'discovered' the anti-globalisation movement.

Starting with the IMF and World Bank meetings in Prague in 2000, WDM has contributed to the counter-summits and social forums which have dogged world leaders over recent years. WDM has also backed many of the protests that are an extension of these social forums, such as at the G8 in Genoa and in Evian, and subsequently found itself with one foot in the protests and counter-summits, and one foot inside what is often know as the 'Red Zone', a generic term for the high-security zone at any major summit.

The official line from many NGOs has been that coverage of the violence of a small minority distracts from the wider issues.[6] However, the possibility of violent protest can be the deciding factor in whether a news programme or paper sends a correspondent to a summit. Major news outlets often call WDM before major summits to ask how likely it is that there will be 'trouble'.

## NEW DEVELOPMENTS

The emergence of the internet, email and digital photography have revolutionised much of WDM's press work making rapid distribution of reports, press releases and photos possible. WDM has also been able to work with anti-GATS (General Agreement on Trade in Services) campaigns worldwide to maximise political impact by engaging in internationally coordinated media campaigns such as a simultaneous global release of leaked WTO negotiating documents on to the internet.[7]

## CONCLUSIONS

Tensions regularly arise between the different internal organisational and campaigning purposes of media work. There may be pressure to focus heavily on human interest stories and details of the impact of policies which are perceived to have a wider popular appeal, than the more technical or political aspects of WDM's campaigns, in order the meet fundraising or marketing objectives.

There can also be conflict between the clear, unambiguous message preferred by the media and the nuances of policy and lobbying work. In 1997 WDM put out a press release that gave the new Labour government's white paper on aid 'One out of 10'. The quotation was displayed prominently on the front page of the *Guardian* but soured relations between WDM and the new Department for International Development for several years.[8]

Engaging with the parliamentary process, submitting evidence to select committees and responding to government announcements all provide WDM with a regular stream of reactive opportunities to gain access to 'on diary' news stories.

Some large NGOs, such as Oxfam and Amnesty International, have assumed the status of official sources. WDM, however, is seen as more radical and its campaigning is more political and directly critical of the UK Government. Consequently the press strategies adopted are highly proactive.

Formulating media strategies for WDM campaigns entails finding a balance between a focusing on the institutional or policy drivers of the problem – IMF Structural Adjustment Policies for example – or focusing on the tangible impact of such policies such as food insecurity and famine. The latter enables WDM to make use of case studies and human-interest stories. Finding a clear connection to the UK in the shape of a domestic company or a government policy is also crucial to avoid the issue being marginalised as a 'foreign' story. Losing a link between institutional cause and real life effect condemns the strategy either to a constant struggle to find mass media appeal or renders it politically impotent.

Attacking a well-known high street or blue chip company over a specific case of exploitation or environmental damage can be an effective way to illustrate the need for large scale reforms covering the activities of all companies and build a political culture more sympathetic to those reforms. This is exactly what WDM tried to do with its 'People before Profits' campaign that ran from 1995 to 2000 which included a series of campaigns on corporate abuses such as cigarette marketing in developing countries, Premier Oil in Burma and mining by Rio Tinto.[9]

A focus on the overseas activities of domestic business might seem attractive as a media strategy but it has two drawbacks: few of WDM's members, potential members or the activist community read the business press. Second, focusing on an individual business can take the political pressure off governments and the international financial institutions they control. WDM seeks changes in the law or in international governance, not just a voluntary change in the behaviour of an individual company.

The key challenge for WDM is to use the impacts of corporate globalisation as a strategy for gaining access to the mainstream media without losing an analysis of the institutional causes of poverty.

## NOTES

1   The *Financial Times*, 10 April 2003, 'Backdrop of war steals the thunder of chancellor, as big theme proves elusive'.
2   WDM press release, Steve Cram joins MPs in 'Race Against Third World Debt', 8 May 2003.
3   'Radiohead rock the boat over global trade rules', *Financial Times*, 19 June 2002.
4   Ellis-Jones, M. (2003) *States of Unrests III: Resistance to IMF and World Bank Policies in poor Countries*, London: World Development Movement.
5   Jeremy Seabrook, 24 July 2001, 'Why Clare Short is wrong', *Guardian*.
6   <http://www.cafod.org.uk/news/g8violence20010720.shtml>.
7   WDM press release, 'Leaked documents reveal UK Government hypocrisy over trade agreement danger', 25 February 2003.
8   *Guardian*, 6 November 1997, 'Short vows to target world poverty'.
9   More about this campaign is available at <http://www.wdm.org.uk/campaign/history.htm>.

# 9

# Peace Activism and Western Wars: Social Movements in Mass-Mediated Global Politics

*Martin Shaw*

In February 2003, some of the largest ever globally-coordinated street protests took place, against the imminent attack on Iraq by the United States and the United Kingdom. In London, maybe 1.4 million people took part (see the careful calculation by Gordon 2003); whatever the correct figure for the number of participants, even the police agreed that this was the largest demonstration on record. By April 2003, however, US and UK forces had launched their attack, deposed the Saddam Hussein regime and 'won' their war. In the same time interval, the peace movement shrank from massive mobilisations to a rump of small political organisations. Certainly, the movement's criticisms of American power reverberated through post-war politics, not least in Britain where the prime minister, Tony Blair, suffered seemingly irreversible political damage. But it had disappeared as a mass political force. Although by general consent the USA's rule in Iraq was ill-prepared, so that the post-war situation was marked by chronic failures in physical and social security, the peace movement offered no coherent voice in this crisis. Politicians, journalists and non-governmental organisations (NGOs) made damaging criticisms of US–UK policy, but the mass activist voice was hardly heard.

How can we explain the paradox of the meteoric rise and fall of street protest? What does this example tell us about the nature and causes of the successes and failures of peace movements? How distinctive was this case, and how far does it fit into a pattern that can be discerned in earlier movements? What is the relationship between the character of current western wars and the dilemmas of peace movements? How far do the politics of the movements and their modes of operation explain their limitations? In what ways does the fact that both wars and movements operate in a globally mass-mediated political environment explain these experiences?

How far are the lessons of peace movements applicable more gener-ally to contemporary social movements? These are some of the ques-tions raised by this case that this chapter will try to explore in a general historical perspective. I write as a sociologist whose work has combined an interest in media and social movements with research on contemporary war and genocide (as well as personal experience as a peace movement activist in an earlier period).

## THE CONTEXT OF IRAQ

Sociologists have often sought to explain social movements in terms of general social characteristics, such as the nature of the social groups that support them (e.g., Parkin's 1968 idea of 'middle-class radicalism') and the general values of their supporters (e.g., Inglehart 1977). However as Mattausch (1989) argued in a study of the 1980s nuclear disarmament movements, these kinds of account 'explain away' the professed causes around which movements campaign, treating them as epiphenomenona of more general social causes. Social science will give a more convincing account of people's actions, he argued, if it takes seriously their manifest, conscious as well as supposed, latent reasons for engaging in them. In the case of the movement against war in Iraq, our first port of call should be to examine the threat by the US and UK to attack Iraq, the rationale and history of the conflict that led to this threat and the reasons why millions of people responded to this threat by taking to the streets and other forms of protest. Clearly the numbers of protestors was of a historically significant order: something very specific must have been going on to make so many people protest. Thus we need to examine both the immediate political context of the threat of war and, behind that, the larger contexts of contemporary world politics and war to which this specific crisis referred.

The outbreak of large protest movements is not easily predictable. Big movements, like the disarmament movements of the early 1980s, often arise as if from nowhere and their rapid success takes even their organisers by surprise. Few who had observed the rather small-scale, muted protests against the 2001–02 war in Afghanistan – or indeed the 1991 Gulf War (for an account of the British anti-war movement then, see Shaw 1996) – would have expected the massive actions against the 2003 Iraq War. Explanations must generally be *post hoc*: it is mainly in retrospect that opposition to the recent war appears to be over-determined, in contrast to these other cases.

However, with this benefit of hindsight, it is quite clear that the war on Iraq was crucially different from other wars in which western states have been involved in recent decades. This western campaign was *not* a more or less direct response to provocative military action by an enemy state or movement, as were the British campaign in the Falklands, the Gulf War, NATO's campaign over Kosovo and the Afghanistan campaign. Uniquely, this was a 'pre-emptive' strike, according to a radical new US strategic doctrine that had little legitimacy outside the US. Partly because of this different context, the war (unlike any of the other cases) had virtually no active support from major states either within or outside the west. Britain's support, resulting from Blair going out on a limb against the weight of opinion in his party and even his government, gave the US a fig leaf of international credibility – but it was not enough, and indeed it provoked intense hostility within the UK. The many months of build-up to war, the failed Blair-led attempts to secure international legitimacy and President Bush's determination to go to war despite the opposition of the UN majority and despite the ongoing weapons inspections, all created an atmosphere of intense crisis.

In this context, the anti-war movements on the streets of the world's cities was able to build up a massive base of support over a series of demonstrations, with an unprecedented political legitimacy. Protestors were cutting with the grain of public opinion (even in the countries where governments gave some kind of support to the war, polls often showed large-scale opposition: of over 90 per cent in Spain, 80 per cent in Italy, 60 per cent in the UK and 40–50 per cent in the US). In all cases they could claim to be speaking alongside the UN majority, and in many cases, such as in France and Germany, they were on the same side as their governments. Because of these various kinds of international and national legitimacy, movements also received unusually favourable media coverage. Indeed many national and regional newspapers echoed their opposition to the war: in Britain, for example, not only the traditionally anti-war *Guardian* but also the tabloid *Daily Mirror* saw the possibility of audience gains through speaking for the opposition to military action.

## FROM 'STOP CRUISE MISSILES' TO 'STOP THE WAR'

In many senses, then, the context for the recent anti-war movement was uniquely favourable. So it was not surprising that this was the largest 'peace' movement since the campaigns against nuclear weapons 20 years earlier. However, unlike those earlier movements, in which mass protests (demonstrations, sit-downs, peace camps, etc. involving hundreds of thousands) built up over about two years from their origins in late 1979 to their 1982 peak, and only gradually subsided after about 1984, the recent movement was, as we have noted, very short-lived. Although it built up over about six months, its decline was extremely rapid.

The reasons for this difference are obviously connected to the nature of the realities against which the movements were protesting. The nuclear disarmament movements of the 1980s took their cue from NATO's November 1979 decision to introduce new intermediate-range Pershing II and cruise missiles into six western European countries. The decisions required several years of preparations, and in some cases parliamentary approvals, to be implemented. Until missiles were actually installed, it remained possible to block their installation on a country-by-country basis. National elections provided focal points for opposition: it was not until after conservative victories in German and British elections in the first half of 1983 that the decisions taken by NATO were clearly secure, and in the Netherlands it was 1986 before there was a national basis to go ahead.

In the case of wars, the dynamics are different from those of weapon deployments. In none of the western wars of the last two decades, to which I referred above, was the build-up period to conflict longer than six months. In all cases, the main phase of armed conflict was even shorter, no more than three months, and military success more or less complete and (apparently) relatively low-cost in terms of life. Despite (or because of) huge and intensive bombardments, only around 150 Americans and 40 Britons were to die in the main phase of combat in Iraq, and many of these were casualties of accidents and from 'friendly fire'. Civilian, non-combatant deaths (in the 'war' phase alone) have been most reliably estimated in the range of 3,200 to 4,300, with Iraqi military deaths in the range of 7,600 to 10,800 (Conetta 2003; but see also Iraq Body Count 2003 for larger figures for civilian deaths, without the adjustments that Conetta makes).

In contrast the Vietnam War had been, of course, prolonged, costly and unsuccessful: the main phase of US involvement lasted a decade, from 1965 to 1975, there were several peaks of fighting, and tens of thousands of US military personnel died, together with hundreds of thousands of Vietnamese fighters and civilians. A huge anti-war movement arose, the most important political movement in the US since the Second World War and one with worldwide ramifications, linked in the minds of many establishment figures to adverse media coverage of this 'first television war'. In fact, academic studies (e.g., Hallin 1986; Mandelbaum 1987) showed that adverse coverage mostly *followed* rather than caused the military difficulties and political opposition to the war.

However, it was from the understanding of the 'Vietnam syndrome' as a product of television coverage, that the US and other western governments concluded that it was necessary to avoid long wars and large-scale casualties, and to manage media coverage to avoid damaging political effects. Hence the (so far mostly successful) preference of the US, UK and NATO for quick military fixes, through intense, mostly aerial bombardment (although in Iraq artillery was also important), risking relatively few military lives. And hence the evolution, through the Falklands, Gulf and Kosovo campaigns, of a model of media management that attempted to direct journalistic attention and massage the effects of western military action on local civilians.

It was this model of combined war fighting and media control that was deployed in Iraq to limit the war. Although the Iraqi resistance in the second week of the war encouraged critics to believe that they would not be so successful this time, in the event the US was able to prevail (to the extent of overthrowing Saddam and gaining overall control of Iraq) even more quickly than in 1991. It seems improbable that any anti-war movement could have made great headway in these conditions: focused on preventing the war, the movements were largely irrelevant once the war was begun; and calling for 'stopping the war', they had little to contribute as Bush's forces sped towards their 'victory'. Thus the difficulties of any anti-war movement in contemporary conditions are starkly underlined. Despite the largest mobilisation in recent history (and huge international political opposition), the US was undeterred. Only if this mobilisation had gained overwhelming ground where it really mattered to Bush (i.e., in US public opinion) would it have been likely to make a difference to the outcome. Alternatively, only if the war had (like Vietnam) lasted years rather than months, had gone badly for the US and had led to very substantial (and apparently pointless) deaths, would the movement have been likely to impact on the actual outcome of the war.

## DYNAMICS OF DEMONSTRATION MOVEMENTS AND
## GLOBAL MASS MEDIA

I have suggested that mainstream media (television, newspaper and radio) coverage of the 2003 anti-war movement was probably uniquely favourable. It has long been an article of faith in all protest movements that 'the media' are a homogenous, hostile force, which misrepresents and distorts their aims. While studies have shown that there is truth in these beliefs (most stations and papers usually take their cue more from governments and corporations than from protestors), they nonetheless obscure the fundamental *dependence* of late modern social movements on mainstream mass media. Without media coverage, would movements – especially protest movements – be able to develop with the rapidity that we saw in the recent Iraqi conflict?

To appreciate the significance of media to late-modern movements let us consider the very different situation a century ago. The first modern social movements, especially labour movements, parties and unions, developed in the nineteenth century at a time when the press was much more restricted and electronic media had not been invented. They developed extensive face-to-face organisation, based on elaborate hierarchical structures of local, regional, national and international organisation. Alongside and through these structures they also developed their own media of communication – labour and socialist newspapers that were widely read in the working class. The German workers' movement, in many ways the prime model, was famously analysed by Roberto Michels (1915) as a state within a state. Later analyses of the western working class in its formative and classical periods before the Second World War emphasised its 'hermetic', closed world (Anderson and Nairn 1965).

Media as well as political developments in the twentieth century transformed this situation. Many historic labour movements, like Germany's, were in any case destroyed or weakened by totalitarianism and war. Electronic media (radio, cinema and television) developed either as state monopolies or as commercial enterprises, largely bypassing traditional workers' movements. Labour papers tended to pass out of movement hands – Britain's *Daily Herald* is the most notorious case, as it metamorphosed into the tabloid *Sun*, the flagship of Rupert Murdoch's media empire. Where workers' organisations survived or revived, they did so utilising their traditional organisational and cultural structures. The functions of labour movements, institutionalised in wage-negotiation, electioneering, etc., enabled such resilience despite often-hostile mass media.

The 'new' social movements that developed from the mid-1950s onwards were of a different type. Although they tended, as Parkin (1968) and others noted, to be strongly based on the 'middle class' (more specifically as Mattausch, 1989, pointed out, the educated, professional and state-employed middle class, including students), their aims were not to represent that class as such. They had no 'natural' social functions embedded in the ongoing self-organisation of a social group, comparable to those of unions, or in institutionalised politics, like parties. Instead, these movements were often organised around specific goals – opposition to nuclear weapons, apartheid and racial discrimination, wars, environmental pollution, etc. – that were in principle of concern to people of any group. Only some 'new' movements sought to organise groups, like women and gays, who were previously largely unorganised, and to represent their specific values and interests.

Because these movements were organised around specific issues, or sought to organise very broad unorganised groups that did not always have 'natural' foci for organisation, they nearly always relied significantly on mass media to gain public attention. The British Campaign for Nuclear Disarmament (CND) for example, the first major anti-nuclear weapons organisation – at the centre of the 1958–63 and 1980–84 movements – was launched through letters in the press. CND's leaders saw it initially as a presence in established institutions – parties, churches, unions, etc. as well as media – and only afterwards did it evolve a local group structure (Taylor 1988). However as CND became the centre of a social *movement*, mobilising people into action on the streets, it also became more rather than less dependent on mass media. Press coverage of demonstrations mobilised new people on to further demonstrations, alongside the sort of direct propaganda (leaflets, local meetings, etc.) that CND itself produced. Interestingly, the direct action favoured by the radical wing of the movement (sit-downs, blockades, etc.) was more likely to have visual impact in the new medium of television (which took off in Britain after 1955) than the more traditional, law-abiding protest initiated by the CND establishment. Although radicals were more suspicious of the media, their mobilisations depended considerably on the notoriety of civil disobedience in the newspapers and television news. Although mainstream media largely represented these events in negative, censorious terms, sympathisers (especially young people) would deconstruct these accounts, so that notoriety only increased their attraction.

Since demonstration-based movements often launched actions at short notice in response to events reported in the media, they were often equally dependent – before the internet – on media to publicise what they were planning. As a local and regional organiser of European Nuclear Disarmament (END) and CND in the early 1980s, I would send out written notices of events and activate 'telephone trees' that would spread urgent information quickly to activists. However I always knew that a mention in the local newspaper or on the radio would be a more effective mobiliser, reaching more people and giving the action more credibility, than publicity via movement channels. Television and the press were vital for building the dynamics of demonstration movements. The success of one march, reported in the media, often led to significantly increased turnouts for future demonstrations. Even negative coverage could draw in wider circles of sympathisers: they learnt that they were not alone, that others were already acting and that action was publicly significant.

There is therefore a cycle of demonstration-coverage-larger demonstration-even greater coverage-even larger demonstration, and so on, up to the point where the maximum marching constituency has been mobilised, or it is clear that goals are not going to be met, or activists become exhausted, or some combination of these. It is noteworthy that Mandelbaum (1987), in generally dismissing the idea that television coverage 'caused' the US failure in Vietnam, nevertheless credited it with one major effect: to fan the cycle of anti-war protests. This demonstration-media cycle also operates internationally, as stories and pictures of demonstrations in one country encourage people in others to follow suit. Thus in the 1960s, the first television decade across the western world, anti-Vietnam War and student protests spread rapidly from the US to Europe, Japan and beyond. These effects could also be seen in the very rapid build-up of protests against the Iraq War: however, the cycle was cut off by the launching of the war and the rapid success of the US and UK forces.

## CHANGING POLITICS, ORGANISATION AND MEDIA OF PEACE PROTEST

Although we can trace big continuities between peace movements in the 1960s and today, much has changed. Developments in the media of communication have certainly facilitated protest. The internet enables activist groups and movement organisations to make their ideas available directly to potential sympathisers, via websites, and to communicate instantly with large numbers of supporters, via email (the telephone tree seems like a technique from another age). Of course, it is very obvious that globalisation of communications has facilitated *global* protest. (The paradox of 'anti-globalisation' activists 'using' globalisation has become a well-worn cliché of journalists writing about the movement.) Movements' web presences may also strengthen their visibility in the mainstream media, since it becomes much easier for journalists to obtain authoritative statements of movement goals, contact activists, etc. Moreover, in the worlds of television and newspapers that are ever more niche-oriented, any sizeable activist cause is likely to find mainstream outlets that will cater for its views and activities.

Nevertheless, the virtual disappearance of the anti-war movement, with which I began this chapter, underlines the fact that technical fixes are not enough, and cannot offset fundamental political difficulties. Peace politics has got more complicated in the last decade, and not only due to the invention of the 'quick fix war'. During the Cold War, the overriding threat of nuclear destruction appeared to simplify much of the politics of peace. The slogan 'Better Red than dead' was maliciously attributed to pacifists, but it did sum up (in a distorted way) the simple fact that the threat of the total destruction of human society seemed to negate any possible political goal for which it might be carried out. Of course, nuclear pacifism still allowed other wars to be fought, and peace politics was divided between pacifists who supported no wars and revolutionaries who supported wars of national liberation and other struggles against western and colonial power. However the Cold War meant that peace politics tended to be the province of those who opposed the west's world role as well as its nuclear strategy.

Even during the Cold War, peace movements struggled with the paradoxes of this position. In the 1980s, the emergence of opposition within the Soviet bloc highlighted the contradictions in the western nuclear disarmament movement's tendency to reduce the Cold War to an 'equal' conflict over weapons. Eastern European oppositionists often demanded that western activists support their demands for human rights and what would now be called 'regime change' (Kaldor 1990). The western movements were increasingly divided between those who emphasised the linkage of disarmament with human rights in dismantling the Cold War (see for example Edward Thompson's 1982 polemic) and those who felt that linkage diluted the core issue of nuclear disarmament. The irony of the decade was that the western movement was largely defeated, and declined after 1984; the Cold War unwound afterwards, as a result of elite détente between Mikhail Gorbachev and Ronald Reagan, beginning around 1986. The seeds sown by the small groups of dissidents grew into the massive democracy movements in countries like East Germany and Czechoslovakia, definitively ending the Cold War in 1989 (and vindicating END's vision). The decade began with mass protest movements against nuclear weapons in western European capitals; it ended with mass democracy movements in Eastern European capitals. The links between the two were essential to ending the Cold War.

This dilemma has been magnified in the 'new wars' (as Kaldor 1999, has called wars that combine international and civil conflict based on identity politics) of the 1990s and 2000s. Anti-war movements have tended to respond to specific western campaigns as discrete events (e.g., the small protest movements against the Gulf, Kosovo and Afghan wars; the huge movement over Iraq). However these campaigns have often been *responses* to crises that lie within state and society in the zone of conflict. And the *effect* of western military intervention is often to transform those crises. Anti-war movements focused exclusively on 'stopping the war' often appear naïve in their attitudes to these underlying conditions. Thus my study of the peace movement in 1990 showed that the movement had no answers to the new problems posed by the Iraqi rebellions and Saddam Hussein's repression, immediately after the Gulf War (Shaw 1996).

Likewise the movement against the 2003 Iraq War was effective in highlighting the lack of legitimacy in the manifest case for war, based on 'weapons of mass destruction'. It did not, however, offer a credible answer to the underlying issue of the war, namely the totalitarian regime of Saddam, and the latent case (often stressed by Bush and Blair) for removing this regime. Hence the demands of western-left and Islamist anti-war activists contrasted with the attitudes of many Iraqi exiles (not to mention activists within Iraq), who willed the US to remove their torturer. The anti-war movement was effective, but it would have been more so if it had actually advocated a credible alternative method of removing Saddam. But that would have taken the movement into the complex politics of the United

Nations, sovereignty and international justice, which was probably impossible for a very loose and broad coalition to achieve.

Likewise, as I pointed out above, a simple demand to 'stop the war' left the movement with little to say when the US predictably did the stop the war, having claimed 'victory' over Saddam, after barely four weeks. This was, of course, the point at which the contradictions of US policy were most sharply revealed. The administration that had spent tens of billions of dollars preparing for war had spent only a tiny fraction of this preparing for post-war administration. The US had not put planning and resources into restoring basic services, so that electricity and clean water continued to be cut off from millions of Iraqis – not for days, but for weeks and months after the 'victory'. Seemingly trigger-happy US troops were quick to shoot Iraqi civilians and ask questions after. Despite the obvious contradictions between different Iraqi factions, the US had little idea of how to go about constructing a new Iraqi government. Law and order proved fragile, and killings both of US soldiers and of Iraqis continued at a serious rate not just in the immediate aftermath of the war, but for a long time afterwards. Almost a year after the overthrow of Saddam, there appears no early end to any of these problems. Thus the continuing crisis of Iraqi society and politics has posed many issues that a peace movement should have contributed to. Once again, however, the seeming necessity of simple focus in 'movement' politics made such a contribution difficult if not possible to achieve.

We could draw the conclusion that a mass demonstration movement is a blunt instrument. In an intense crisis, which poses one seemingly simple question above all others, such a movement allows large numbers of people to offer an answer and influence more conventional political processes in parliaments, governments, etc. But when issues become more complex, and the single question is replaced by many questions, this kind of movement becomes less relevant. Indeed we could posit a functional specialisation, since while movements as such often don't offer more complex answers, clearly organisations that are related to and overlap with them – NGOs – do develop more sophisticated and complex analyses and recommendations, and offer alternative, more consistent modes of ongoing pressure. The history of activism, like that of media, in the last two decades could be seen as a movement towards more sophisticated, diverse and specialised forms of action and organisation.

However, an alternative conclusion from the limitations of protest movements is that, even within these constraints, they often suffer from over-simplified politics. As in the 1980s, it actually weakens the cause of peace if movements don't offer alternatives to war, rather than a simple 'no'. In the twenty-first century, the protagonists in local conflicts, like Saddam's regime, are often perpetrators of gross human rights abuses, or even genocidists. It is not enough to say that the west should not wage war against them, and to say this is an issue for their own people: they need to be removed from power and the world community has a duty of solidarity with the oppressed. A simple anti-western politics, such as fuelled much of the organising of anti-war protests, is not enough.

## ANTI-WAR AND OTHER SOCIAL MOVEMENTS

This chapter started by arguing that we need to take the specific characters of social movements seriously: a 'one size fits all' analysis will not work. However, it is obvious that anti-war movements do not exist in a vacuum, unrelated to other kinds of contemporary social movement. The movement against the Iraq war mobilised networks and constituencies that had already been mobilised, not only by earlier campaigns against the US war in Afghanistan, but also by the 'anti-globalisation' movement which had organised a new generation of young activists since the late 1990s. Indeed, this relationship repeated a general pattern throughout the history of 'new' social movements in the second half of the twentieth century. There has been constant cross-fertilisation of ideas, tactics and activists, so that one movement often leads to another.

However, the specific form of each movement depends on its aims and the structural conditions to which it responds. As I have argued elsewhere (Shaw 1994), some movements, like the movement against the Iraq war, respond to very specific crises. This means that they tend to be narrowly focused and find it difficult, as movements, to go beyond their initial objects. Other movements (women's movements are good examples) are more broadly based in a range of issues. Clearly the 'anti-globalisation' movement is closer to the latter model, which may be why it has lasted longer than the anti-war movement. However the 'anti-globalisation' movement was initially very incoherently focused, since 'anti-globalisation' was an inherently implausible idea – not just because activists needed the technology and infrastructure of globalisation, but also because global change also offers possibilities for progressive development. Not surprisingly, movement thinkers and activists have increasingly preferred to call it instead the 'global justice movement'.

## CONCLUSIONS

This chapter has used a discussion of the anti-Iraq war movement to advance arguments about the changing relations of social movements, media and global politics. In the nineteenth and early twentieth centuries, *modern* social movements were strongly rooted in subordinate classes in national societies. Their aims centred on class interests and international issues in relation to these; they were closely linked to class-based parties; and their modes of action integrated their social bases through face-to-face organisation and print media. In the second half of the twentieth century, *late modern* ('new') social movements were based primarily among educated middle-class youth. Their aims centred on universal, chiefly global issues; they integrated their bases both through more flexible modes of organisation and via television and other mass media; and they were often successful to the extent that they pursued single issues free from party agendas.

This chapter has suggested that in the post-1989 *global* era, simultaneous changes in political and media contexts have created a crisis of movement activism, with major new challenges and opportunities. I have argued that so far movements have responded better to new media than to the transformed political and ideological conditions of the global era. While some herald a new era of movement activism in the twenty-first century, I contend that movement politics remains in crisis. The changed political environment has created political and organisational dilemmas that movements have not and may not overcome.

## BIBLIOGRAPHY

Anderson, P. and T. Nairn (1965) *Towards Socialism*, London: Fontana
Conetta, C. (2003) *The Wages of War: Iraqi Combatant and Noncombatant Fatalities in the 2003 Conflict*, Project on Defence Alternatives Research Monograph 8, <http://www.comw.org/pda/0310rm8.html>
Gordon, D. (2003) 'Iraq, war and morality', *Economic and Political Weekly*, XXXVIII, 12 and 13, 1117–20, <http://www.epw.org.in>
Hallin, D. (1986) *The 'Uncensored War': The Media and Vietnam*, New York: Oxford University Press
Inglehart, R. (1977) *The Silent Revolution: Changing Values and Political Styles among Western Publics*, Princeton: Princeton University Press
Iraq Body Count (2003) <www.iraqbody.count.net> [accessed 2 September 2003]
Kaldor, M. (1999) *New and Old Wars: Organized Warfare in the Global Era*, Cambridge: Polity
—— (1990) *Europe from Below: An East-West Dialogue*, London: Verso

Mandelbaum, M. (1987) 'Vietnam: the television war', *Daedalus* III, 4, 157–69

Mattausch, J. (1989) *A Commitment to Campaign: A Sociological Study of CND*, Manchester: Manchester University Press

Michels, R. (1959 [1915]) *Political Parties: A Sociological Study of the Oligarchical Tendencies of Modern Democracy*, New York: Dover

Parkin, F. (1968) *Middle Class Radicalism: The Social Bases of the British Campaign for Nuclear Disarmament*, Manchester: Manchester University Press

Shaw, M. (1996) *Civil Society, Media and Global Crises: Representing Distant Violence*, London: Pinter

—— (1994) 'Civil Society and Global Politics: Beyond a social movements approach', *Millenium: Journal of International Studies* 23, 3, 647–68

Taylor, R. (1988) *Against the Bomb: The British Peace Movement, 1958–1965*, Oxford: Clarendon Press

Thompson, E. P. (1982) *Beyond the Cold War*, London: European Nuclear Disarmament

# Part III

# Global Activism and Activist Media

# 10
# Activist Media, Civil Society and Social Movements

*John D. H. Downing*

In an era in which global civil society, transnational social movements, and corporate globalisation are focusing the attention of socialist researchers and activists more intensively than ever, the varying roles of alternative media within this scenario become of paramount importance. What do alternative media enable to happen? Where should activists concentrate their efforts? Do the 'social justice experts' who throw their energy into developing strategies and programmes to combat the effects of corporate globalisation and human rights abuses, sufficiently pause to analyse how alternative media activism needs to be part and parcel of their work? Furthermore, do alternative media activists sufficiently recognise the ways media may be used by entirely negative, or traditionalistic, social movements, as well as by constructive social forces?

To answer these questions, I will focus on three contrasting case studies of alternative media uses in global civil society developments: the global anti-apartheid movement; India's *Hindutva* movement among non-resident Indians worldwide and the *Falun Gong* (*Falun Dawa*) movement of Greater China and the Chinese diaspora. These movements, in partially different periods, represent very different political positions but all have depended on media strategies. The intention here is, by contrasting each of these very different movement/civil society media operations with each other, to illuminate two key issues: the different communication possibilities open transnationally to contemporary social movements from those previously available; and to probe terms such as 'civil society' and 'alternative media' for their implicitly constructive and socialist aura. A common problem with accounts of civil society (e.g., Howell and Pearce 2001; Kaldor 2003; Keane 2003) is the weakness of their attention to media, communication and social networking issues. This chapter hopes to make some contribution to flagging and remedying this signal weakness.

## THE GLOBAL ANTI-APARTHEID MOVEMENT

As a local force, the anti-apartheid movement began some one hundred years ago. Following a decade's activity by the African Political Organisation, the African National Congress (ANC) was founded in 1912 (under an initially different title). As a global force, the movement gathered particular momentum after 1948 when the National Party came to power in South Africa in a virtually Whites-only election and proceeded to systematise the standard state racism which the British had organised in South Africa. Against the general backdrop of the 1950s shift away from in-your-face colonialism to neocolonial structures, South Africa increasingly stood out as suffering from a militantly retrogressive White minority regime. As a result, the international anti-colonial movement came to focus more and more closely on it.

Anti-Apartheid began as an organisation in Britain in 1959. Its history has been written in part, especially as regards its activities and influence in the USA (Massie 1997; Thörn 2003). We will focus here on two aspects of the story, the ANC underground radio station and the global publications and communication links of the anti-apartheid movement. Together with the informal underground communication networks inside South Africa,[1] and the roles of newspapers such as *The Sowetan* and, until 1985, the *Rand Daily Mail*, followed by the *Weekly Mail* (in so far as they were permitted to function under the regime's censorship rules), these two were among the primary communication nodes in the anti-apartheid struggle.

The radio station was named *Radio Freedom*, founded in 1967. There were heavy penalties for being found listening to it, namely a five- to eight-year jail sentence. It broadcast initially from Zambia and Tanzania, and later also from Angola and Ethiopia in the 1980s, aided by heavy Soviet influence at that time in those two countries' regimes. It awaits a comprehensive study,[2] as do the internationally circulating anti-apartheid print and other media. The archive[3] of the British Anti-Apartheid Movement lists 35 nations worldwide that boasted anti-apartheid organisations, some lasting only a few years but others resembling the British and lasting for decades. The Netherlands, in particular, had three organisations, each with its own emphasis, and was a particularly strategically placed nation, given the Dutch origins of the Afrikaner community. In Australia the anti-apartheid movement strongly resonated with the generational shift away from the 'White Australia' mentality so prevalent in the first two-thirds of the twentieth century and before, and played a significant symbolic role in that process of national self-redefinition. Another active nation was Denmark, whose government was the first one to fund the southern African liberation movements directly, and thereby made it more possible for other governments to be pressured to do the same. And of course the US, given its pre-eminent role in the Cold War, was a vital but reactionary link in the chain in terms of the majority of its corporate and governmental elites.

The archive lists a quite extraordinary range of global activities, running from international sporting, cultural, academic, consumer, investment, weapons sales and tourism boycott campaigns, to campaigns for political prisoner release (especially Nelson Mandela), for death row inmates and for those unjustly tried and/or detained. All involved media uses of one or more kinds, and thus listed in the archive as well are the regularly appearing magazine *Anti-Apartheid News* (1965–94), documents concerning press relations (1960–94), numerous photos, a selection of 18 videos of varying lengths from varying sources, the works displayed in 14 photo-exhibitions, artwork, lapel-badges, banners, shopping bags and T-shirts. Admittedly the British organisation was one of the most enduring and energetic, but if one imagines a global archive of these materials from even just the 35 nations with active anti-apartheid groups, the sum total of media dynamism involved in this movement was really quite extraordinary, in both its variety and its persistence as well as the scale of its transnational diffusion.

And this is before we acknowledge the tremendous impact of particular media items, notably three: *Naught For Your Comfort* (a personal account by an Anglican monk, Trevor Huddleston, of the devastation wrought under apartheid, published in 1956); and two documentaries shot clandestinely in South Africa, *End of the Dialogue* (1970)[4] and *Last Grave at Dimbaza* (1973).[5] Huddleston's book was excerpted in *Reader's Digest*,[6] surprisingly given the magazine's fierce anti-communism. Both documentaries were shown very widely across the world, not only in anti-apartheid campaigns or film programmes, but also in colleges and schools, where they were bought or rented for regular use in classes. They were also screened on a number of television channels internationally, including the BBC, over howls of protest from the regime's London embassy.

The earlier documentary argued that the apartheid regime was not one with which any dialogue about social justice or democracy was feasible; the later one documented the never-ending physical removals of African urban communities and their typical abrupt relocation in remote and barren places with no amenities of any kind whatsoever, including housing.

This is not to discount the impact of some feature films which successfully dramatised the brutal enforcement of the apartheid system, such as two made earlier on in the struggle, *Cry The Beloved Country* (1951) and *Come Back Africa* (1959), and two in its latter years, *Cry Freedom* (1987) and *A Dry White Season* (1989), all of which received substantial international distribution. Although no global listing has been compiled, a mass of television documentaries as made across the planet with the intention of exposing conditions of life for the Black majority in South Africa.

So far I have focused only on the scale and diffusion of media coverage of apartheid. A different study would need to engage precisely with content: for example was the coverage one simply of moral disgust at a repressive system, or did the political economy of global corporate and governmental involvement get adequate play as well? Clearly, too, the apartheid regime was energetically pumping major funds into its own public relations campaign, both directly and implicitly (e.g., in tourism advertising and sports coverage). The relation between the global anti-apartheid campaign and the regime's publicity machine would also be important to analyse. However, the key issue remains the extraordinary duration and scope of this global movement, facing off as it did against western corporate priorities and sullied as well as assisted by the funds poured into anti-apartheid activity by the USSR. All this was done pre-internet, so that the technical capacity for very rapid and widespread mobilisation was in no way comparable with the possibilities globally available after the final demise of the apartheid regime in 1994. While the internet can be a splendid mobilising tool as well as an information archive, the truly vital resources are collective energy and commitment to transnational campaigning and the absence of fatalism in facing down Goliath. Indeed Thörn (2003) rightly stresses the very considerable importance of networking at international conferences, and especially of continual speaker-tours by South African visitors and exiles, 'spiders in the webs of global anti-apartheid activism' (2003:25).

## HINDUTVA

This term is used by ultra-rightist Hindu organisations, such as the RSS (Rashtriya Sevak Sangh) and the VHP (Vishwa Hindu Parishad),[7] to assert that India is a one-faith nation, the implication being that its 12 per cent Muslim, 2 per cent Sikh and 2 per cent Christian population should convert to Hinduism. In the case of Muslims, a frequently used slogan within these extremist groups is translated as 'Muslims should go to Pakistan/Or to the Cemetery' (the Hindi words for Pakistan and cemetery rhyme). This phenomenon, so radically different from the anti-apartheid movement, is nonetheless substantially a transnational movement as well as a local one. Non-resident Indians (the standard term used in India for the Indian diaspora), especially in the US, Canada and Britain, have been very significant donors to the RSS and VHP, though not always aware that their charitable donations to Indians in need have been diverted into the coffers of these groups.[8]

The communal conflicts between Hindus and Muslims in modern India go back to the colonising invasions of the subcontinent by Muslim warlords some thousand years ago. Like Christian invaders elsewhere, the Mughal emperors quite often destroyed other religions' shrines or in some cases seized them for Muslim use. Especially toward the close of the twentieth century, extremist Hindu demagogues seized upon such actions as still-living symbolic defeats for the Hindu majority's entitlements, which the militants asserted both the gods and human pride demanded be at last avenged and righted. This came to a head in December 1992 with the razing, by a fanatical mob, of the Babri Masjid, the Emperor Babar's mosque at Ayodhya, the supposed birthplace of the immensely popular deity Ram (Rajagopal 2001:151–211, 284–91). In Mumbai there were immediate Muslim–Hindu confrontations in which the police largely sided with Hindu mobs, and the following month, January 1993, there were anti-Muslim pogroms incited by the rightwing extremist organisation Shiv Sena. By the end of those two months in Mumbai some 900 were killed, nearly two-thirds of them Muslims. In March 1993 a series of bombs were set off in the city, killing over 250 more.[9] In January 2002 in Gujarat State, the conflicts surged to the fore again, with the murders of some 60 Hindu pilgrims to Ayodhya in a blaze deliberately set in their train carriage. This appalling act was followed by a massacre of some 2,000 Muslims, men, women, children and the aged, in and around Ahmedabad,

Gujarat's capital, greenlighted by the State's extremist Governor (Chief Minister).[10] Furthermore, throughout the period since independence, the state of Kashmir, overwhelmingly Muslim, has been the centre of tension and intermittent wars between the Indian and Pakistani governments, even to the point of nuclear sabre-rattling in 2002. Yet the thousand-year history of relations between Muslims and Hindus was multi-faceted and went through different phases of accommodation and conflict over the centuries. The story was far from one of unrelieved mutual hatred.[11]

Vinay Lal[12] has discussed the outpouring of falsified history in US-based internet sites.[13] Articles are given a scholarly veneer by citing the names of sources, though not the location of the text in question. Some sites however, such as Hindu Unity, Sarvarkar Darshan, Soldiers of Hindutva, Mabharati, Hindu Women versus Muslim Women, the Saffron Tigers – described by one commentator as the 'stormtroopers' (Gupta 2001) – went far further, often prominently displaying exhortations to eliminate physically the supposed enemies of *Hindutva*.

These multiple levels of communication, ranging from the superficially scholarly to religious ceremonial information services (the Hindu University Resource Center) to the literally lethal, are characteristic of many ultra-rightist movements (see Billig 1978, on Britain's neo-Nazi National Front). Some analysts have emphasised this facet of the Hindutva movement in particular connection with the widespread US fund-raising organised through the internet and in a number of US temples, often in the name of philanthropic outreach to impoverished groups[14] in India. The largest and most respectable of such groups in the US is the IDRF (India Development and Relief Fund), which funneled at least US$4 million in 2000 to Sangh Parivar foundations and groups in India. The full extent of monies transferred by the IDRF, temples and other groups, and the purposes for which they are appropriated in India, is far from transparent. The VHPA (VHP America) and its offshoot, the blandly-titled Hindu Students Council (its leaders ceased being students many years ago), are other leading US bodies within this panoply. A number of temples sent money to the groups that razed the Babri Mosque and constructed the Ram temple in Ayodhya. Connecticut-based lawyer Sunil Deshmukh attests that extreme right-wing Indian Hindus in America tend to be more staunch than those in India: 'Their silence on the violence in Gujarat was deafening. What is more alarming is the feeling among them that with their money power, they can do anything.'[15]

In Britain, similarly, the group AWAAZ – South Asia Watch's publication *In Bad Faith? British Charity and Hindu Extremism*[16] has identified two major organisations directly linked to the RSS (the HSS and Sewa[17] International UK) which have concealed their affiliation in raising considerable public donations for earthquake relief and other causes. In India itself, the RSS and linked groups have frequently been active in denying help to non-Hindus, and in threatening other agencies endeavoring to offer them assistance (AWAAZ 2004). Accounts of similar phenomena in Canada, Australia and other locations of the NRI Diaspora such as Malaysia or the Gulf states were not available to the author at the time of writing, but the combination of internet links and certain temple networks makes it inconceivable that the *Hindutva* transnational movement communication between India, the US and Britain outlined here is restricted to those three countries. This communication has the most direct of consequences, virtually all of them totally inimical to the rights of Muslim and other subordinate groups in India.

## FALUN GONG

Our third example of global civil society media use is sharply different again from the first two. *Falun Gong* is a religious movement drawing from Daoism and Buddhism, although on occasions its leader, Li Hongzhi, has also been sharply critical of certain aspects of Buddhism. It has roots (Sinclair 2002a) in popular religious ('White Lotus') movements in China, stretching back many centuries, many of which were as energetically repressed in the Imperial era as is *Falun Gong* currently. It is very suspicious of modern western science, very concerned with meditation and bodily health exercises and highly respectful of Chinese cultural traditions. Its emergence was probably aided by the official blessing the PRC (People's Republic of China) regime accorded the traditionalist *Qigong* health and fitness cultivation movement in the 1980s, of which it is in many ways a variant.

It may also be, as Thornton (2002) suggests, that within the cultural framework of *Qigong*, the assertion of independent body-mind cultivation in the philosophical premises of *Falun Gong* is easily construed as a fundamental critique of the regime, both by its practitioners and the regime alike. Heberer (2001) argues that its adherents inside the PRC may largely be drawn from those – the elderly, the unemployed, minor government officials – who have lost out in the shift to aggressive marketisation undertaken by the Chinese Communist Party leadership, but who find themselves straitjacketed by the continued political authoritarianism of the regime. Far and away the best recent account of *Falun Gong's* philosophy and media activism is Zhao (2003), upon which I have drawn extensively.

*Falun Gong* began in 1992 in the PRC and initially sought registration as a licensed organisation. This was repeatedly refused, making it clear it would not only never be granted, but also signaling that it needed to shed the normal signs and appurtenances of an organisation if it was to avoid further unwelcome attention from the state. In response, one major association (*Falun Dafa*) was disbanded in 1997 and activities within the PRC were decentralised. While it is not an organisation or a religion in the sense of having a divinity and clergy, it is capable of a surprising degree of mobilisation. In April 1999, out of seemingly nowhere, it mounted a large silent demonstration of between 10,000 and 30,000 people right outside Zhongnanhai, the Beijing zone reserved exclusively for top leaders, shocking them into banning the movement and the harsh repression of its devotees. There were claims the demonstration was significantly organised through email, though Tong (2002:647) cites official PRC media sources claiming that the primary communication technology used was the telephone, along with some 80 websites. In response to the arrests of many demonstrators, protests were staged in some 30 Chinese cities (Landler 1999; Lum 2001). Tong (2002:636) cites a PRC source claiming *Falun Gong* organised no less than 307 protest demonstrations from the end of April to the end of July 1999.

Sinclair (2002a) identifies the motivation for the regime's all-out assault on the movement as twofold. One is concern that *Falun Gong's* deep identification with Chinese nationalism might offer a popular ideological alternative to the Chinese Communist Party's own nationalism – which among the ashes of Maoism constitutes its sole claim to the public's loyalty – and would thereby contest its monopoly of power. The other is that in the deeply contradictory relation of the US elite to China – scrambling to invest, but terrified of the rebalancing of Chinese power *vis-à-vis* the US – the repression of *Falun Gong* has been a useful stick with which to beat the Chinese regime for its human rights abuses. However, cynicism about the US elite's commitment to human rights in no way justifies the Chinese regime's savage prison policies towards *Falun Gong* adherents.

The history of communist regimes shows that *any* domestic movement with independent mobilising power is automatically defined
as a serious threat. Heberer (2002:22) argues that the subterranean
organisational style of *Falun Gong* is all too reminiscent of the underground organisation of the communist party itself before 1949, and
may therefore be particularly worrisome to the regime. He cites one
US-based analyst as describing the regime's dilemma: 'It's like a giant
fighting a ghost ... You know it's there and it's hunting you. But
you don't know exactly where you need to grab it or where it is
grabbing you.'

Tong (2002:636) describes *Falun Gong* as an 'evolving and clandes-
tine social organisation with changing features and practices, sur-
vival structures and camouflage mechanisms'. Its media response
has been extensive, both in radio and even television. In summer
2000 it began international broadcasts from the US into China for
an hour a day over short wave radio, in the late evening by Beijing
time (BBC News Media Reports 2000). Up to 50 million Chinese citizens are said to use short wave radio to access non-national broadcasting. But this initiative did not carry the symbolic weight of what
would happen two years later.

In 2002, a series of *Falun Gong* 'video-break-ins' was confirmed by
the Chinese authorities (*Computer Weekly* 2002; McDonald 2002).
These took the form of videocassettes smuggled into a series of
provincial television stations and substituted by staff *Falun Gong*
practitioners for the designated tapes, or patched into local cable
networks. On at least one occasion, using the satellite then in service
through the end of 2004 (its successor would most likely be proof
against this), sympathisers even managed not only to acquire the
necessary codes and passwords, but also to insert their tapes into the
satellite ground station transmission on two or three occasions, or to
drown out its signal with a very powerful mobile ground station
located in or very near China (whether they used the latter or the
former tactic is currently unclear). The satellite transponders in
question served the remoter rural areas, but symbolically speaking,
cutting off nine national channels and ten provincial stations – even
if the tape they broadcast was cut off after only 20 seconds – was a
first for an unofficial group and a blow to the regime's prestige. One
report suggests that on another occasion a tape ran off the satellite
feed for as much as 15 minutes (Pan 2002).

A newspaper 'hijacking' also occurred about the same time
(Reuters 2002), with two four-line poems by Li Hongzhi inserted on

to an economics page of the major south China *Guangzhou Daily*. Zhao (2003:217) indicates that *Falun Gong* 'has a massive and extremely sophisticated presence' on the world wide web. Porter (2003:207–21) has examined the movement's internet use in a little detail, focusing somewhat on its operations before the PRC government's major assault on the movement in July 1999, but rather more on how the movement has worked with the internet since. His study principally addresses a group of *Falun Gong* practitioners in the US whom he interviewed as part of his extended anthropology master's thesis.

The PRC-based websites were nearly all hacked into after September 1999, and thereafter became inaccessible or inoperative. The government, as is well known, has been a world leader in endeavoring to control internet communication within its frontiers (Sinclair 2002b:13–28), although its initiatives have only been possible as a result of the kindly technical support and advice provided by hungry and conscience-free western informatics firms (Sinclair 2002b:16).

As of the early 2000s, a number of western-based *Falun Gong* sites have been in operation, some offering similar materials in Mandarin and English on mirror-sites. Some are general interest, such as clearwisdom.net, and others offer more specific materials for devotees (e.g., <pureinsight.org>). Porter (2003) proposes an eightfold typology of their standard contents: conversion stories; 'karmic' retribution stories (Porter's term); stories to correct the record against PRC distortions; reprints of PRC news articles with key terms changed in parentheses to switch from negative to positive loading; PRC jail stories; devotees' insights; photo reports of *Falun Gong* meetings or demonstrations; and editorials. By 'karmic retribution' Porter has in mind accounts of persecutors who proceed to meet a sticky end, or at least a very agonising illness or accident. The movement's worldview takes a very affirmative position on the typicality of the universe 'balancing out' through retribution for wrongs meted out.

Noteworthy too is the publication from 2000 on in New York City of the newspaper *Epoch Times*. Zhao (2003:218) notes the paper had grown to be able to run local editions with a common core in 'thirty U.S. states, as well as in Canada, Australia, New Zealand, Japan, Indonesia, Taiwan, Hong Kong, and major Western European countries'. There were also Websites associated with the newspaper. It ran ordinary news, current affairs and entertainment material along with attacks on the PRC regime and special in-depth *Falun Gong* materials.

Uncertainty continues regarding the actual numbers of *Falun Gong* practitioners inside and outside the PRC, the true number of demonstrators outside Zhongnanhai, and the full scale of both internet use and 'television break-ins'. We need to recognise that both the regime and *Falun Gong* may have a common interest, based on entirely different motivations (Tong 2002), in representing the movement at large. In the regime's case this is because its ability to define *Falun Gong* to the national and international public as a political menace to China's stability and needing to be repressed depends in part on its size and most particularly, its capacity to mobilise independently. This has led the regime to group *Falun Gong* with Tibetan and Taiwanese independence activists, and with 'anti-China' elements internationally, as forces intent on wrecking China's growth to global economic and national power. Indeed Zhao concludes:

> one of the most tightly controlled modern media systems in the world has bred one of the most powerful counter-ideological communication networks. Compared with the 1989 prodemocracy discourse, Falun Gong's challenge against the Chinese media system and state power is more profound in its substance, more widespread in its societal reach, much globalized in its structure, and more sustained and militant in its efforts. (2003:221)

She notes too how important to the group's internet activism are servers located in western nations. However, just as the Iranian opposition movement was eventually hijacked by Ayatollah Khomeini and his followers in 1979 and deprived of political freedom for its many strands, so too it is entirely conceivable that if *Falun Gong* nurtures its strength ever more successfully through its western-based international media activism, its own brand of orthodoxy could come to dominate the course of events in China for a while – and today, that means not only in China. On the other hand, the aggressiveness of *Falun Gong*'s unsolicited internet approaches to US and Canadian residents with Chinese names began in 2003–04 to become a major point of contention by those targeted.[18] Its political language, too, had not it seemed liberated itself from the hectoring and absolutist traditional style of the Chinese communist media (Zhao 2003:221).

## CONCLUSIONS

Each of these three movements demands much more detailed and intensive research than given here. Their uses of media and internet communications (where relevant) have been hard to track down with the desirable degree of precision and breadth. Nonetheless, the variations between these three movements – locational, ideological, media-technology-related – clearly indicate that unless we are to identify global civil society only with those aspects of it with which we feel at ease in identifying, the contemporary upsurge in horizontal international linkages is, to say the least, multi-faceted. Of these three movements, the author can identify only with the anti-apartheid movement and its media, and it is hard to think that adherents of any one could whole-heartedly subscribe to either of the others.

Nonetheless, the mobilising power of the internet is clearly considerable when enmeshed with the energy of the *Hindutva*, the *Falun Dawa* and kindred movements. It is a power of both direct on-call information, of sharing information, of reinforcing collective identity on a virtually as-needed basis, and of summoning up collective actions through ideological reassertions and calls to action. It is further strengthened through combination with books, videos, satellites, demonstrations and other expressive media. But it is not magic: it is hard to imagine that apartheid would have fallen much faster if the internet had been available, simply because the line-up of western forces behind the apartheid regime was so colossal for so long (despite their sickening assertions of moral scruple) and the military ruthlessness of the regime was so unqualified. Rather like free speech, it is better to have the internet's potential than not to have it, but we should not disguise to ourselves its contradictory facets, its necessary limitations or its dangers (the *Hindutva* movement, which could destabilise south Asia for generations, with untold consequences for the subcontinent's poor). One final consideration is particularly sobering, however: the strenuous attempts of both the PRC regime and of transnational corporate capital to hijack or corral the internet's potential, remind us that the foes of global civil society (in Kaldor's, Howell's and Pearce's sense), are multiple in shape.

### NOTES

1   The text of a whole range of magazines, newsletters, pamphlets and other alternative print media from the apartheid regime era has been digitised and is accessible at <http://disa.nu.ac.za>. See also Sibeko (1977). For a selection of texts of pamphlets, fliers and radio broadcasts circulating at intervals in South Africa during the apartheid years, see

<http://www.anc.org.za/ancdocs/history/ug/>. For a CD with some of the music and other material broadcast by Radio Freedom, see *Radio Freedom: Voice of the African National Congress and the People's Army Umkhonto We Sizwe*. For a compilation of popular insurrectionary songs circulating underground during the struggle, there is a 2-CD set entitled *South African Freedom Songs*.

2  Professor Ruth Teer-Tomaselli of Natal University has confirmed to me that this is the case.

3  <http://www.bodley.ox.ac.uk/dept/rhodes/aam/aam.html>

4  Produced by a multi-racial and multinational crew: Antonia Caccia, Chris Curling, Simon Louvish, Nana Mahomo, Vus Make and Rakhetla Tsehlana.

5  Also directed, scripted, shot and edited by Nana Mahomo.

6  Where this author first learned about apartheid.

7  Gandhi's assassin was a member of the RSS, convinced that Gandhi was pro-Pakistan and therefore anti-India; the country's prime minister, Vajpayee, through the turn of the millennium, was a long-term RSS member, leader of the intensely conservative BJP party. The VHP organisation, sometimes referred to as the Sangh, has been responsible for some of the most atrocious acts of violence in defense of extreme reactionary positions on a whole number of issues.

8  *The Foreign Exchange of Hate* (2002), Sabrang Communications & Publishing, Mumbai, <http://www.sabrang.com/hnfund/sacw/index.html> [accessed 21 April 2003].

9  For the Mumbai tragedies, see the official report by Justice Srikrishna <http://www.altindia.net/srikrishnareport.htm> [accessed 21 April 2003].

10  See the two-volume report *Concerned Citizens Tribunal – Gujarat 2002*, issued by the monthly magazine *Communalism Combat*, <http://www.sabrang.com/tribunal/index.html> [accessed 21 April 2003]; and also *Communalism Combat* 76 (March–April 2002), <http://www.sabrang.com/cc/archive/2002/marapril/index.html> [accessed 21 April 2003].

11  To begin to understand the contemporary dynamic of communalism in India requires taking on board an appreciation of the nation's intensely complex political and economic formation. Rajagopal (2001) carefully weaves together its main strands: (a) the decline into inefficacy and corruption of the long-established Congress Party, which took over the government of India from the British, and its escalating attempts during the 1980s to appeal to voters *as Hindus* to shore up its popularity; (b) the stagnation of the national economy and consequent growth of immiseration; (c) the onset of neo-liberal globalisation as a vaunted economic cure-all, yet with its usual severely dislocating impact on many sectors; (d) the rightists' successful political exploitation of what Rajagopal terms the 'split public', namely the secular Anglophone elite versus the Hindi-speaking mass of the public; (e) the rapid emergence of a non-resident Indian global elite, especially in the US and Canada, many of whom were passionate supporters of a militarily strong India, and some of whom defined the islamophobic Hindu rightist party (the BJP) as the best instrument to that end; and not least (f) a major media event over the period 1987–90, the immensely popular television serialisation of

the ancient Hindu religious epic, the *Ramayana*. This last was a pivotal cultural turn, for a nation whose official political orthodoxy had constantly proclaimed its secular foundations. Rajagopal's study exemplifies the multi-pronged analysis that comprehension of socio-religious conflicts and their media representation demands. His study has been critiqued for its focus on Delhi and the cultural-political realities of northern India, tendentially omitting the complicated vectors of southern states. Nonetheless, it is a remarkable *tour de force* of media-political analysis.

12  Vinay Lal, *The History of History: Politics and Scholarship in Modern India*, Oxford University Press, 2003, excerpted in the article 'Domain Name Hindutva' in the *Indian Express* (6 August 2003), <http://www.indianexpress.com/full_story.php?content_id=29019>.

13  A Google search (8 April 2004) under the heading 'Aryan invasion, India', produced virtually nothing except denunciations of the 'myth' of the Aryan invasion in the first five pages. Sometimes defined as a leftist invention, sometimes as a British colonialist invention, the assertion of a purely Hindu-origin India certainly seemed to dominate the internet on this topic at the time of writing.

14  There is a disquieting twist to this aspect of the story, which can only be flagged here but not explored. Some of the impoverished groups targeted by fundraisers are Indian tribal groups, often referred to as *adivasi*, and sometimes bracketed with the 'untouchable' castes (the *dalit*) as the collectively excluded. As part of the strategy of India's rightist governing party, the BJP, to expand its support-base, there have been a series of outreach projects aimed at the *adivasi*, previously shunned by middle and upper caste Hindus. They also get renamed as *vanvasi* (forest people, signifying they are original Hindus, not survivors of the Aryans' conquest). What is especially troubling is that some *adivasi* elements in the huge anti-Muslim pogrom organised by the Gujarat State government in 2002 were among the most rabid and vicious lumpenproletarian elements in perpetrating its outrages, not unlike the poor southern US Whites who were mobilised against Black civil rights protestors. (My thanks to my Southern Illinois University colleague Dr Jyotsna Kapur for advising me on sources and also clarifying the meaning of *vanvasi* to me.)

15  A. K. Sen 'Deflections To The Right', in <OutlookIndia.com>, <http://www.outlookindia.com/scriptur11w2.asp?act=sign&url=/full.asp?fodname=20020722&frame=VHP+%28F%29&sid=1&pn=3>. See also Mathew and Prashad (2003) and Rajagopal (2001) for analyses of the phenomenology of many NRI technical professionals in the US, caught between racism and individualised anonymity on the one hand and consumerism and a private search for collective identity on the other:

> The slow process of interpellation draws the participant into a dynamic whereby the messages and idioms begin 'talking to you' (to the person on the net for a weekly identity fix). At your computer, you are an Indian, escaping the homogeneity of corporate America and talking ... to other faceless people who seem to encounter a similar problem. (Mathew and Prashad 2003)

16  http://www.awaazsaw.org/ibf/. My thanks to Dr Kamala Viswesaran of the Anthropology Department, University of Texas at Austin, for drawing my attention to this report.

17  *Not* to be confused with the Indian women's self-help organisation *Sewa*.

18  I am grateful to Cao Yong, my doctoral research assistant in the College of Mass Communication and Media Arts, Southern Illinois University, for drawing my attention to this and for feeding me information on other aspects of these matters.

## BIBLIOGRAPHY

Atton, C. (2001) *Alternative Media*. London: Sage

AWAAZ (South Asia Watch) (2004) 'In Bad Faith? British charity and Hindu extremism', <http://www.awaazsaw.org/ibf/ibfhires.pdf>

*BBC News Media Reports* (2000) 'Banned sect broadcasts to China', 1 July, <http://news.bbc.co.uk/1/hi/world/monitoring/media_reports/814848. stm>

Billig, Michael (1978) *Fascists: A Social-Psychological View of the National Front*, London: Jakanovich

*Computer Weekly* (2002) *'Falun Gong* group hijacked Chinese satellite', 9 July, <http://www.computerweekly.com/Article113997.htm>

Diani, M. and D. McAdam (eds) (2003) *Social Movements and Networks: Relational Approaches to Collective Action*, Oxford: Oxford University Press

Downing, J. (1996) *Internationalizing Media Theory: Transition, Power, Culture: Reflections on Media in Russia, Poland and Hungary, 1980–95*, London: Sage

Downing, J. (2001) *Radical Media: Social Movements and Rebellious Communication*, Thousand Oaks, CA: Sage

Gupta, A. S. (2001) 'Bigots on the Internet', *People's Democracy* XXV.43, <http://pd.cpim.org/2001/oct28/2001_oct28_snd.htm>

Heberer, T. (2001) 'Falungong – Religion, Sekte oder Kult? Eine Heilsgemeinschaft als Manifestation von Modernisierungsproblemen und sozialen Entfremdungsprozessen', University of Duisberg, *Duisberg Working Papers on East Asian Studies*, 36, <http://www.let.leidenuniv.nl/bth/falun.htm>

Howell, J. and J. Pearce, (2001) *Civil Society and Development: A Critical Exploration*. Boulder, CO: Lynne Rienner Publishers

Huddleston, A. S. (1956) *You are Wrong, Father Huddleston*, Amsterdam: Culemborg

Kaldor, M. (2003) *Global Civil Society: An Answer to War*, Cambridge: Polity Press

Keane, J. (2003) *Global Civil Society?* Cambridge: Cambridge University Press

Landler, M. (1999) 'China Imposes Ban on *Falun Gong* Sect', CN-mall.com News, <http://www.cn-mall.com/news/items/50.html>

Lum, T. (2001) 'China and *"Falun Gong"'*, *Congressional Research Service*, 1 August, <http://www.globalsecurity.org/military/library/report/crs/RS20333. pdf>

Massie, R. K. (1997) *Loosing the Bonds: The United States and South Africa during the Apartheid Years*, New York: Doubleday

Mathew, B. and V. Prashad (2003) 'The saffron dollar', Forum of Indian Leftists website, <http://www.foil.org/politics/hindutva/nridollar.html>

Mattelart, T. (ed.) (2002) *La Mondialisation des Médias Contre la Censure: Tiers Monde et audiovisual sans frontiers*, Brussels: De Boeck

McDonald, H. (2002) '*Falun Gong* invades China's TV airspace', *The Age* (Melbourne, Australia), 5 October, <http://www.theage.com.au/articles/2002/10/04/1033538773097.html>

Pan, P. (2002) 'Banned *Falun Gong* Movement Jammed Chinese Satellite Signal', *Washington Post*, 9 July, A18, <http://www.washingtonpost.com/ac2/wp-dyn/A41297-2002Jul8?language=printer>

Porter, N. (2003) '*Falun Gong* in the United States: an ethnographic study', Anthropology Master's Thesis, University of South Florida, <http://www.lib.usf.edu/ETD-db/theses/available/etd-06122003-113105/>

Rajagopal, A. (2001) *Politics After Television: Hindu Nationalism and the Reshaping of the Public in India*, Cambridge: Cambridge University Press

Reuters (2002) '*Falun Gong* slips poems into Chinese newspaper', 4 April, <http://www.rickross.com/reference/fa_lun_gong/falun260.html>

Rodríguez, C. (2001) *Fissures in the Mediascape*, Cresskill, NJ: Hampton Press

Sibeko, A. (1977) 'The underground voice', *The African Communist* vol. 68, republished in S. Siegelaub and A. Mattelart (eds), *Communication and Class Struggle 2: Liberation, Socialism*, Bagnolet, France and New York City: International General, 1983: 203–07

Sinclair, G. (2002a) 'Nationalism and ethnicity', <http://www.geocities.com/gelaige79/flg.pdf>

Sinclair, G. (2002b) 'The Internet in China: information revolution or authoritarian solution?', <http://www.geocities.com/gelaige79/intchin.pdf>

Thörn, H. (2003) 'Anti-apartheid, "new social movements" and the globalization of politics', paper presented in the conference *Perspectives on the International Anti-Apartheid Struggle: Solidarity and Social Movements*, 31 May 2003, St Antony's College, Oxford

Thornton, P. (2002) 'Framing dissent in contemporary China: irony, ambiguity and metonymy', *China Quarterly* 171: 661–81

Tong, J. (2002) 'An organisational analysis of the *Falun Gong*: structure, communications, financing', *China Quarterly* 171: 636–60

Zhao, Y. (2003) 'Falun Gong, identity, and the struggle over meaning inside and outside China', in N. Couldry and J. Curran (eds) *Contesting Media Power: alternative media in a networked world*, Lanham, MD: Rowman and Littlefield: 209–23

# 11
# If it Leads it Bleeds: The Participatory Newsmaking of the Independent Media Centre

*Kate Coyer*

Democracy is a pain in the ass.

(KILL Radio manual)

## FROM WHENCE IT SPRANG

'The culture of a consumer society is mostly about forgetting not learning' (Bauman 1998:82).

Not long after the mass demonstrations against the WTO (World Trade Organisation) and corporate capitalism in Seattle, 1999, Gap stores featured a window display with fake graffiti that was to look as though someone had spray-painted the words *Revolution* and *Freedom* across the giant glass windows as if attempting to liberate the khaki trousers off the mannequins. One of the offending Gap stores in downtown Seattle was located next to the infamous Starbucks, whose smashed windows became one of mainstream media's most oft-repeated images, sparking frustration over the disproportionate focus on broken glass over the level of police violence perpetrated against protestors and the larger peaceful mission of the vast majority of those present.

Ironically, if a legislator in neighbouring Oregon had had his way, violence against Starbucks would have been considered a hate crime, thereby protecting a commercial coffee brand with the same language used to enact harsh sentences on those who commit racist attacks.

Then there is the video game *State of Emergency*. It is billed as an urban riot game set in the near future in which 'fascist, capitalist oppressors have finally locked down the whole town' and it is up to an underground group of masked youth to fight for freedom in the street against 'The Corporation'. Players accrue points by killing security forces in riot gear, busting glass windows and looting.

Video punch-ups and lattes aside, this is the backdrop of cultural clutter amongst which activists and independent media makers have created their *own* space rather than vie for inclusion within the mainstream. For transformations in communication to occur, however, both the technical possibilities and social needs must be addressed. Necessary attention has been afforded to the role of the internet in taking alternative media and activism to new levels of accessibility, participation and efficacy. But despite everything new technology has to offer, the revolution may be televised from a digital media centre, but it is not so revolutionary if it relies on the same old structural models. Equally, as Tony Dowmunt cautions, there is 'no simple guarantee that because a production process is "alternative" it will transparently communicate a radical message to its desired audience' (1998:1). Consequently, the Independent Media Centre, or Indymedia, is a project born out of the aspiration for the organisational structure to represent its values.

Indymedia is both a global network and over 120 (at the time of writing) local, autonomous Indymedia organisations offering 'grassroots, non-corporate coverage'[1] of major protests and issues relevant to the global anti-capitalism and anti-war movements. IMCs can be found across North America, Europe and Australia, as well as in Israel, Palestine, South Africa, Indonesia, Nigeria, Russia, Brazil, Cyprus, Croatia, India and Colombia. The effectiveness of Indymedia has established a model that has since been replicated many times around the globe by activists who want to cover their own local demonstrations and issues, and as a forum to create media centres for coverage of large-scale global protests.

Indymedia has continued to grow exponentially since its inception in 1999, both in size and scope. The philosophy of Indymedia informs each aspect of the global network and local collectives, from its anti-authoritarian decision-making processes, to its open publishing, flexibility as an organisation, decentralisation and commitment to local autonomy. London-based activist Marcus 'Sky' Covell adds:

> It is impossible to calculate how many people are involved, as participation in the volunteer-run group runs the gamut from those who work full-time to keep the infrastructure running, to those who post a single story during a specific event. The IMC has no world headquarters, but if it can be said to be located anywhere, that location is at the convergence of several critical trends: the rebirth of activism, the maturation of the Internet and the

crystallisation of what participants see as a new evil in the form of out-of-control corporatism. (as quoted in *We Are Everywhere*, 2003)

Since 2002, there has been a semi-explosion of academic writing on Indymedia, most notably those by Nick Couldry, John Downing, DeeDee Hallick, Dorothy Kidd and Graham Meikle, in addition to powerful first-person accounts in *We Are Everywhere: The Irresistible Rise of Global Anti-Capitalism*. What is perhaps unique in this body of work is the level of involvement among many of its storytellers, myself included; somewhat reflective of the kind of fluid and participatory media environment it is. The weakness is the potential for over-romanticisation or an 'alternative utopianism'. However, the high level of self-reflexivity among Indymedia activists seeks to avoid that kind of pitfall. As Downing concludes: 'The IMCs are not heaven-sent. They are ours, us at work, to act as best we can to make them empowering agencies and fora – not uniquely so, but as part of the tapestry' (2003:254). This chapter loosely draws on each of these significant pieces and, along with interviews conducted with Indymedia activists and my own participation, seeks to offer a broad overview of the Indymedia phenomenon.

Indymedia is a participatory and hence more democratic form of media. It is media created by activists, participants and observers – media activism seeking to use independent media as a form of direct action and as an alternative to the corporate media system. It is media that cuts across issues and borders, and is a project of experimentation with network structures, both digital and social. Indymedia is a project of negotiating tensions both practically and philosophically. There are countless nuances to the vision. 'Indymedia is many things to many people. It is no ONE thing' (Herndon 2003:5). Views may seem divergent from each other, but perhaps it is more accurate to say they represent the multiple interests of a dynamic group of people.

## EMBEDDED JOURNALISTS AND THE COMMONS

Indymedia's organic development is situated within the evolutionary history of alternative media, social movements and DIY activism. Its emergence is a logical next step for activists in an online world.[2] In Britain, for example, the Indymedia banner provided a useful organising structure in preparation for the May Day 2000 demonstrations, though a similar online media space was created prior to

Seattle during the massive Carnival Against Capitalism protests on 18 June 1999. Some involved with Indymedia cite inspiration from the Zapatista movement in Mexico, in particular Subcomandante Marcos' widely distributed video communiqué in 1996 urging the international progressive community to build a global media network:

> We have a choice: we can have a cynical attitude in the face of media ... (or) we can ignore it and go about our lives. But there is a third option ... (and) that is to construct a different way – to show the world what is really happening – to have a critical worldview and to become interested in the truth of what happens to the people who inhabit every corner of this world. (as quoted in We Are Everywhere 2003)

The Indymedia project is thus borne out of the particular experience, knowledge, passion and energy of those involved, combined with a touch of serendipity among cross-continental convergences of technical resources and timing.

The first Independent Media Centre was built in the months prior to the WTO demonstrations. Activists rented a storefront in downtown Seattle only blocks from where the main demonstrations were to take place. Computer equipment was donated and borrowed, open source server software obtained and a multi-media production complex and internet broadcast facility was built in less then two months. The goal was, as co-founder Jeff Perlstein put it, to create a 'community-based peoples' newsroom, a space where people who had never worked together could all collaborate' (2003:231).

During the protests in Seattle, 500 independent media makers provided up-to-the minute reports online in print, video, audio and photo – most footage uploaded and edited from the Indymedia space downtown. Information was dispatched from the street by walkie talkie, mobile phone and from people racing back to the IMC with news or fresh footage to upload. A series of five video documentaries was produced and uplinked via satellite to public access television stations each day of the protests. A daily newspaper was distributed on the streets of Seattle. Internet radio station, *Studio X*, broadcast online and there were a number of pirate radio stations broadcasting throughout the city. People around the world went to the website to find out what was actually happening. The site received more then 1.5 million visitors during the week, outperforming CNN's website during the same period (Perlstein 2001).

People found out about the site from alternative media coverage such as the progressive syndicated radio programme *Democracy Now!*, activist listserves and networking channels and word of mouth, in addition to mainstream media outlets. Indymedia was called a 'surprisingly effective news organisation' and a 'glimpse of what lies ahead for journalism in the new century ... we wouldn't be surprised if one or two IMCs developed into a major source with their open source reporting model' (indymedia.org).

This media making occurred while urban warfare took place just outside their door, and many activists themselves sought refuge in the media centre from the chaos, police brutality and tear gas on the streets. The potency of live coverage from Indymedia resonated especially when mainstream broadcasters reported police were not firing plastic bullets, while there was already footage up on the Indymedia site of people on the street with large welts on their bodies holding up plastic bullets (Perlstein 2003:240). The city of Seattle later settled a lawsuit filed by protestors resulting from the level of police violence.

Most of the work within Indymedia occurs under far less dramatic conditions, yet the process of piecing together temporary hi-tech media centres remains a remarkably similar collaborative project. Indymedia convergence spaces have since begun morphing into a model of both news reporting and training centres, or polymedia labs. In 2003, Indymedia was home to 'Tidal Wave Cancun' in Mexico for the fifth Ministerial World Trade Organisation meeting, which was an alternative media convergence where those participating could share in the collective work of building the necessary infrastructure of the space, like rigging the rented building with wireless internet, to workshops in radio production, video editing, web page authoring and antenna and transmitter building for micro radio broadcast. It was an 'all hands on deck' environment, resplendent with the kind of colourful chaos you would expect of such a major production where people with technical skills simultaneously do and train, and people without them learn by doing.

Nevertheless, it is no accident that so many Indymedia centres were created in preparation for large global actions. As Seattle activist and Indymedia co-founder Dan Merkle put it:

When there's going to be a lot of attention, it's easier to create an IMC because it's something real that's happening, so it gives us the opportunity to get away from the drudgery of meetings and things that are so far off in the distance. Most people want to do something real. They don't want to stuff envelopes. They don't want to talk about stuff. They want to do stuff. (From personal interview.)

Merkle calls this the 'chasing the spotlight' strategy. On the other hand, there is an 'obsession with the collective present' (John Jordan as quoted in McKay 1998:11) and concern that perhaps we fetishise the moment in focusing single-mindedly on coverage of the dramatic global actions instead of everyday news reporting. Graham Meikle articulates the concerns with such a strategy: 'This focus on speed and immediacy, on being the first on the scene, leads to news that is all event and no process' (2002).

This is an area Indymedia is working to improve upon though, something which speaks to the distinction between the global and the local sites, both in terms of function and utility. In the UK, the site has been broken into regional subsections, such as Indymedia London, Indymedia Sheffield, etc., in hopes of encouraging greater local generation of news and facilitation of a stronger sense of community amongst participants. To that end, the London collective produces a weekly radio programme on local community radio station *Resonance FM*. Other local Indymedias produce similar programming in their area. These shows offer progressive Indymedia content to a wider audience outside the website and serve as a particularly local organising tool outside the immediacy of live event coverage and favours more in-depth reportage. There are also community internet radio stations such as *KILL Radio* in Los Angeles and *Radio Volta* in Philadelphia, and pirate FM stations that have emerged from local Indymedia collectives either directly or indirectly.

## ALL NEWS IS FIT TO PRINT

Open publishing is at the heart of the IMC project because it ensures a place for everyone's voice and participation and is a key to what makes Indymedia a participatory and thus inherently more democratic medium. Anyone who comes to the site can post video, audio, print, or photography, or publicly comment on any other posting without going through an editor. As the site itself describes: 'Open publishing means the process of creating news is transparent to the readers.' The process of 'how to' is self-explanatory and postings appear as they are published on the newswire. Dorothy Kidd explains:

> The Network has begun to move away from the reactive mode of much of 'alternative media' which focuses only on countering the hegemonic messages of the corporate and state media. Instead the IMCs' emphasis on the direct witness of 'open publishing,' and on the self-rule of local sites, begins to prefigure autonomous communications centred in the dreams, realities and communications needs of each locale. (2003:4)

For the London collective, open publishing has 'allowed the streets to enter cyberspace [and] brought technology to the streets' in the form of public access terminals located along protest routes so people could literally post a piece right there from the demonstration.[3]

The success of Indymedia brings an ever-increasing number of people publishing stories and opinions, which means new postings are quickly pushed off the front page. For example, Indymedia UK averaged 19 postings a day in 2002, by 2004, they received over 150 each day. Los Angeles Indymedia participant Marc Herbst puts it this way:

> There's that political rant I've heard a thousand times but maybe it's the first time that person has had the space to say it and maybe they think no one has heard it before. Hopefully if they spend enough time on the site, they'll see that other people may be thinking the same things and engaged in the same political discourse. And maybe then they'll get the notion of collectivity. (Personal interview.)

Indymedia is thus an open network where access and participation are instrumental to the process of newsmaking, even if it makes for a 'messier' process. Open publishing puts greater responsibility on the reader to negotiate their way through the number and quality of postings, a facet that brings with it critique from traditional journalistic quarters. In the *Columbia Journalism Review*, Gail Beckerman comments: 'An open, representative form of media may be a worthy ideal, but in reality is often a messy thing' (2003). She is absolutely correct, but so can it then be argued that sorting out bias and influence in corporate and state media is far messier, indirect and coercive in nature. Indymedia, while far from perfect, at least makes the issues and process visible whereas mainstream media systematically operates towards denial of its inherent flaws. Indymedia represents a form of citizen's media, rather then consumer media through a transparency of process in blurring lines between producer and audience, rather then the blurring of lines between editorial and advertising or funding.

This is not to say there is no editorial policy or filters within Indymedia. For example, open publishing sites are notoriously favoured by purveyors of racist and hate speech. In terms of editorial control, each Indymedia has the ability to 'hide' a posting in adherence to their local guidelines, and such guidelines usually include the removal of hate speech. In the UK, like most Indymedias, racist remarks are subsequently hidden from view. Such a policy is not without controversy, however. Some have argued it inhibits freedom of expression and opens a Pandora's box of editorial control. Others respond there is no reason to keep such speech visible as it goes against the mission and spirit of the project, and opens the sites up for an increasing number of such postings. Contrast that with Indymedia Germany where all postings must be reviewed prior to upload because German law forbids publication of hate speech. What it comes down to is how network decisions affect the structure of local autonomy and non-hierarchical decision-making and the legalities of the countries they operate within. There is recognition that with autonomous entities all sharing the same virtual identity, there exists mutual dependency, shared risk and shared responsibility.

The other question endemic of the open publishing structure is the balance between media activism and alternative news production. The role of Indymedia is two-fold. The first is to present news and information from activists around the world and to provide alternative perspectives and voices. The second is to serve as an organising tool within the activist community to disseminate information about upcoming events and protests and to help activists stay in touch with the worldwide movement. That most Indymedia participants see themselves as both activists and journalists is fundamental to the project vision, and is representative of new forms of community building around media activism.

It is also a direct challenge to the myth of objectivity permeating American media culture.[4] For activist news media, context should be everything and the bias worn on the proverbial sleeve. In Chris Burnett's words: 'The corporate media presents news as symptomatic and without context. We are presented with problems but no ability to solve them, which results in alienation from information. It is a very subjective decision to not provide context' (personal interview). Interestingly, the public debate over definitions of newsmaking within Indymedia was sparked at the annual *Webby Awards* in San Francisco, a pseudo Oscars-style awards show to highlight and promote the internet industry. Indymedia was nominated for an award in the 'Activism' category. During the presentation of the 'News' category award, an activist ran on stage, grabbed the news award from the podium and shouted 'Fuck Corporate Media'. He later said: 'If Indymedia is an activist site, mainstream media like CNN and ABC are activists for corporate and rich elites.'

This debate speaks to the rise in popularity and acceptance of more informal sources of news and information which themselves offer forms of resistance to the sites of traditional media power. Indymedia, and activist media in general, serves as a kind of witnessing and this role should not be undervalued. At the same time, I would suggest the problem may be that within debates surrounding news value, objectivity and fact are being conjoined. The quest to improve standards of reporting is essential for an independent media source. Seklar states: 'We have to look credible. If we don't look credible they'll say, ah, they're just kids. They'll grow out of it. They're just going through a phase right now' (personal interview). Factualness matters, but it is not the same as objectivity.

## DEMOCRACY IS THE RULE OF THE ORATORS

Indymedia is, in effect, a space where the 'hyper-global' and 'hyperlocal' meet. For example on the global Indymedia site, a story from Melbourne details coverage of a videotape broadcast on Australian SBS TV documenting the burning of villages, churches and schools in West Papua, Indonesia, by local armed forces. A collaborative piece on asylum seekers in Britain includes a report from Scotland's Dungavel Detention Centre. This neighbourhood-based reporting model advocates that those affected by the news provide a unique capacity for reporting on it as well. At the same time, there is a wide range of people interested in accessing locally situated news from other places. By sharing stories, a global movement is built.

The global Indymedia network is a horizontal network (Perlstein 2001; Downing 2001) composed of working groups who meet primarily online and share information and decision-making. Discussions are often archived on the Indymedia site and can be accessed by all.[5] Working groups are primarily open to anyone and to join one simply signs up to the listserve and theoretically jumps right in. The digital network that allows for communication via email and electronic sharing of documents makes it possible to develop relationships and infrastructure without having to attend face-to-face meetings. Whereas ultimate consensus rests with the local IMCs who maintain their own individual editorial guidelines, formulation of network structure and policy takes place in the global online Indymedia world. Global online communities exist but are balanced by local collectives. Burnett describes one practical application:

> On the local level, you can see each other face to face and know who is who and suss out instigators. They are usually quite obvious and disruptive. You can't deal with the freaks or those who are abusive in a virtual environment. An unknown person wouldn't carry any clout in a local IMC meeting. (Personal interview.)

Inevitably, with such a decentralised network of individual actors involved, there exists a kind of tyranny of structurelessness. Not enough people want to do the ground work, too many complain about problems without stepping in to solve them, bureaucratic tyranny grows out of excessive benign structure, too many listserves flood mailboxes in the computerised world and the 'tyranny of the loudest voice' can develop when power vacuums form, even within anti-authoritarian settings. There is also concern surrounding the dominance of American collectives and English as the primary, often only, language on global lists and online discussions, though efforts are underway to add more translation. Beneath these geographic divides, however, lie fundamental questions of control and process.

In 2002, the global Indymedia project was awarded a grant from the Ford Foundation for $50,000 (Beckerman 2003). But Indymedia activists in Argentina, Brazil, Italy and others opposed taking the money because of its connection to the corporate world, and because the legacy of Ford Motors is tied with the former brutal dictatorship in Argentina (Beckerman 2003). Others, especially many in the US, felt the money should be taken, as there were no strings attached. In the end, the grant was turned down. It was a bitter lesson for some, and for others proof that Indymedia's survival depends on working through these kinds of tensions and fissures. This may in fact also be the crux of how Indymedia embodies a new vision of alternative media, where process and consensus matter more then short-term prosperity, financial or otherwise.

## WHO CONTROLS THE CODE CONTROLS THE FUTURE

'Um, you sit down at a computer for six hours and you type, basically. You type and try not to make typos and hope it works' (Kawakami, personal interview).

Indymedia is both a social and technological phenomenon. In addressing the dualism between the digital and social networks, Rheingold asks: 'If we decided that community came first, how would we use our tools differently?' (2001). The original software that ran the Indymedia sites was developed by Matthew Arnison for the Community Activist Technology (CAT) collective in Sydney, an organisation he co-founded. The software, called *Active*, was created in response to a number of local needs and personal interests within Sydney's activist community, but quickly made its way to organisers in Seattle planning for the WTO protests.[6] CAT and the Active software are part of the larger movement for free and open source software that seeks to defy corporate control over ownership and copyright. It is free software, which not only means anyone can use the source code without charge, but anyone can make changes to the code and adapt it for their specific needs.

Inevitably, those with technical skills often carry heavy weight at meetings and on discussion listserves, despite an anti-authoritarian ethos. More significantly, they must be trusted members of the collective. Los Angeles Indymedia programmer John Kawakami puts it this way: 'No one wants to create the boss [but] it's a heavy responsibility. You've got to trust the person enough because they will have complete access to the whole machine' (personal interview). Not only that, but there is also a 'tyranny of techies' that exists. Because Indymedia is a voluntary entity, work is done based on who is willing to do it. And because so much of the online Indymedia infrastructure is dependent on computer programming, techies are invaluable in a way previously unseen in alternative media projects.

Decentralisation, however, is a key part of the matrix of Indymedia. Technically, decentralisation increases the reliability of the network because there are numerous computer servers hosting the actual Indymedia sites and controlling the flow of information, so that if one server falters, data is automatically rerouted to another computer. The software lacks a password system by design. Indymedia does not collect information on its visitors and has stopped keeping back-end logs all together. This change occurred after the US Federal Bureau of Investigation (FBI) subpoenaed logs from Seattle Indymedia after a death threat against President Bush was posted. Indymedia successfully denied the FBI's request on the grounds the logs they had requested had nothing to do with who was visiting the site, but rather who was administering the site and actually working on the machine. It should be noted that the person who posted the threat did not do so anonymously and even provided their email address.

Even so, are security concerns overplayed for existing IMCs? In Genoa, the day after activist Carlo Giuliani was killed by Italian police, police raided the Indymedia convergence centre, which was located inside a public building rented out by organisers from the city. Police raided the building in the middle of the night: 'IMC journalists stood with their hands against the walls ... Some were kicked while they were sleeping ... Computers and phones were then smashed and hard drives and video tapes confiscated, and all the papers were ransacked.'[7] Had IMC servers been located in Italy during the protests, they most certainly would have been confiscated. Burnett feels it is naïve to think Indymedia does not have enemies but that sites are monitored and meetings infiltrated. Paranoia does not rule Indymedia, rather, it feels like a distrust and disdain for the system fuelled with the desire to prove that security and openness do not have to be mutually exclusive.

## FINAL THOUGHTS

'Where there is no rich, healthy public sphere we should support anarchistic communicative techniques. Where there is a rich, healthy public sphere, we must take an honest, unromantic account of the costs of such anarchy' (Siva Vaidhyanathan, open Democracy.net).

So, is Indymedia the wave of the future, as some media analysts have proclaimed? Burnett answers: 'If we are careful how we design structure, the model the IMC offers can be proliferated around the world. Indymedia could rival the power of corporate media, but it could serve as a social model for organising which is much more interesting' (personal interview). At this moment, Indymedia appears interested in ensuring their sustainability by working out ideological differences and structural development rather then feeling complacent about their successes. And in the end, it may be useful to have both those who are most passionate about content and those who are most passionate about negotiating collective responses to technological and social needs.

I would also conclude by restating the significance of access and participation with respect to the wider movement for community media. At a time when the UK is on the verge of creating a third tier of broadcasting in the form of community radio (and similar efforts for expansion of such service continue in the US), demands for community media support increase around the world.

## NOTES

1 From Independent Media Centre (IMC) mission statement at indymedia.org
2 Kidd (2002, 2003) and Downing (2003), for example, offer insightful examinations of the precedent movements informing Indymedia, and the socialist anarchist tradition, respectively. Meikle (2002) as well provides useful historical context, especially of the origins of the initial software running the sites.
3 By IMC activists 'Annie' and 'Sam', <http://docs.indymedia.org/view/Local/ImcUkWritingMd2>
4 See Nick Couldry's piece (2004) for further discussion of open publishing, objectivity and media power.
5 <http://lists.indymedia.org>
6 See Graham Meikle's Future Active for extensive history of Community Activist Technology (CAT) and Active software. Of particular interest to me is the importance of historicising local uses of global technologies: 'The routine emphasis on the global nature of the Net means it's easy to overlook the significance of *local* applications of computerised communications' (Meikle 2002:91).
7 There is evidence suggesting the raid occurred because the IMC had footage of police dressed as Black Bloc anarchists leaving a police station then later throwing rocks at officers in attempt to incite the crowd. Irrespective of whether or not the IMC has this footage, it is a tactic police have used to instigate violence at large demonstrations. Others have suggested the raid was in search of footage of Guiliani's killing. Source is <laweekly.com/printme.php3?&eid=267>.

## BIBLIOGRAPHY

Amoshaun, personal interview (2003)
Bauman, Z. (1998) *Globalization: The Human Consequences*, New York: Columbia University Press
Beckerman, G. *Columbia Journalism Review* (2003)
Burnett, C. personal interview (2001, 2003)
Calloway, C. personal interview (2002)
Couldry, N. and J. Curran (eds) (2003) *Contesting Media Power: Alternative Media in a Networked World*, London: Rowman and Littlefield

Downing, J. (2003) 'The Independent Media Centre Movement and the Anarchist Socialist Tradition' in N. Couldry and J. Cunan (eds) *Contesting Media Power: Alternative Media in a Networked World,* Rowman and Littlefield
—— with T. Villarreal Ford, G. Gil and L. Stein (2001) *Radical Media: Rebellious Communication and Social Movements,* London: Sage
Dowmunt, T. (1998) 'An alternative globalization: youthful resistance to electronic empires', in D. Thussu (ed.) *Electronic Empires,* London: Arnold
Halleck, D. (2002) 'Gathering Storm: The Open Cyber Forum of Indymedia', paper presented at *OurMedia II Conference,* Barcelona, Spain, July 2002, <http://www.ourmedianet.org/eng/om2002/papers2002.html>
Herbst, M. Personal interview (2001)
Herndon, S. Personal interview (2001, 2002)
—— 'Barranquilla Presentation/Notes', as presented at *OurMedia III Conference,* Barranquilla, Colombia, May 2003, <http://www.ourmedianet. org/eng/om2003/om2003.papers_eng.html>
Kawakami, J. Personal interview (2001)
Kidd, D. (2003) 'Carnival and Commons: the Global IMC Network', draft paper presented at *OurMedia III Conference,* Barranquilla, Colombia, May 2003, <http://www.ourmedianet.org/eng/om2003/om2003.papers_ eng.html>
—— 'Which Would You Rather: Seattle or Porto Alegre?' paper presented at *OurMedia II Conference,* Barcelona, Spain, July 2002, <http://www. ourmedianet.org/eng/om2002/papers2002.html>
McKay, G. (1998) 'DiY Culture: notes towards and intro', in D. McKay, *DiY Culture: Party and Protest in Nineties Britain,* London: Verso
Meikle, G. (2002) *Future Active: Media Activism and the Internet,* New York and London, Routledge and Annandale, London: Pluto Press
—— 'Indymedia and The New Net News', *M/C: A Journal of Media and Culture,* <http://www.media-culture.org.au/0304/02-feature.html>
Merkle, D. Personal interview (2001)
Notes from Nowhere (ed.) (2003), *We Are Everywhere: The Irresistible Rise of Global Anticapitalism,* London: Verso
Perlstein, J. (2001) 'The Independent Media Center Movement', *MEDIAFile,* Volume 20, Number 1, January/February
—— interviewed in *We Are Everywhere: The Irresistible Rise of Global Anticapitalism,* London: Verso, 2003
Quinton, P. Personal interview (2003)
Rheingold, H. (2001) <edge.org/documents/questions/q2001p.html>
Seklar, J. Personal interview (2001, 2003)
Shumway, C. (2001) 'Participatory Media Networks: A New Model', *Reclaim the Media,* <http://www.reclaimthemedia.org/stroeis.php?story=02/05/ 21/6042306>
Starr, A. (2000) *Naming the Enemy: Anti-Corporate Movements Confront Globalization,* London: Zed Books
Starr, S. Personal interview (2002)
Vaidhyanathan, Siva, openDemocracy.net <http://www.opendemocracy. net/home/index.jsp> [Accessed April 2004]
Zelmer, A. (1979) *Community Media Handbook,* second edition, London: Scarecrow Press

# 12
# Transgender Activism and the Net: Global Activism or Casualty of Globalisation

*Kate O'Riordan*

Transsexuality and transgender are contested terms which signify in a range of ways. This chapter does not seek to destabilise different experiences of transgendered or transsexual subjects. However, it does question some models of transsexual identity – as a passive subject (Hausman 1995) or pathologised – and some ideas of transgender articulated in popular cyberculture, by contextualising trans-activism as a social movement. It also questions the use of transgender to signify an 'ideal' queer subject (e.g., Halberstam 1998).

The focus of the chapter is female-to-male transsexual (ftm or transmen) organisations online. It examines how organisations and individuals represent themselves and communicate through the internet and draws on three structuring elements. These are that:

- The internet, in addition to other media, has a significant role as an actualising agent (or site of subjectivity) in identity formation;
- alternative media has a role in challenging hegemonic discourses of sex and gender disseminated through broadcast and print media and in mobilising political action through:
  - representation, and
  - communication/information;
- the intersection between different accounts of trans identity and political priorities from the US, Europe and the UK raises problems, as well as momentum, for those trying to address political trans issues in national contexts.

### SOCIAL MOVEMENTS, IDENTITY POLITICS AND THE MEDIA

Naomi Klein (2000) argues that the identity politics of the late 1980s and early 1990s 'amounted to a rearranging of the furniture whilst the house burned down' (2001:123) and more critically perhaps that identity politics feed global capitalism. This commentary intersects with Joshua Gamson's (2003) argument that LGBT (lesbian, gay, bisexual, transgender) online media has become part of the corporate media industry in its own right and the relationship between LGBT media and LGBT activism is non-existent rather than contingent. That the media industries have an ability to commercialise successfully the images of identity is a well-established tenet in media theory. The niche markets provided through the visibility of identity politics is thus a problematic dynamic, because on the one hand representation is necessary. On the other hand, it is vital for collective identity and political agency for activists to own media intervention, as well as experience assimilation and re-packaging through corporate media ownership. However, the mediascape is not such a straightforward either/or environment.

There is a large global market for LGBT media and thus there are global corporate media infrastructures constituting and capitalising on that market, particularly in print and publishing (e.g., Millivres Prowler Group). Online media fits into this economy at present in the shape of PlanetOut Partners, as documented by Gamson (2003). Like other media structures however, monopolies do not necessarily mean totality. The commodification of identity does not mean that political activism has been erased or that activists no longer have a place in, or use for, the media. Broadcast and print media coverage of current political activism in the early twenty-first century often focuses on anti-capitalism and anti-war campaigns with an eye for the dramatic and a tendency toward a male dominated 'warrior' image of civil disobedience. Such portrayals elide the strong presence of feminist and LGBT involvement in May Day and other anti-capitalist demonstrations (such as the UK-based Out Against the War) as well as the historical context of the civil rights movements.

Academic writing on social movements also contributes towards this elision. Women's activism does feature in media and social movements writing (Larana et al 1994; Downing 2001). It has a high profile in internet literature such as Cherny and Weise's (1996) *Wired Women*, Harcourt's (1999) *Women@Internet* and Consalvo and Paasonen's (2002) *Women and Everyday Uses of The Internet*. However, other politics of gender and sexuality are absent from much social movements writing (e.g., Atton 2002; Larana et al 1994; Meikle 2002). There is also a tendency toward a lack of historicism in the discursive construction of new social movements. Downing's (2001)

*Radical Media* is an important corrective to this and he carefully elucidates an alternative media history taking Sojourner Truth as an iconic starting point. Other writings on global media and social movements link online media with European social history of English feudalism (Kidd 2003), as a way of providing a historical context for theorising public communication spheres. However, in this literature there are very few clear links made between the histories of feminist and LGBT activism and current social movements and there is very little sense of LGBT activism having a space in current images and theories of social movements.

Transactivism, like other social movements, deploys alternative media forms to contest the images disseminated through multinational corporate ownership and to mobilise politically. Other alternative forms such as video, newsletters and independent film are used to generate alternative discourses of transgender. The internet has become a set of central forms, both in terms of visual representation and in organisational/individual networking and communication. Readings of some of this web-based media, including elements of visual culture such as the Brandon Exhibition (1998–99) and the work of individual artists, and local, national and international organisations, highlight the diversity of discourses produced within and around transactivist media itself.

## FTM TRANSGENDER

As referenced above, Gamson (2003) argues that LGBT online media no longer relates to activism. This follows in the case of the lesbian and gay monopolies he describes. However the Transgender in LGBT is not re-packaged by the organisations that he details, except as an ideal cool/queer subject such as that invoked by Bornstein (1994). Corporate gay and lesbian media is very much about a 'mainstream' gay or lesbian subject despite the diversity of identities referred to on PlanetOut websites.[1] Transgender is a contested term and a minority culture in the LGBT coalitions, and despite the inclusion of the 'T' in LGBT, transgender does not necessarily refer to a queer subject. Female-to-male transmen (ftms) are somewhat isolated in these coalitions as they have both a minority voice within transgender as a whole and an uneasy relation to feminism.

Hemming (2002) argues that both bisexual and transsexual subjects have been positioned similarly in relation to queer politics; they are situated either as the ideal queer subject at the 'centre' of queer, or as the partly straight subject marking the boundary of queer. Thus, the fluid, free-floating performative ideal can be one version of queer trans. Equally, an ftm who passes and makes a female object choice can be positioned as straight and thus not queer. Within feminist discourse ftm identity can be positioned as signifying both sexism and homophobia as it can be used to symbolise the repudiation of the female and lesbian body. Within heteronormativity ftm identity can be positioned as transgressive, and therefore punishable, as it destabilises both normative and legal definitions of masculinity and femininity. Transphobia and discrimination are thus issues for ftms, as also is the use of ftm to signify the ideal queer subject. Trans is thus contested by other stakeholders and needs also to be examined on its own terms. Ftm trans and online media have a close connection at a number of levels. One of the first online exhibitions (as opposed to an online catalogue) by a global art institution was the Brandon Exhibition hosted by the Guggenheim Museum (New York). This exhibition was organised by artist Shu Lea Cheang. The interactive exhibit was concerned with boundaries and borders between actual/virtual and male/female and the interplay of gender and sexuality. It also questioned hegemonic and institutional bias towards the clearly defined and conformist body. It deployed the metaphor of the panopticon and re-staged the court sessions of the Brandon Teena case. Concerned with the rape and murder in 1993 of Brandon Teena, the case has also been discussed in the press, documented in *The Brandon Teena Story* (1998) and popularised in the film *Boys Don't Cry* (1999). Brandon Teena was a biological female who 'passed' as male for much of the latter part of his life. Born in 1972 and killed in Nebraska in 1993, Brandon has become a figure associated with LGBT rights and the case has become iconic in these movements as it is thought that the action of 'passing' – specifically as ftm – was directly causal to the occurrence of violent death.

The Brandon Exhibition was used to explore interactions between law, sexuality and identity. Allucquere R. Stone and Del LaGrace Volcano, who had involvement with the design of this site, make direct connections in their work between the boundaries of actual and virtual and those of gender. Stone's theoretical work on actual/virtual/multiple identities (Stone 1995; Benedikt 1991) is symbolically correlated to Brandon's identity through this site. The theme of performativity, as lived experience, is actively explored through representation and interaction. This theme can be seen across work on identity more generally and the tensions between essential, constructed and performed models of identity are also in evidence here. The performance of bodies through representation on these sites could be seen in part, as a virtual embodiment of these theoretical tensions.

The exhibition was an example of the merging of form and content in virtual representation and of the difficulty in distinguishing between agent and text. The interactive elements of the Brandon site drew in observations and commentary from participants and combined them with pre-designed 'text' of the site. The exhibition is now archived. The Brandon Exhibition intersected with a specific political agenda, around a conceptual re-figuring of the body and society. It brought into focus some of the issues with which the transgender movement is concerned and some of the themes of cyberculture. The construction of gender through legislation, bureaucracy and consensus was highlighted in this project and conformity to this construction of the body questioned. The connection that one informant, involved with the site, made between the virtual/actual tension and gender performance was that virtuality allowed the exploration of different gender identities. This is a theme that has been reiterated by many other critics of cyberspace and the notion that online media can be used to play out social issues that are difficult to pursue in physical spaces is confirmed by other research (Munt et al 2002). The suggestion that the internet can facilitate an understanding of trans through its virtual ontology has been pursued in fictions such as Scheirl's (1998) *Dandy Dust*, and Bornstein and Sullivan's (1996) *Nearly Roadkill*. The relationship between a virtual ontology and identity was also a theme of that which Silver has termed 'second generation' cybertheory, which includes some of Stone's theoretical work (Silver 2000). Online identity has historically been central to cybercultural studies. Earlier work in the 1990s brought with it the idea that identity could be disengaged from the body. This move appeared to have liberatory potential in the hands of some theorists, but ultimately has little to offer in terms of political identity, especially in the context of trans, which is often about sexed identity and embodiment.

The context of the symbolic links between transgender and online environments co-joins to the conceptualisation of transgender as global movement, because this context has been part of a momentum of representation exemplified in the Brandon Exhibition. In other words, the popularisation of cyberculture has contributed to a greater awareness around the idea of transgender as a social theme. However, less usefully, this has also contributed further to the queering of trans and helped also to substantiate the myth that trans hinges on disembodiment.

In the context of this chapter the links between cyberspace and transgender that I articulate are not those of identity play and gender subversion. I am not concerned here with subjectivity and the internet but with identity and the internet. The use of the internet, described by individuals as part of their ability to negotiate a trans identity is the central point here (Nestle et al 2002). Other works exploring interviews with ftm transpersons include Devor (1999) Johnson (2001a and b) and Ringo and Freeman (2002). The internet is one set of technologies, along with other media, images and communication technologies, that contributes to identity, mobilisation and networking.

The media are central to, and probably most powerful in, their ability to actualise identities (Grossberg et al 1998). Trans identity has not traditionally appeared in national broadcast and print media as a self-determined identity, but as the subject of medical and technical discourses. This passive subject position is repeated in academic representations of trans such as Hausman's (1995) *Changing Sex: Transsexualism, Technology, and the Idea of Gender*. The hostility with which trans was represented in Raymond's (1979) *Transsexual Empire*, contributed to the deep limitations in and absence of trans feminist discourses.[2] The internet has become relevant in constituting and enhancing an active political subject position in transgender mobilisation. It has been used to circumvent these issues to build on and develop a series of transgender networks from inside transgender communities, as well as a mode of representation.

## BEYOND REPRESENTATION

Online media hinges only in part on representation, and the development of the web into a visual environment is a point of continuity with other media forms. Media as activism is a more discontinuous aspect of the web and transgender as a politics in all three of Vegh (2003) typologies is in evidence.[3] Visual representation can be seen as an aspect of 'awareness/advocacy' on the web. However, trans activists and artists, organisations and individuals also use the web to mobilise, inform, disseminate and gain information about transition and trans identity. Reactions to legislation and calls for lobbying and petitions to change legislation are published through the Press For Change, International Lesbian and Gay Association (ILGA) and GenderPAC websites. Information about conferences, gatherings and support groups is circulated, as well as information about sympathetic members of the medical profession, how to deal with local medical services and how to access human rights and legal information. ILGA publishes information about the global context and on a national level Press For Change, for example, gives the UK context.

Local, national and international trans organisations have a developed web presence and individual ftms use the web to gain and disseminate information about support groups and the processes of transition. There is a tension between the processes of transition and the global reach of the internet, however. Medical and legal establishments regulate transition and these establishments have specific conditions depending on the place in which they apply. Law remains largely a national structure, although increasingly there can be recourse to the human rights framework in Europe. Medical processes are also embedded in national structures and rights to care differ in Europe according to region and country.

Trans identity and experiences are multiple and differ from transgender theory, art and activism as well as intersecting with them. One obvious example of disjuncture between experience and discourses of activism is that the latter come in part from queer cultures but experience of ftm does not necessarily invoke a queer identity. Nineteenth-century categorisations of sexual deviance such as the works of Kraft-Ebbing and Ellis conflate (and create) categories of deviance, seen as varying from a norm of heterosexuality (Foucault 1979). Although these medical discourses are contested by twentieth-century LGBT liberation movements, this conflation continues to re-occur today with the positioning of transsexual and transgender into a rhetoric of queer that, with radically different intent, also conflates everything (that is not normative heterosexuality) with the radically queer.

The alternative media produced in the circulation and dissemination of transactivism and networking is substantially web-based. There are a number of functional reasons for this and in addition to global reach, a significant one is anonymity. Like subscription magazines the internet can be used in a semi-private and intimate environment such as the home. This can be regulated by readers to a greater extent than dissemination through newsagents or video outlets, which are in a more public sphere of consumption. Even subscription and postal mail based distribution can go through a number of gatekeepers from customs, the post office and other people in the same abode. Discrimination and transphobia are realities that require careful negotiation. So also is the desire to pass, and the use of the internet as an alternative media form allows the individual some control and an ability to stratify audiences of their trans identity whilst simultaneously reaffirming and consolidating that identity.

Local transsexual organisations support individuals who identify as transsexual or transgender and provide information, space and networks to affirm transsexual identity. Some of these organisations are non trans-specific in their approach. Spectrum, for example is a local group in southeast UK but as the name implies it is an LGBT organisation not trans specific. This also occurs on an international level with an organisation such as the International Lesbian and Gay Association (ILGA). In this case the title is specific but the mission statement of the organisation includes 'lesbians, gay men, bisexuals and transgendered people'. However there are many specific groups in the UK such as Press For Change, the Gender Trust, the Gendys Network and the FtM Network. All of these organisations have a web presence and use email groups. They collate significant amounts of information and use the web to actualise a network by bringing these together and creating links to other sites and sources. Also contributing to these networks are the sites created by individuals. These intersect and link to each other, also making use of web rings. There are also discussion lists, both directly linked to these organisations but also as general internet groups such as those hosted by Yahoo.

Press For Change, a national UK organisation, focuses on action and news about the judiciary and legislative change. This organisation defines the community it serves as 'all transgendered people in the United Kingdom'. Its mission statement is: 'to achieve equal civil rights and liberties for all transsexual and transgendered people in the United Kingdom, through legislation and social change' (Press For Change website). This is a human rights orientated organisation and it carves out completely different discursive space when compared to US transactivism. Press For Change articulates a transsexuality that is dependent on sex-reassignment and, in this sense, shares the same semiotic field as Hausman's (1995) *Changing Sex*.

This organisation uses its website to describe transsexuality as 'an internationally recognised condition, and not a form of sexual or political rebellion' (Press For Change website) which strongly contrasts with Califia's (1997) concluding statement in *Sex Changes: The Future of Gender and Transgenderism*: 'Welcome to the gender revolution, indeed.'

GenderPAC, a national US organisation, also focuses on legal status but its mission statement aim is to 'end discrimination and violence caused by gender stereotypes' (GenderPAC). The organisation's director Rikki Anne Wilchins was the founder of the Transexual Menace activist organisation and is also the author of *Read My Lips: Sexual Subversion and the End of Gender* (Wilchins 1997). The Transexual Menace, GenderPAC and Wilchins' work have all been influential in what might now be termed a global transactivism. The language used by GenderPAC diverges from Press For Change because the former mobilises individual rights and visibility discourses whilst the latter engages in human rights in tandem with non-visibility. The differences in the language used by these organisations highlights the issue of visibility in transactivism. For many ftms what is important is to pass, that is for society to read you, as you identify. This is not necessarily about visibility, or being out as a transman but about being read as a man. This is not universally true and many ftms are out as transmen but ftm transsexual experience and desire is of course varied. There are as many different experiences of ftm as there are ftms. Press For Change attempts to tread the line between affirming successful transition and thus invisibility and simultaneously making visible the, 'fact that this quiet and invisible group of people are among the most cruelly discriminated of all citizens in the United Kingdom' (Press For Change website). However, like the public face of any movement there is a political value to be had in strategic positioning and the language deployed in literature open to a non-specified audience is clearly tempered by such stratagem.

Global transactivism then, is made up of local, national and international organisations, and a variety of individuals pursuing different goals, creating and mobilising competing discourses about what constitutes trans. Individual, largely US based activists include Leslie Feinberg (Transgender Warriors 1996), Kate Bornstein (Gender Outlaw 1994), Pat Califia, Loren Cameron and Del LaGrace Volcano. The websites, literature and images produced by these individuals can be defined as radical. They use the internet to display images and information and to invite collaboration with their forms of activism.

On a local and national level there are organisations working to secure legal rights and to support trans persons. These organisations, in the UK, rarely have direct links to these activists and are more likely to have local council and government links. Press For Change is discursively distanced from these 'gender terrorist' (Del LaGrace Volcano) associations through the language used on the Press For Change website already quoted. Dr Stephen Whittle, vice president of Press For Change, and long-term activist, is often cited in broadcast media and contributes to this more 'moderate' image of transsexuality. He also describes himself as part of a 'new political movement' which positions his activism as a more embedded social process than the 'revolutionary' evocations of Bornstein, Califia and Feinberg.

ILGA has a specific strategy for negotiating cultural difference on a global scale. When initiating a protest action 'the basic precondition for initiating an action is a request from a member group based in the country with which the action is concerned' (Ramakers 1994:837). This highlights one of the methods through which global/local interfaces can be successfully negotiated in NGO organisations. This structure is also used by animal welfare organisations such as the International Fund for Animal Welfare (IFAW), for example, which lends the funding and support of an international organisation to local groups in times of local crisis. This kind of 'bottom-up' structure can avoid then the colonisation of the agenda that occurs within a top-down structure. This is important in the case of transgender activism where the needs of local organisations differ radically according from the local political climate.[4]

## DISCUSSION

This chapter has examined a range of primarily ftm trans organisations and individuals and the web-based media that circulates in relation to transactivism. It has also tried to clarify the connections between cybercultural theory and transgender whilst highlighting the dysfunctionality of any conflation between the tropes of cyberculture and the experience of trans. At the time of writing the UK government had just produced the 'Draft Gender Recognition Bill 2003' (11 July 2003). The UK and Albania are currently the only European countries that do not legally recognise the reassigned sex of transsexuals. This legislation can be welcomed as an attempt to allow legal recognition of the sex change of a person and is framed in a positive light by Press For Change. However, although legislative change is needed, this legislation reifies a male/female binary and continues to position transsexuals as subjects of surgery and treatment. It is normative in the sense that it allows transsexuals 'in' to a dominant heterosexual paradigm, inscribed in law.

It is at the level of policy change that competing trans discourses intersect and shift from their circulation through alternative media forms to an inscription that has legal power to act upon bodies. Many other European countries already recognise transgendered persons as legal subjects and allow the production of official documentation to reinforce the sex of choice. The influence of a linear trans 'disorder' narrative – disorder, diagnosis, referral, treatment, reassignment, recognition – is the one that is also becoming embedded in UK law.

If this narrative is the outcome of activism and policy at the national and European levels there remains a question about which other perceptions of trans are closed down by this legislation. The other discursive directions discussed, produced at other levels by other areas of activism, do not intersect with these moves. Fitting the complexity and variety of transsexual experience into a legislative shape is not an easy task. However, a definition that only admits surgically reassigned individuals as trans closes down a variety of other needs and goes beyond facilitating transition, to the discursive imposition of medical treatment upon transsexuals, and thus defining and re-constituting it through a discourse of medicine.

As Devor (1999) notes after interviewing 45 ftm transsexual identified people, transgender is not only and always about wanting to be reassigned. Many ftms experience a transgendered identification, rather than a male identification, and hope to see social changes that acknowledge a range of ways of interpreting sex and gender. In this context of desire the 'revolutionary' approaches of US activists meets the needs of some ftms (although such a direction problematically risks contributing to a constitution of trans as choice based). The ability to be recognised as other than m or f is perhaps that which is potentially closed down by gender recognition legislation. However, this kind of legislation is vital in the UK, which so far fails to recognise the rights of transgendered persons with any legal equity.

## CONCLUSION

The internet as a global form has become indispensable in facilitating the affirmation of individual transsexual experience, and contributes to the structuring of a coalition of global movements activating political change. However, negotiating the variety of different objectives of transsexual and transgender organisations, across different national structures of medicine and law, raises radical differences. The point at which transgender activism becomes a casualty of globalisation is the point at which it is elided from discourses of political action. Transgender activism continues to move from the representational politics of individuals, to the mobilisation of identities in active politics. This is facilitated by global communication networks of alternative media, which support the growing momentum of transactivism and may help, as Dr Stephen Whittle expresses it, to find a way out of 'the issues of body fascism' (Press For Change), that face all bodies.

Whilst this work is neither a call to arms nor a plea for inclusion, in the current political climate access to global media can constitute effective political mobilisation. It is vital that gender, sex and sexuality are recognised as political issues, far beyond the exploitation of the commercialisation of identity, and an acceptance that difference always remains is still crucial. Corporate investment in niche markets should not distract from the identity politics, which continue to be at stake. Noting the different agendas of trans organisations emphasises the point that politics is always about the differences raised by identity, and not only about finding common ground. In negotiating a hope for global social justice it is the constant and ongoing interface between different identities, which can perhaps negotiate the friction between local and global.

To borrow from Featherstone (1995), global flows can move outwards, expanding and homogenising existing cultural formations, simultaneously producing heterogeneity through proximity of difference. In this context, transgender activism can be seen to be an effect of both of these processes and a terrain under continual renegotiation; on the one hand presenting greater public engagement, but on the other contested within its own terms. In terms of both individual and human rights the contesting discourses of trans representation, engagement and activism have yet to be entirely homogenised. This lack of closure can be used as strategy to maintain an open discourse and allow new openings, but at the same time concrete political moves need to be made to allow rights and equity to be developed. It is these tensions that continue to be played out in the various local, national and international public spheres, now also facilitated by online communication.

## NOTES

1 As noted by Gamson (2003) this is often a white, young middle-class subject.
2 The absence of feminist attention to trans is also problematised by Johnson (2001a) and Hines (2002).
3 'Awareness/advocacy; organisation/mobilisation; and action/reaction' (Vegh 2003:72).
4 For a comprehensive discussion of sexual politics, NGOs, lobbying and government interfaces in Europe see Beger (2001).

## BIBLIOGRAPHY

Atton, C. (2002) *Alternative Media*, London: Sage
Beger, N. (2001) *Que(e)ring Political Practices in Europe: Tensions in the Struggle for Sexual Minority Rights*, PhD Thesis, University van Amsterdam; forthcoming 2004 Manchester University Press
Benedikt, M. (ed.) (1991) *Cyberspace: First Steps*, Cambridge: MIT Press
Bornstein, K. and K. Sullivan (1996) *Nearly Roadkill: An Infobahn Gender Adventure*, London: Serpent's Tail
Bornstein, K. (1994) *Gender Outlaw: On Men, Women and the Rest of Us*, New York, London: Routledge
Califia, P. (1997) *Sex Changes: The Future of Gender and Transgenderism*, San Francisco: Cleis Press
Cameron, L. (1996) *Body Alchemy: Transsexual Portraits*, San Francisco: Cleis Press
Cherny, L. and E. R. Weise (eds) (1996) *Wired Women: Gender and New Realities in Cyberspace*, Washington: Seal Press
Consalvo, M. and S. Paasonen (2002) *Women and Everyday Uses of the Internet: Agency and Identity*, New York: Peter Lang Press
Devor, H. (1999) *FTM: Female-to-Male Transsexuals in Society*, Indiana: Indiana University Press
Downing, J. (2001) *Radical Media: Rebellious Communication and Social Movements*, London: Sage
*Draft Gender Recognition Bill* (2003) London: The Stationery Office
Ellis, H. (1933) *Psychology of Sex*, London: William Heinemann
Featherstone, M. (1995) *Undoing Culture: Globalization, Postmodernism and Identity*, London: Sage
Feinberg, L. (1998) *Trans Liberation: Beyond Pink or Blue*, Boston: Beacon Press
—— (1996) *Transgender Warriors: Making History from Joan of Arc to RuPau*, Boston: Beacon Press

Foucault, M. (1979) *The History of Sexuality: Volume 1* (translated by R. Hurley), London: Penguin Books

Gamson, J. (2003) 'Gay media inc.: media structures, the new gay conglomerates, and collective sexual identities', in M. McCaughhey and M. D. Ayers (eds) *Cyberactivism: Online Activism in Theory and Practice*, London, New York: Routledge

Grossberg, L., E. Wartella and D. C. Whitney (1998) *Mediamaking: Mass Media In A Popular Culture*, Thousand Oaks, CA: Sage

Halberstam, J. (1998) *Female Masculinity*, Durham: Duke University Press

Harcourt, W. (1999) *Women@Internet: Creating New Cultures in Cyberspace*, London, New York: Zed Books

Hausman, B. (1995) *Changing Sex: Transsexualism, Technology, and the Idea of Gender*, Durham: Duke University Press

Hemming, C. (2002) *Bisexual Spaces: A Geography of Sexuality and Gender*, London, New York: Routledge

Hines, S. (2002) 'Absent Subjects: Feminist Discourse and Trans Masculinities', paper at the *Gendys Seventh Gender Dysphoria Conference, Hulme Hall*, University of Manchester, England 31 August–1 September 2002

Johnson, K. (2001a) *Being Transsexual: Self, Identity and Embodied Subjectivity*, London: Middlesex University PhD thesis

Johnson, K. (2001b) 'Studying transsexual identity: a discursive approach', in F. Haynes and T. McKenna (eds) *Unseen Genders: Beyond the Binaries*, Eruptions Series, New York: Peter Lang Press

Kidd, D. (2003) 'IndyMedia.Org: a new communications commons', in M. McCaughhey and M. D. Ayers (eds) *Cyberactivism: Online Activism in Theory and Practice*, London, New York: Routledge

Klein, N. (2000) *No Logo, No Space, No Choice, No Jobs: Taking Aim at the Brand Bullies*, London: HarperCollins

Krafft-Ebing, R. von (1978) *Psychopathia Sexualis: With Especial Reference to the Antipathic Sexual Instinct* (translation), New York: Scarborough Books

Larana, E., H. Johnston and J. Gusfield (eds) (1994) *New Social Movements: from Ideology to Identity*, Philadelphia: Temple University Press

Meikle, G. (2002) *Future Active: Media Activism and the Internet*, London, New York: Routledge

Munt, S., C. Bassett and K. O'Riordan (2002) 'Virtually belonging: risk, connectivity and coming out On-line' in J. Alexander (ed.) *Queer Webs: Representations of LGBT People and Communities on the World Wide Web, International Journal of Sexuality and Gender Studies* 7, 2/3

Nestle, J., C. Howell and R. Wilchins (eds) (2002) *Genderqueer: Voices From Beyond: The Sexual Binary*, Los Angeles: Alyson Publications

Ramakers, M. (1994) 'The International Lesbian and Gay Association five years later', in M. Blasius and S. Phelan (eds) *We Are Everywhere: A Historical Sourcebook of Gay and Lesbian Politics*, London, New York: Routledge

Raymond, J. (1979) *The Transsexual Empire: The Making of The She Male*, London: The Women's Press

Ringo, C. L. and P. Freeman (2002) *Media Roles in Female-to-Male Transsexual Identity Formation*, MA Dissertation, University of Wisconsin

Silver, D. (2000) 'Looking backwards, looking forward: cyberculture studies 1990–2000', in D. Gauntlett (ed.) (2004) *Web.Studies: Rewiring Media Studies For The Digital Age*, London: Arnold

Stone, A. R. (1995) *The War of Desire and Technology at the Close of the Mechanical Age*, Cambridge: MIT Press

—— (1991) 'The empire strikes back: a posttranssexual manifesto', in K. Straub and J. Epstein (eds) *Body Guards: The Cultural Politics of Gender Ambiguity*, New York: Routledge

Vegh, S. (2003) 'Classifying forms of Online Activism: The Case of Cyber protests against the World Bank' in M. McCaughey and M. D. Ayers (eds) *Cyberactivism: Online Activism in Theory and Practice*, New York: Routledge

Wilchins, R. (1997) *Read My Lips: Sexual Subversion and the End of Gender*, Ann Arbor: Firebrand Books

## FILMS

Muska, S. and G. Olafsdottir (1998) *The Brandon Teena Story*, USA, production: Bless Productions, Distribution: Zeitgeist Films

Pierce, K. (1999) *Boys Don't Cry*, USA, production: Hart-Sharp, Independent Film Channel, Distribution: Fox Searchlight

Scheirl, A. H. (1998) *Dandy Dust*, UK/Austria, production: Dandy Dust Filmproduktion, Distribution: Peccadillo, ACMI

## WEBSITES

Del LaGrace, Volcano <http://www.disgrace.dircon.co.uk/Frame1.htm>
FTM Network <http://www.ftm.org.uk/>
GenderPAC <http://www.earstohear.net/GenderPac.html>
Gender Trust <http://www.gendertrust.org.uk>
Gendys Network <http://www.gender.org.uk/gendys/>
Guggenheim Museum <http://www.Guggenheim.org/>
International Lesbian and Gay Association (ILGA) <http://www.ilga.org/>
Loren Cameron <http://www.lorencameron.com>
Press For Change <http://www.pfc.org.uk/>

# 13
# Bridging the Gap: From the Margins to the Mainstream

*Pollyanna Ruiz*

St George's Hill in Weybridge, Surrey, is currently the site of one of the most 'exclusive private estates in Britain' (Platt 1999, see website). Even the humblest dwellings on the estate sit in at least an acre of land and enjoy the protection of private security guards. One could argue that the golf course and fast cars, the mansions and wealthy neighbours epitomise the worst or the best excesses of the capitalist dream. However, even this degree of moneyed exclusivity has failed to protect the estate and its residents from the radical past of St George's Hill.

In 1649, in the midst of the political and social turmoil that followed the beheading of King Charles I, Gerrard Winstanley led a group of landless peasants on to St George's Hill and occupied the land. The Diggers built shelters and planted crops in defiance of both their traditional foes, the local landlords and their erstwhile friend,

*Photo 3* Banging the same drum (Rebecca Tanyar)

Oliver Cromwell, for whom they had just helped fight and win the English Civil War (see website).

In 1912 the public, that had used St George's Hill recreationally as a place to walk and picnic, were denied access when the land was bought by WG Tarrant and developed into the estate that exists today. However activists commemorating the Diggers movement and campaigning for land reform in Britain today reoccupied the land in 1999. As we enter a new millennium the question Gerrard Winstanley first asked in the mid-seventeenth century remains potent and as yet unanswered: 'Was the earth made to preserve a few covetous, proud men to live at ease, and for them to bag and barn up the treasure of the Earth from others, that these may beg or starve in a fruitful land, or was it made to preserve all her children?' (Winstanley quoted by Platt 1999). This chapter will examine the way in which this question is being asked by some of those involved in the anti-globalisation movement today.

## THE GAP

There is a feeling among some in the anti-globalisation movement that international organisations such as Greenpeace and Friends of the Earth are in someway 'playacting' at protest and have therefore become 'ineffectual' in their efforts to force environmental change (Dom quoted in Atton 2002:84). Indeed there are those who go even further arguing that NGOs are now so closely intertwined with global capitalism that they have become an essential part of the very system they once sought to change. It is therefore increasingly necessary to make a distinction between 'professional activists' engaged in 'large scale actions to raise awareness of issues through media exposure' and 'ordinary people' trying to effect change in a far more immediate and personal capacity (Atton 2002:84). These groups of 'ordinary people' invariably reject the bureaucratic professionalism of NGOs in favour of what George Mckay, amongst others, has described as a more 'Do it Yourself' approach to political change (1998). As a result, these organisations tend to concentrate less on the creation of desirable but intangible shifts in public opinion and governmental policies, preferring instead to focus on achieving single clearly defined goals such as stopping the construction of a particular road or supermarket.

Partly as a result of their differing aims, DIY groups tend to be characterised by organisational forms that set them apart from the mainstream. Thus, 'professional' environmental groups usually share many of the elements that characterise corporate society as a whole, such as hierarchy, standardised procedures and uniformity of voice. DIY groups on the other hand tend to occupy what Deleuze and Guattari have described as 'smooth space' (Goodchild 1996:165) and are therefore less 'structured' than 'rhizomatic' in their approach to politics. This organisational looseness enables DIY groups to accommodate a multiplicity of contradictory voices and actions whilst maintaining a real sense of ideological unity. Indeed some commentators argue that the fluctuating and fractured coherence of the DIY movement is a defining feature of both alternative politics in general and the alternative media in particular. Thus, DIY politics celebrates 'self-organisation' and 'bricolage' as a source of both strength and inspiration (Atton 2002:82).

These groups tend to have developed along anarchist lines and are therefore far smaller and more flexible than most mainstream organisations. This enables them to 'ebb and flow, group and regroup' (Ward 1972:137) with a fluidity of movement that frequently confuses and confounds its opponents in the mainstream. This flexibility also has important and far-reaching ideological and political implications. It has enabled these groups to move away from the traditional Marxist emphasis on a disciplined party primed to seize control of the organs of power and towards a more anarchist concept of revolution. As Blunt and Wills point out, an anarchist view sees it not as a single paradigm shifting event but as an ever ongoing 'process; a process of undermining all existing institutions and relationships' (Rigby 1990:54). This emphasis on process frees protesters from the traditional obligation to provide a replacement ideology for the current system and allows them to be far more 'outrageous' (Monbiot, 30 October 2003, see website) and eclectic in their political style.

Whilst the emergence of new organisational forms may indicate a degree of dissatisfaction with the larger NGOs, DIY movements are not trying in any way to replace the larger organisations. Indeed, as Purkis points out, these smaller groups frequently aim to attract and influence 'the more mainstream non-governmental organisations' as well as 'governments, businesses and the general public' (2000: 94). Thus during the Newbury bypass protest smaller, more anarchic groups of protesters arrived first and drew attention to themselves by occupying the land and skirmishing with the authorities. These groups were then followed by more established organisations bringing an entirely different set of resources and expertise. For example, when Friends of the Earth arrived in Newbury it set up an office space from which it could manage public interest in events on the ground (Ruiz 1999). In this way their differing approaches to protest complement rather than compete with each other, enabling both organisations to utilise their strengths and maximise their impact on the public sphere.

DIY philosophy is based very much in the here and now allowing protesters to act with an invigorating sense of energy and optimism frequently denied to those more institutionally involved in politics. Inevitably, there are problems associated with DIY politics. As Mckay points out, while this 'culture of immediacy' (1998:15) is immensely liberating it can at the same time lead to a debilitating loss of both the past, with all its histories and traditions, and the future, with its sense of continuity and strategies for development. I would argue that many DIY organisations are becoming increasingly aware of this problem and have built supportive outer structures that contain and develop individual actions without constraining their creative flexibility.

## THE LAND IS OURS

'The Land Is Ours' was established in 1995 as an umbrella organisation for many disparate land rights campaigns and has organised actions to promote awareness of land issues all over Britain. These include occupying land on Shirburn Hill near Watlington in order to highlight the Earl of Macclesfield's neglect of the chalk downs, and derelict land in Wandsworth to illustrate the 'appalling misuse of urban land, the lack of provision of affordable housing and the deterioration of the urban environment' (Monbiot 1998:174). The Land Is Ours describes itself as having its ideological roots in the seventeenth century Diggers movement while working towards 'a future of land for decent secure homes, community food production and a renewed sense of belonging to the land' (TLIO website, campaigns page, 31 July 2002). Thus the value of the past and the future is recognised by The Land Is Ours as an umbrella organisation, whilst individual actions enjoy the freedom and flexibility offered by action in the here and now.

However, notwithstanding its sense of continuity and embeddedness in both time and land, The Land Is Ours does not actually exist as an organisational body. It has no offices, staff or permanent structures and is simply made up of the people taking part in whatever particular actions happen to be taking place on the ground. When there are no actions The Land Is Ours withdraws into the suitably ethereal realm of the internet and becomes a diary of campaigns and associated writings. The group's single concession to traditional organisational forms is a statement of principles, which was adopted in an attempt to prevent emerging hierarchies, and reads as follows: 'The Land Is Ours campaigns peacefully for access to the land, its resources and the decision making processes affecting them for everyone – irrespective of race, age or gender' (Monbiot 1998:176). Beyond this bricolage of movements and people, there is nothing.

This type of organisational form is typical of the wider anti-globalisation movement and has been most influentially exemplified by the Zapatistas. While the Zapatistas began as an organisation committed to furthering the rights of Mexico's indigenous population, it quickly broadened its remit to include the interests of anyone – 'as long as they thought of themselves as outsiders' (Klein 2001:13). The Zapatistas resist any attempts to 'compartmentalise the community into workers, warriors, farmers and students' preferring instead to organise their communities 'as a whole across sectors and across generations' (Klein, the *Guardian Magazine*:13 March). In doing so they deny the vertical linkages which typify corporate culture and can be found in most political, social and even, apparently, counter-cultural organisations, creating instead a system of horizontal linkages that bind one into a web of interconnected political aims and aspirations.

This contrasts sharply with mainstream organisations, such as Greenpeace and Friends of the Earth, which usually campaign on a number of broadly related, ranked issues arranged so as to make up an ideologically coherent whole. Those involved in these more formal, departmental campaigns may consider the rather chaotic and sometimes even contradictory plurality of voices found in DIY politics to be a destabilising and potentially destructive force. Indeed some would argue that notions such as DIY politics and the anti-globalisation movement have become so 'elastic as to be devoid of virtually any signification' (Abel 1997:79). However, commentators such as Downing and Atton maintain that this emphasis on lateral communication is one of the most empowering elements of alternative organisations (Downing 2001; Atton 2002). Thus many DIY organisations revel in the 'ragged' (TLIO website, campaigns page,

31 July 2002) nature of their actions seeing the 'refusal to grant primacy to any particular site or mode of struggle' as a sign of increased flexibility and strength (Welsh and Mcleish quoted in Atton 2002:82).

## THE OCCUPATION OF ST GEORGE'S HILL

On Saturday 3 April 1999, 300 protesters celebrated the 350th anniversary of the Diggers movement by marching on the super-exclusive enclave of St George's Hill in Weybridge, Surrey. A smaller group of activists then set up a 'communal settlement' on a piece of land the Diggers had originally occupied in 1649, and refused to leave until a 'permanent and publicly accessible home' was found for a carved stone commemorating the first historic encampment. Protesters were served an eviction notice five days later on 8 April, but were able to hold a celebratory 'open day' on the Sunday 11 April, before peacefully leaving the site on the Thursday. This was one day before their formal eviction date, which had been set for 16 April.

Direct actions, like any other form of civil disobedience, depend upon the twin 'logics' of 'truth force' and 'bearing witness' (Seel, Paterson and Doherty 2000:1). According to these logics, the moral force of activists' opinions draws the public's attention to the inherent wrongness of a situation and in doing so shames perpetrators into redemptive action. This dynamic enables protesters to break the law with a considerable degree of moral impunity, provided that they are seen to be motivated by a principled desire to expose the bad behaviour of those in authority. As a result, the media is now routinely used by those on both sides of any action's political divide to either promote or denigrate events as they unfold on the ground. According to Brian McNair there are usually two stages to winning public legitimacy. The first is simply 'to be seen and heard in the public sphere', while the second stage depends upon protesters' ability to secure 'qualitatively favourable coverage, which accentuates the positive and downplays negative features' (1998:52).

In order to achieve these ends, groups which pride themselves on their flexible, transitory, leaderless systems must reach out and connect with far more traditional, formally-structured organisations. The problems created by this mismatch in systems can be illustrated by examining the normally uncontroversial role of spokesperson. As a rule, groups involved in the anti-globalisation movement eschew the notion of spokesperson preferring to remain anonymous where possible and speak collectively when necessary. This contrasts sharply with the needs of journalists who want a single, named contact who is 'close at hand, reliable, well informed and ... newsworthy' (Curran 2000:31), as well as being charismatic, articulate and, most importantly of all, photogenic. In this particular instance journalists seemed to have found the perfect candidate for such a role in one of The Land Is Ours founding members, George Monbiot.

One could argue that George Monbiot was ideally placed to act as spokesperson being a journalist himself and having a life-long interest in land reform issues. However, such is the anti-globalisation movement's ambivalence (some would say outright hostility) to the press that he soon found himself the target of virulent criticism from the more spiky end of the alternative press (Monbiot 1998). Monbiot was quick to step away from the role of unofficial spokesperson, however the difficulties experienced by The Land Is Ours surrounding the role of spokesperson illustrate the depth of the organisational gulf between the radical left and the mainstream media. I would argue that despite this gap activists are discovering increasingly imaginative and efficient ways to bridge the divide. There are two ways in which activists have attempted to engage with journalists' professional needs without compromising their ideological integrity. The first concerns their use of journalist-friendly demonstrative events, such as The Land Is Ours Easter Sunday picnic on St George's Hill, while the second focuses on activists' use of internet pressrooms to manage journalists' interest and secure 'qualitatively favourable coverage' (McNair 1998:52). These actions do more than simply bridge the gap between activists and journalist: they actually create rare and temporary space in which alternative and traditional structures and ideologies can coexist. Thus for a moment the standardised rigidity of straited space and the rhizomatic flux and flow of smooth space overlap allowing information to pass, almost unnoticed, from the margins to the mainstream.

## DEMONSTRATIVE EVENTS

The preference of anti-globalisation movements, including The Land Is Ours, for land occupations to make manifest their political position can be interpreted as a way of binding the many variously-motivated individuals involved in these protests into a single, practically focused action. This viewpoint interprets space as the 'constant', providing some semblance of order in an otherwise 'floating world of ideas' (Smith and Katz 1993:80). However, while some traditionalists undoubtedly view space as 'the missing foundation for everything else in flux', others, such as Smith and Katz, point out that it is precisely this sense of 'fixity and inertness that makes a spatial grammar so fertile for metaphorical appropriation' (1993:71). The notion is a particularly fruitful line of enquiry as it introduces the notion of the physical occupation of space as a way into exploring the symbolic implications of protesters' actions.

We can understand The Land Is Ours' St George's Hill 1999 Easter Sunday picnic in a variety of ways. On one level, it demonstrated the depth of public feeling in a very traditional way, by mobilising large numbers of supporters. However, it also worked on a more complex level in that it served to make manifest the political and ideological principles behind The Land Is Ours' occupation of St George's Hill. Protesters invited residents, journalists and the public at large to enjoy a day of discussion, interactive drama, story telling, wicker weaving and face painting at the camp. In doing so, they were also inviting them to compare two contrasting modes of existence. The capitalist mode of being, represented by St George's Hill (enclave of the super-rich) and the communal mode of being, represented by St George's Hill (ideologically sound eco-village). Moreover, this event demonstrated The Land Is Ours' criticisms of corporate society without individual protesters having to articulate them formally to the public or the press.

The implications raised by this type of demonstrative event can be further understood by analysing the food that activists provided for their guests. A picnic was gathered from skips that shops had filled by emptying their shelves of perishable goods, in preparation for the Easter weekend. This juxtaposed the 'blatantly wasteful' nature of corporate society with a more 'ecologically sound and socially just' alternative. It also returns us to the notion of spatial metaphors whereby the 'strange is rendered familiar, but the apparently familiar is made equally strange' (Smith and Katz 1993:71). Thus, the oddity of eating discarded food is normalised by the nostalgic simplicity of a Sunday picnic while the usually unobjectionable notion of sell by dates and public health and safety is suddenly exposed as blatantly and extravagantly wasteful. In this way activists are able to feed their guests while also providing journalists with an engagingly quirky *and* ideologically-loaded story.

Thus, the camp on St George's Hill can be read in a variety of different ways, all of which hinge upon the DIY movement's belief in the public's ability to be converted by the 'truth force' of positive example. One can interpret protesters' actions from an anarchist viewpoint, in which case their occupation of St George's Hill becomes part of the ongoing revolutionary process of 'undermining all existing institutions and relationships' (Rigby 1990:54). Similarly, one can also view the encampment as a Zapatistian attempt to create a counter-cultural space, which 'simply by existing as [an] alternative', constitutes a critique of corporate culture in itself (Klein 2000:13). Both these understandings depend upon the notion of reclaimed land as a place through which to 'think about alternative possibilities' and experiment with different, enlightening forms of utopia (Lefebvre 2000:21). Moreover, by using the picnic on St George's Hill as a spatial metaphor, protesters were able to illustrate the inequities of the current system in an interesting and news-friendly way.

## INTERNET PRESSROOMS

The Land Is Ours exists either on the ground, in the form of various loosely related campaigns, or on the internet, in the form of various articles and campaign diaries. Its internet presence includes an article by George Monbiot entitled 'An Activist Guide to Exploiting the Media' and a pressroom in which to put that knowledge into practice. The pressroom is particularly significant in that it provides journalists with a permanent point of contact for an otherwise intangible and sometimes completely inaccessible organisation. It also enables protesters, who follow Monbiot's detailed advice on the content and presentation of press releases, to channel information into the mainstream. As Paul Patton points out, 'the manner in which a given occurrence is described determines it as a particular type of event' (2000:28). This is of particular significance to those on the radical left because media outlets generally 'pander to the prejudices of their billionaire proprietors' (Monbiot 2003, see website) and are therefore invariably hostile to those attempting to challenge the system. Fortunately protesters are becoming increasingly aware of the need to communicate clearly with the journalists who control their representation in the public sphere and are therefore becoming more successful in the inevitable 'struggle' (Patton 2000:28) over the way in which events are described.

If the St George's Hill open day was a carefully controlled event designed to win support on both a local and a public level, its success was very nearly jeopardised by events entirely beyond protesters' control. On Monday 5 April, one week before the picnic was scheduled, an assault took place on the encampment. Within hours of the assault, The Land Is Ours posted a press release on the internet which carefully managed every aspect of this potentially damaging story. The press release begins with a 'short, pithy and to the point' headline of less than eight words; 'Campaigner Attacked At St George's Hill Diggers Community'. This is followed by an apparently straightforward account of the incident. However, the facts given are all carefully chosen to frame the story in a particularly helpful and generous way. Thus the unnamed assailant arrives in a slightly sinister sounding 'black four-wheel drive vehicle', punches and knocks down the named protester in an 'unprovoked assault' and then leaves at an implicitly dangerous 'high speed'. This reckless behaviour is contrasted with the 'many other local residents' who 'have visited and are supportive' of the camp. In this way, activists manage what could easily have turned into another 'violent protest' story and ensure that their interpretation of events is heard.

The Land Is Ours is similarly careful in its management of witnesses to the incident. As George Monbiot points out, journalists on an encampment 'will be having enough trouble crossing the cultural divide as it is' and therefore need to be steered towards people who are 'charming, persuasive and well-briefed' (TLIO website, 27 October 2003). In the light of this advice, journalists were given the name and contact numbers of two witnesses to the assault. Both witnesses were placed casually but firmly on the respectable side of the law when they were described as being former residents of St George's Hill estate. Thus by choosing their own witnesses The Land Is Ours is able to bypass the usual vertical forms of communication and replace them with their own more empowering 'horizontal linkages' (Downing 1995:241). Thus the practical implications of organisational form both produce and confirm ideological principle, and vice versa.

## THE OVERLAP

On some levels, this protest clearly failed in that activists were evicted without securing public access to, or a permanent position for, their memorial stone on the site of the original Diggers encampment at St George's Hill. However, the stone was accepted by Elmbridge museum and one could therefore argue that they succeeded in positioning their stone within a mainstream narrative. Moreover, there is no doubt that by engaging and forcing a reaction from those in power, even if that reaction was to serve an eviction notice, protesters succeeded in drawing 'the whole of society with its officials and citizens' into dialogue (Herngren 1993:14). While these achievements are unlikely to have caused the residents of St George's Hill many sleepless nights, it is important to remember that protesters were not attempting anything as comprehensive as the overthrow of the status quo. Instead they were working, slowly and by example, towards a different way of being. Thus I would argue that while the occupation of St George's Hill lasted only a short time, protesters did succeed in their attempts to 'subvert existing cartographies ... and urban spaces ... according to different experiences, desires and values', albeit temporarily (Pinder 2000:34).

The occupation of St George's Hill was also more than a physical means to a practical end – it was also an 'enormously important symbolic action' (*Guardian online*, 5 April 1999). On this more symbolic level, protesters succeeded in securing and controlling media attention. Numerous, generally positive, stories appeared in the local press and a few articles even appeared in the national broadsheets ('Levels of Optimism', *Guardian*, 24 March 1999 and 'Enclosure fight reopened', *Guardian*, 5 April 1999). Thus, while The Land Is Ours may have failed to inspire the well-healed residents of St George's Hill to cast off their material wealth and join the Diggers community in 'working to restore this country's land to the benefit of all its inhabitants' (TLIO website, 31 July 2002), it did succeed in provoking debate on the ground, in the courts and in the press regarding the uses and abuses of public land. While it would be more than a little optimistic to claim that The Land Is Ours succeeded in actually converting the opposition, protesters did succeed in 'confronting, challenging and perhaps even shaming' (Mckay 1998:29) the opposition into an important moment of self-reflection.

As a result I would argue that The Land Is Ours' use of demonstrative events and internet pressrooms first to attract and then to control journalistic interest was in many ways successful. Moreover, that this type of campaign has been, and is being, replicated all over the country by a myriad of other low-key DIY protests. Furthermore, the forms of these campaigns are as significant as their content in so far as they illustrate the possibility of thinking, and therefore doing, things differently. Clearly each campaign in isolation does not pose any serious threat to the established ways of doing and being; however, given time, it is possible that these many campaigns will create a 'swarm' of protests (Klein 2001:13) and eventually impact forcefully on the mainstream.

The organisational forms that produce and in some ways define the anti-globalisation movement are in contrast to, and sometimes in direct conflict with, the mainstream. Despite this, many of those involved in DIY politics express an explicit interest in communicating with the mainstream, describing themselves as 'writing to the bridge' (Beale quoted in Atton 2002:92). Regardless of the problems inevitably caused by the clash of systems and ideologies, protesters are becoming increasingly adept at bridging the gap between the radical left and the mainstream media.

The space created by demonstrative events and internet pressrooms allow the organisational contexts of both activists and journalists to temporarily overlap. In this way journalists are able to access the rather chaotic and complex world that is DIY politics, while activists are able to assert and maintain some level of control over their representation in the mainstream. This is not to maintain that these spaces solve all – or any – of the problems commonly associated with the radical left's attempts to communicate with the mainstream media. But to suggest that these spaces temporarily unfix the meanings usually ascribed to them, thus enabling 'each interested party' to attempt 'to place their discourse onto it' (Purkis 2000:216). In these spaces, contradictory systems can momentarily be caught and made compatible before they become mutually incomprehensible once again.

Somewhat ironically it could be argued that activists' media strategies have been deeply and beneficially influenced by the effects of global capitalism. Economic circumstances have encouraged corporate news organisations to move away from costly and time-consuming investigative journalism in favour of reprocessing the slick information packages supplied (with care and for free) by many resource-rich organisations. While the anti-globalisation movement cannot compete with these organisations economically, its unusually developed levels of technical know-how and artistic flair have enabled the movement to engage with the mainstream press in other ways. Thus small spaces are constantly being created where the organisational forms – and by implication the ideological impulses behind those forms – of the radical left are being exposed and hopefully understood by those 'outside' them.

## CONCLUSION

This chapter has addressed the issues raised by groups that have rejected the bureaucratic professionalism of NGOs, such as Friends of the Earth and Greenpeace, in favour of more loosely structured actions organised around a single clearly defined goal. I have argued that this invariably temporary and narrow focus frees protesters from the obligation to provide an all-encompassing replacement ideology and creates a space in which to experiment with different types of utopia and could therefore be said to constitute a critique of the corporate world in itself. I have proposed that the interactions of activists and journalists during demonstrative events and in internet pressrooms establishes a dynamic through which both organisational structures can exist not in opposition to but in relationship with each other. I have concluded by suggesting that this overlap produces a space in which the flux and flow of protest culture and the standardised rigidity of the mainstream can momentarily be caught and made compatible, thus creating a conduit for ideas to pass from the alternative to the corporate world.

## BIBLIOGRAPHY

Abel, R. (1997) 'An alternative press why?', *Publishing Research Quarterly*, 12:14, Winter 1996–97: 78–84
Atton, C. (2002) *Alternative Media*, Thousand Oaks: Sage
Blunt, A. and J. Wills (2000) *Dissident Geographies: An Introduction to Radical Ideas and Practice*, Singapore: Prentice Hall
Curran, J. (2000) *Media Organisation and Society*, London: Arnold
Downing, J. (1995) 'Alternative media and the Boston Tea Party', in J. Downing, A. Mohammadi and A. Sreberny-Mohammadi (eds) *Questioning the Media*, Thousand Oaks, London, New Delhi: Sage: 240–1
—— (2001) *Radical Media: Rebellious Communication and Social Movements*, Thousand Oaks: Sage
Goodchild, P. (1996) *Deleuze and Guattari: An Introduction to the Politics of Desire*, Thousand Oaks: Sage
Klein, N. (2000) 'The Unknown Icon', *Weekend Guardian*, 3 March 2001: 9–13
Lefebvre, H. (2000) *Writing on Cities* (Trans) E. Kofman and E. Lebas, Oxford, Massachusetts: Blackwell.
Mckay, G. (1998) *Party and Protest in Nineties Britain*, London and New York: Verso

McNair, B. (1998) 'Journalism, politics and public relations: an ethical appraisal', in M. Kieran (ed.) *Media Ethics*, London and New York: Routledge: 49–65

Monbiot, G. (1998) 'Reclaim the fields and country lanes!' The Land Is Ours campaign, in G. Mckay (ed.) *Party and Protest in Nineties Britain*, London and New York: Verso: 174–86

Patton, P. (2000) *Deleuze and the Political*, London and New York: Routledge

Pinder, D. (2000) 'The Situationists International', in A. Blunt and J. Wills (eds) *Dissident Geographies: An Introduction to Radical Ideas and Practice*, Singapore: Prentice Hall: 33–5

Purkis, J. (2000) 'Modern millenarians?' in S. Benjamin, M. Paterson and B. Doherty (eds) *Direct Action in British Environmentalism*, London and New York: Routledge: 93–111

Rigby, A. (1990) 'Lessons from anarchist communities', in I. Cook and D. Pepper (eds) *Anarchism and Geography, Contemporary Issues in Geography and Education* 3, 2: 52–6

Ruiz, P. (2000) *The Internet, Politics and the Independent Media Center*, Sussex MA Dissertation

Seel, B., M. Paterson and B. Doherty (2000) *Direct Action in British Environmentalism*, London and New York: Routledge

Smith, N. and C. Katz (1993) 'Grounding metaphor; towards a spatialised politics', in M. Keith and S. Pile (eds) *Place and the Politics of Identity*, London and New York: Routledge: 67–80

Ward, C. (1972) *Anarchy in Action*, London: George Allen and Unwin

**WEBSITES**

Brooks, L. 'Latter-day Diggers claim piece of an up-market golf course', *Guardian Unlimited*, <http://www.guardian.co.uk/uk_news/story/0,3604,309378,00.html> [Accessed 5 April 1999]

Monbiot, G. 'An activists guide to exploiting the media', The Land Is Ours, <http://www2.phreak.co.uk/tlio//pubs/agm2.html> [Accessed 30 October 2003]

Platt, S. 'Levels of Optimism', *Guardian Unlimited*, <http://www.guardian.co.uk/guardiansociety/story/0,3605,307968,00.html> [Accessed 24 March 1999]

'About the Diggers Community', The Land Is Ours, <http://www2.phreak.co.uk/tlio//campaigns/diggers/d350ab.html> [Accessed 31 July 2002]

'In 1649 to St George's Hill', The Land is Ours, <http://www2.phreak.co.uk/tlio//campaigns/diggers/d350pr.html> [Accessed 31 July 2002]

# 14

# Civil Society Organisations and the Internet: The Case of Amnesty International, Oxfam and the World Development Movement

*Anastasia Kavada*

Hailed as the medium which will breathe a new life into civil society and the public sphere, the internet and its political potential have been the source of ardent optimism. Optimists hope that the internet will increase the pluralism of voices within the public sphere by providing a space for non-mainstream and fringe organisations to publish their opinions. Its networking capabilities can also be used to strengthen the bonds between different organisations, fostering solidarity and a sense of mutual support. Furthermore, by encouraging participation and online deliberation the internet can deepen the involvement of the public with civil society organisations.

But is this optimism well founded or just a passing fad? This chapter aims to provide a reality check for the above claims by examining the actual purpose and functions of the websites of three civic organisations. This analysis will further enable us to make some inferences about the impact of the internet on civil society and the public sphere.

## BACKGROUND: THE POLITICAL POTENTIAL OF THE INTERNET

At the heart of the optimism around the internet and its political potential lays a belief in its publication and networking capabilities. As a publication medium, the internet provides a space for political organisations to publish their opinions and gain a foothold in the public sphere. Its effectiveness lays in its low production and administration costs, particularly for reaching large audiences, which extend far beyond national boundaries (Benoit and Benoit 2002). Furthermore, information can be presented in much livelier ways online, as the web can incorporate sound, text, video and interactive features, such as online games or search engines. In addition, specific pages of the site can be tailored to meet the needs of particular target groups, such as volunteers or the press, offering more customised and personalised information. Organisations can also use the internet to release the latest news on campaigns and actions, as the web can be updated more easily and more rapidly than the traditional media.

But most importantly, the internet allows organisations to communicate directly with their audiences, bypassing the mechanisms and commercial bias of the mainstream media (Hill and Hughes 1998:22). This means that online organisations can diffuse information about issues that the traditional media would not normally cover and present their own point of view to the public, avoiding the distortions of mainstream journalism. Given the media-centric nature of today's politics, this feature is of crucial importance for political organisations.

But apart from a new publication medium, the internet is also a powerful networking tool. As such, the web can lead to a more integrated civil society as it can be used to build and strengthen internal and external organisational links (Gibson and Ward 2001:29). The internal linkages consist of those between the headquarters and their local groups. External links include those between the civic organisations and other bodies, such as interest groups, government departments or media outlets. Through these hypertext links, civic groups 'can build "one-stop shops" to their internal branches from their central web site or link to like-minded organisations across the world' (Gibson and Ward 2001:29–30).

Furthermore, the participatory and interactive features of the internet, such as email lists, newsgroups or chatrooms, can be used to foster solidarity within the organisation and deepen the public's involvement with its cause. Newsgroups and chatrooms can operate as spaces of debate, where people can freely exchange their views on the goals and activities of the organisation, becoming a more integrated social network (Diani 2001:121). Interactive features can also serve as a means to gauge public opinion and solicit feedback from users and supporters.

This participatory function is particularly important in the current political climate, whereby the professionalisation of NGOs has raised questions about their democratic potential. Critics often regard such organisations as protest businesses, arguing that the majority of their membership is just 'cheque book' activists who simply donate funds but do not participate in protests or decision-making (Ward 2001:3).

Also termed as 'credit card participation' (Richardson 1994:25), this phenomenon has led to the alienation of the membership base from the decision-making centre of the organisation. In that respect, the participatory functions of the internet can be used in an effort to restore the relationship with the membership base and strengthen its commitment.

Civic organisations can further use the internet to mobilise support and generate resources more cheaply and efficiently. Providing membership and donation forms online is only one way of getting people to contribute, while new fundraising techniques are currently explored. Finally, the internet has created opportunities for innovative campaigning and activism, as it constitutes a space for organisations to extend their existing repertoires of action or create new ones. With repertoires of action we mean 'the set of strategies, tactics or forms of protest' (Pickerill 2001:149) employed by the organisation. The most common of these new repertoires is 'electronic civil disobedience' which borrows its tactics from the tradition of non-violent direct action, such as sit-ins or blockades, and tries to apply them on the net (Wray 1998). Flooding a company with emails or crushing a website's server with too many requests for information are examples of this technique (Pickerill 2001:146). Such tactics transform the Internet infrastructure from a means towards or a site of communication to an object or site of action (Wray 1998).

However, the effectiveness of the internet as a new publication and networking medium is limited by its 'pull' nature which suggests that online it is the users who have control of the interaction and can easily choose to avoid political coverage. In other words, the 'pull' nature of the internet entails a completely different communication dynamic, demanding from political organisations to try to 'pull' visitors to their websites through promotion and advertising, instead of 'pushing' their message to an unsuspecting audience.

Furthermore, the information overload on the net constitutes an additional problem for political organisations, as it hinders the users' efforts to find the information they are searching for. As a result, users typically rely on search engines or on links from the outside of cyberspace to lead them to the sites they are looking for. However, search engines are also induced with commercial bias, while the number of links leading to a site depends on the size and prominence of the organisation. Thus, even in cyberspace it is still the well-resourced organisations which have a better chance of getting the user's attention.

In addition, organisations with better resources usually have more sophisticated websites. In fact, internet costs are 'directly tied in to some of the potential advantages of this medium' (Benoit and Benoit 2002), as multimedia and interactive features, personalisation, adaptation and constant updating are the most expensive features. But are civic organisations making the most of the internet's potential? And which are the limitations they face? The next section attempts to answer these questions by examining the actual functions and performance of the websites of three cause organisations.

## RESEARCH FINDINGS

The civic organisations examined in this study were Amnesty International, Oxfam and the World Development Movement. The research used a combination of qualitative and quantitative methods for the in-depth examination of the sampled cases. First, content analysis of the organisations' websites analysed the functions of the website and gave an indication of how well they performed. The content analysis categories were based on the schedule developed by Gibson et al (2001). To complement the findings of the content analysis, semi-structured interviews with the web coordinators of the sampled organisations revealed the thinking, strategy and problems concerning the websites.

### Information provision

Content analysis showed that all of the studied organisations use their websites to provide in-depth information about their goals and mission, successes, history and structure. The internet is thus transformed into an ideal reference information point, providing complete information archives as well as the latest news on campaigns and actions. Yet the internet is used more as an extension of the offline than as a medium in its own right, as it mainly provides texts developed for the offline to be downloaded online.

According to the interviews, the provision of up-to-date, accurate and in-depth information is indeed a top priority for all the examined organisations. This is because the function of information provision is considered crucial for retaining the commitment of the existing supporters and for gaining new ones.[1] Furthermore, it allows cause organisations to promote their own point of view to the public and to the media, as journalists are a primary audience of online communication. This is particularly the case for issues that

*Table 14.1*   Information provision

| | Amnesty | Oxfam | WDM |
|---|---|---|---|
| Organisational history | ✓ | ✓ | ✓ |
| Structure | ✓ | ✓ | ✓ |
| Values/ideology | ✓ | ✓ | ✓ |
| Policies | ✓ | ✓ | ✗ |
| Documents | ✓ | ✓ | ✓ |
| Newsletters | ✓ | ✓ | ✓ |
| Media releases | ✓ | ✓ | ✓ |
| People/who's who | ✗ | ✗ | ✗ |
| Event calendar | ✓ | ✓ | ✓ |
| Frequently asked questions | ✓ | ✓ | ✗ |
| Privacy policy | ✗ | ✓ | ✗ |
| Article archive or library | ✓ | ✓ | ✓ |
| News | ✓ | ✓ | ✓ |
| Work opportunities | ✓ | ✓ | ✓ |
| Annual report | ✓ | ✓ | ✗ |
| Campaigns information | ✓ | ✓ | ✓ |
| Information about successes | ✓ | ✓ | ✓ |

are already on the agenda, as users go online to get more in-depth information about something that triggered their interest offline.

### Resource generation

Content analysis of the websites revealed that all of the surveyed organisations have the option of an online transaction for donations and membership. Furthermore, online selling of merchandise or publications is also developed, while all the organisations offer the option of an online enquiry about volunteering.

However, interviews reveal a slightly different picture, as according to their web coordinators online fundraising does not constitute a major priority for the studied organisations. This is often translated into a lack of a comprehensive fundraising strategy or of clear quantitative goals regarding the funds expected to be raised through the website. Of course retaining the existing members and attracting new ones is an important function of the website. But this is mainly achieved by providing timely information and increasing the accessibility of the organisation to the public, particularly in locations where there is not a strong local group.

According to the interviews, there are several reasons for this lack of interest in online fundraising. First, the internet is still a new medium and, due to limited resources, organisations are developing only those functions which are considered essential to their overall strategy. Furthermore, the internet is not yet very cost-effective for recruiting participants. This is because of its 'pull' nature, which means that, in order to get people to donate, online organisations should first invest in promoting and advertising their websites. Nevertheless, it is worth noting that, according to evidence from political parties,[2] the medium shows potential, particularly for the target groups of young people and students, as well as people leaving in localities where the grassroots organisations are quite weak.

### Networking

All websites have hyperlinks to their local groups and international branches. This indicates that the internet has led to a greater decentralisation of the information provision process. At the same time, it has provided a platform for local groups to speak their mind. This potential could be particularly problematic for organisations wishing to keep a tight control of their message and image, since the local groups' websites may lack up-to-date information, be poorly designed and deviate from the organisation's official position. Yet none of the surveyed organisations has tried to control centrally the design and content of the grassroots' websites.

In the case of partisan links, meaning the links to other parties or organisations that are supportive of the organisation's goals (Gibson and Ward 1998), most of the sampled organisations link only with the ones they cooperate or co-manage a certain project. Oxfam has taken this approach a step further, aiming to help its partners in developing countries to move online by providing consultation and technical support.[3] Reference links, meaning the links to neutral or

*Table 14.2*  Networking

|  | Amnesty | Oxfam | WDM |
| --- | --- | --- | --- |
| Internal links | >100 | 11–20 | 1–10 |
| Members-only area | – | – | – |
| Partisan links | 0 | 21–50 | 11–20 |
| Reference links | 0 | 0 | 1–10 |
| Commercial links | 0 | 0 | 0 |
| Opponent links | 0 | 0 | 1–10 |

Figures represent the number of links.

news/educational sites, are even fewer. It is also worth noting that none of the studied organisations has links promoting business services.

Civic organisations have a very cautious and tight policy of external links. According to the interviews, this is partly because of the additional workload that finding and monitoring these external links would imply. What is more, competition for the users' attention is stiff, so organisations try to keep the number of external links to a minimum in order to prevent visitors from drifting to other organisations' websites.

Finally, none of the examined organisations offers a password-protected area for its members, even though all of them have expressed the desire to do so. Ultimately, this is a decision which depends upon the availability of resources.

### Participation

Most websites are quite open to the public, in terms of the number of email contacts to distinct units or branches within the organisation listed on their sites. This large number of email addresses can be attributed to the organisations' effort to decentralise the process of information provision, connecting directly the members of the public with the appropriate person to answer their enquiries.

However, none of the surveyed organisations fares well in terms of interaction. Most of the websites do not offer any interactive features, apart from some games, even though all of them have expressed the desire to do so. For instance, Amnesty International

*Table 14.3*    Participation

|  | Amnesty | Oxfam | WDM |
|---|---|---|---|
| Openness | 19 | 23 | 10 |
| Feedback | 2 | 1 | 1 |
| Opinion polls | ✓ | – | ✓ |
| Interaction | 1 | 1 | 0 |

Openness: Count of email contacts to distinct units or branches within the party or organisation listed on site.

Feedback: (1) email address on the site; (2) email address explicitly focused on soliciting comments; (3) an online form to submit views offered.

Opinion polls: ✓ = present, – = absent.

Interaction: (1) games/gimmicks to play; (2) bulletin board or guest book to post views; (3) chat room for real-time discussion.

would like to launch a discussion group within the members' area it plans to create, whereby the members of committees or working groups will be able to communicate with other members of their group.[4] Oxfam maintains a discussion group for the high-level activists, managed by the campaign's team,[5] while WDM is also thinking of launching a discussion group, even though for the time being their focus lays in creating more email lists for the public.[6]

Thus, it seems that the examined organisations have just extended some of their participatory functions online, such as the process of dealing with enquiries. However, none of them seems to benefit from the unique capabilities of the internet to increase participation and interaction. Possible reasons for this reluctance include the high costs of developing and maintaining the interactive features. In that respect, it seems that unless organisations become convinced of the benefits of this greater interactivity, they will not be willing to make the required investment. It is also possible that, since the internet is still a relatively new medium, organisations have not yet had the time to develop any communication functions which suit its interactive characteristics. However, it is questionable that they ever will, as this greater interactivity may be unsuitable for their communication culture. This is because interactivity increases the control of the user on the communication and information flows and challenges the existing dynamic of communication. This could prove very problematic, particularly for organisations with tighter and more centralised systems of information management.

## Campaigning

In terms of campaigning, all of the surveyed organisations offer their offline leaflets and campaign documents to be downloaded.

*Table 14.4*   Campaigning

|  | Amnesty | Oxfam | WDM |
|---|---|---|---|
| Election site/sites for specific campaigns | ✓ | ✓ | ✗ |
| Negative campaigning | ✗ | ✗ | ✗ |
| Cookie | ✗ | ✗ | ✗ |
| Join an email update list | ✓ | ✓ | ✗ |
| Become online campaigner/send an email/sign an online petition | ✓ | ✓ | ✗ |
| Download logo/wallpaper | ✗ | ✗ | ✗ |
| Download offline leaflets/propaganda | ✓ | ✓ | ✓ |
| E-cards | ✗ | ✗ | ✗ |

This is the most basic campaigning function as it involves material which was already developed for offline campaign actions. Indeed, for organisations with limited resources, such as WDM, this is the only online campaigning activity they are involved in.

Furthermore, all of the studied organisations provide users with the option to join an email update list, as most of them have several email lists focusing on different campaigning issues.[7] Organisations use those lists not only to keep the participants up to date with the latest developments, but also to draw more people to the website in a strategy which is suitable to the 'pull' nature of the medium. These lists are essentially top-down communication from the organisation to its supporters[8] and their discussion elements are minimal, as supporters use them very rarely for communicating between themselves.[9]

As for online activism, both Amnesty International and Oxfam provide users with the option to become an online campaigner by signing a petition or sending a protest email. However, web co-coordinators have voiced their concerns about the effectiveness of such techniques. Specifically, a government official can easily mass delete protest emails, ignore them or use an alternative address.[10] This is the reason why WDM has not yet extended its letter-writing protests online[11] and why Oxfam is considering new modes of campaigning actions.[12]

Another major problem with internet campaigning is the difficulty of disseminating the campaign message to people who are not already familiar with the organisation. In that respect, the offline can be more effective in generating support, as offline it is easier to contact people personally and to take advantage of their local or personal networks. This means that the size of the internet audience should increase in order for public campaigning to be more successful.[13] One way of doing this is viral marketing which, in its simplest form, asks the members of an email list to forward an email sent by the organisation to the people listed in their address book.

### Delivery

As for website delivery, it seems that the examined organisations do not make the most of the distinctive capabilities of the medium to provide information in new and innovative ways. Personalisation of the message is underdeveloped, while the use of multimedia, interactive features, and narrow casting is also very limited. In addition, most of the organisations do not fare well in terms of access

(Table 14.5). In practice, however, greater accessibility is achieved by avoiding gimmicks and Flash, as well as applications needing many 'plug-ins'. On the contrary, most of the organisations fare well in navigability, as all of them have search engines and a fixed menu bar on all pages. As for freshness, all of the organisations update their websites daily, apart from WDM who does it every one to six months. In terms of visibility, the number of links from other websites to the site of the organisation, as counted by Google, shows that Oxfam has the most visible website, followed by Amnesty International, while WDM has the lowest visibility of all. This order seems to simulate their exposure in the offline or mainstream media.

*Table 14.5*   Website delivery

|  | Amnesty | Oxfam | WDM |
|---|---|---|---|
| **Glitz and Multimedia** | | | |
| *Homepage design* | | | |
| Graphics | ✓ | ✓ | ✓ |
| images/photos | ✓ | ✓ | ✓ |
| Frames | | | |
| moving text/images | | | |
| *Multimedia index* | | | |
| Sound | | ✓ | ✓ |
| Video | | | |
| live streaming | | | |
| **Access** | | | |
| no frames option | | | |
| text only option (entire site) | ✓ | | |
| text only documents to download and print | ✓ | ✓ | ✓ |
| WAP/PDA 'wireless' enabled | | | |
| foreign language translation | | | |
| blind/visually impaired software | | | |
| **Navigability** | | | |
| Navigation tips | | | |
| No. of search engines | ✓ | ✓ | ✓ |
| Homepage icon on lower level pages | ✓ | ✓ | |
| Fixed menu bar on lower level pages | ✓ | ✓ | ✓ |
| Site map/index | | | |
| **Freshness and Visibility** | | | |
| Freshness | Updated daily | Updated daily | Updated monthly |
| Visibility (Number of links to the site) | 2070 | 4210 | 1340 |

## CONCLUSIONS

What the foregoing analysis showed very clearly is that the internet is used more as an extension of the offline media rather than as an autonomous medium with its own strategy and techniques. This is the case for all the examined websites and is particularly obvious in the functions of participation and campaigning.

The interviews suggested several reasons for this bland and unimaginative use of the internet. First, the internet is still a young medium which has not yet convinced civic organisations of its political potential. Organisations are thus unwilling to make the required investment in internet applications. They are also unwilling to engage in a costly 'pull' strategy, investing in promotion and advertising in order to attract more audiences to their websites. But as long as organisations do not make the required investment, the political potential of the internet is bound to remain unrealised.

However, the lack of resources and confidence in the new medium are not the only obstacles to its innovative utilisation. A closer look at the goals and strategy of the best-resourced organisation of our sample confirms this view. Specifically, Oxfam, which has the largest web team, is indeed driven more towards innovation but this innovation concerns mainly the functions of information provision and campaigning. On the contrary, the more interactive and participatory functions are largely ignored, as they are currently excluded from Oxfam's priorities.

Thus, what could be an equally pertinent explanation is that the use of the new medium varies between different organisations, depending on their goals and mission, culture and degree of institutionalisation. This means that the sampled organisations are currently developing only those internet functions that are considered instrumental for the achievement of their goals. In addition, the scope and ability of experimentation of the studied organisations is limited by their high degree of institutionalisation, as they are established political organisations with years of campaigning experience and large membership bases. This means that they have already established ways of treating the media and communicating with the public, which cannot easily be altered to suit the demands of a new medium. Besides, the nature of this new medium may not be suitable to the communication culture of these established organisations. This is particularly the case for the more interactive functions of the internet which increase the control of the user on the information and communication flows of the organisation. This indicates that the 'pull' nature of the medium itself demands a change of attitude from political organisations, as in order to lure more people to their websites they should yield part of the information control to the user. It is worth noting, however, that some of the civic organisations of our sample seem willing to move towards that direction.

It seems that all of the organisations under research link extensively to their internal departments and local groups. This is a result of their drive to decentralise the information provision process, in order to decrease the workload of the central office. Yet this development may bring a much deeper effect than the one initially expected. This is because the internet has the potential to tighten the bonds between the different parts of the organisation and transform their internal operation to a more network-like form. On the other hand, it still remains to be seen whether this greater decentralisation will increase the power of the grassroots groups and their influence to the central decision-making process at headquarters.

When it comes to the impact of the new medium on the public sphere, it is obvious that the internet constitutes a new political space which is open to all organisations to publish their opinions. It is thus characterised by a plurality of voices, allowing even fringe organisations to present their views. However, not all voices are equally strong, as organisations with better resources have more sophisticated websites and possess a greater degree of visibility on the net, in terms of links to their websites. Thus, to a lesser extent, the internet seems to replicate the power structures of the offline media.

Furthermore, the internet has not led to a greater integration of civil society, as, judging by the organisations of this study, it has neither intensified the links between civil society organisations nor increased the information and communication flows between them. An indication of this is the tight policy of external links adopted by all the examined organisations and designed to prevent visitors from drifting to other websites. This is because organisations are unwilling to take on the additional workload of finding and monitoring those external links. In addition, the time visitors spend online is limited, hence competition is stiff.

On a deeper level, what seems to be missing is a spirit of trust and solidarity that is essential for these tighter bonds of communication to exist. This means that, in order for visitors and political information to circulate freely between different websites, organisations need to show a deeper commitment towards transparency and cooperation. This involves a much more profound shift in the political system than the technical potential of the internet would imply. It ultimately demands from cause organisations a total change of mind and attitude and a dismissal of old practices in favor of a more open and collaborative communication space.

## NOTES

1   Interview with Anna Zhora, responsible for the Supporters' Services at the World Development Movement, 12 July 2002.
2   Interview with Mark Pack, Communication and Internet Officer of the Liberal Democrats, 31 July 2002.
3   Interview with Duane Raymond, member of the Innovations Unit of Oxfam UK, 16 July 2002.
4   Interview with Susie Wright, Web Coordinator/Information and Publicity Manager of Amnesty International UK, 20 June 2002.
5   This does not show in the content analysis because a link to it did not appear in the public site of the organisation.
6   Interview with Anna Zohra, see above.
7   WDM has an email list which is restricted for its high-level activists. This email update list does not show in the content analysis results as it is not provided as an option on the WDM website. (Interview with Anna Zhora, see above.)
8   This was verified by all the web coordinators interviewed.
9   Again this was verified by all the web coordinators interviewed.
10   Interview with Susie Wright, see above.
11   Interview with Anna Zohra, see above.
12   Interview with Duane Raymond, see above.
13   Interview with Duane Raymond, see above.

## BIBLIOGRAPHY

Axford, B. and R. Huggins (eds) (2001) *New Media and Politics*, London: Sage

Benoit, W. L. and P. J. Benoit *The Virtual Campaign: Presidential Primary Websites in Campaign 2000*, <http://acjournal.org/holdings/vol3/Iss3/rogue4/benoit.html> [Accessed 17 July 2002]

Bucy, E. P. et al (1999) 'Formal features of cyberspace: relationships between Web page complexity and site traffic', *Journal of the American Society of Information Science* 50, 13: 1246–56

Castells, M. (2001) *The Internet Galaxy: Reflections on the Internet, Business and Society*, Oxford: Oxford University Press

Clift, S. (2000) *Democracy is Online*, <http://www.publicus.net/ebook> [Accessed 7 July 2002)

Coleman, S. (ed.) (2001) *Elections in the Age of the Internet: Lessons from the United States*, London: Hansard Society

Diani, M. (2001) 'Social movement networks: virtual and real', in F. Webster (ed.) *Culture and Politics in the Information Age: A New Politics*, London and New York: Routledge

Dordoy, A. and M. Mellor (2001) 'Grassroots environmental movements: mobilisation in an Information Age', in F. Webster (ed.) *Culture and Politics in the Information Age: A New Politics*, London and New York: Routledge

Gibson, R. and S. Ward (2001) 'The politics of the future? UK parties and the Internet' in S. Coleman (ed.) *Elections in the Age of the Internet: Lessons from the United States*, London: Hansard Society: 29–35

—— (2000) 'A proposed methodology for studying the function and effectiveness of party and candidate Web Sites', *Social Science Computer Review* 18, 3: 301–19

—— (1998) 'U.K. political parties and the Internet: "politics as usual" in the new media?', *Harvard International Journal of Press/Politics* 3, 3: 14–38

Graham, F. (2000) *The Potential: Attracting Activists Online*, Fundraising UK Ltd, <http://www.hitdonate.net/1environment/1potential.htm> [Accessed July 2000]

Hacker, K. L. and J. van Dijk (eds) (2001) *Digital Democracy: Issues of Theory and Practice*, London: Sage

Hill, K. A. and J. E. Hughes (1998) *Cyberpolitics: Citizen Activism in the Age of the Internet*, London, Boulder, New York, Oxford: Rowman & Littlefield Publishers

Jones, S. G. (ed.) (1998) *Cyber Society 2.0: Revisiting Computer-Mediated Communication and Community*, London: Sage

Karmack, E. (2002) *Campaigning on the Internet in the Off Year Elections of 1998: A Snapshot in Time*, <http://siyaset.bilkent.edu.tr/Harvard/karmack.htm> [ Accessed 17 July 2002]

Keys, J. *Environmental Internet Campaigning of NGOs*, Greenpeace International, Amsterdam, <http://www.isep.at/internet_ws/keys.html>

Margolis, M., R. Gibson, D. Resnick and S. Ward (2001) *Election Campaigning on the WWW in the US and UK: A Comparative Analysis*, revised paper first prepared for presentation at the 97th annual meeting of the American Political Science Association, SanFrancisco, 29 September 2001, <http://www.esri.salford.ac.uk/ESRCResearchproject/papers/apsapaper.html>

Margolis, M., D. Resnick and J. D. Wolfe (1999) 'Party Competition on the Internet in the United States and Britain', *Harvard International Journal of Press/Politics* 4, 4: 24–47

Melucci, A. (1996) *Challenging Codes: Collective Action in the Information Age*, Cambridge: Cambridge University Press

Norris, P. (2001) *Digital Divide*, Cambridge: Cambridge University Press

Oxfam UK website <http://www.oxfam.org.uk>

Pickerill, J. (2001) 'Weaving a green web: environmental protest and computer-mediated communication in Britain', in F. Webster (ed.) *Culture and Politics in the Information Age: A New Politics?*, London and New York: Routledge

Richardson, J. (1994) 'The Market for Political Activism: Interest Groups as a Challenge to Political Parties', *Jean Monnet Chair Papers 18*, Florence: European University Institute

Rodgers, J. (2001) *NGOs and e-Activism: Institutionalizing or Extending the Political Potential of the Internet?*, paper presented in the ISA Hong Kong

Convention of International Studies, 26–28 July. Panel: Globalization and the Internet: Practices and Political Transformation

Sparks, C. (2001) 'The Internet and the Global Public Sphere', in W. Bennett and R. Entman (eds) *Mediated Politics: Communication and the Future of Democracy*, Cambridge: Cambridge University Press

Tsagarousianou, R., D. Tambini and C. Bryan (eds) (1998) *Cyberdemocracy: Technology, Cities and Civil Networks*, London and New York: Routledge

Ward, S. (2001) *Political Organisations and the Internet: Towards a Theoretical Framework for Analysis*, paper prepared for the ECPR Joint Sessions, Grenoble, 6–11 April 2001, <http://www.essex.ac.uk/ecpr/jointsessions/grenoble/papers/ws3/ward.pdf>

Weare, C. and W. Y. Lin (2000) 'Content analysis of the World Wide Web: opportunities and challenges', *Social Science Computer Review* 18, 3: 272–92

Webster, F. (ed.) (2001) *Culture and Politics in the Information Age: A New Politics?*, London and New York: Routledge

Wray, S. (1998) *Electronic Civil Disobedience and the World Wide Web of Hactivism: A Mapping of Extraparliamentarian Direct Action Net Politics*, <http://www.nyu.edu/projects/wray/wwwhack.html.> [Accessed November 1998]

# Notes on the Contributors

**Sarah Berger** was a 'Ban the Bomb' Aldermaston marcher at age 14, and in CND as a teenager. She was active at Greenham Common Women's peace camp, Anti-Apartheid Movement, the Labour Party and the socialist group Big Flame. After combining family and local community activism, she again joined anti-war campaigns. Sarah has worked as a charity manager in mental health, substance misuse and older people's services. Recently, she has protested at world summits on trade justice and debt.

**Kate Coyer** is a refugee from commercial radio and is currently a PhD student and visiting tutor in the Department of Media and Communications at Goldsmiths College, University of London, where she writes about community media. She has been producing radio and coordinating activist media projects since 1986.

In 2004 **John Downing** was named Director of the new Global Media Research Center in the College of Mass Communication and Media Arts, Southern Illinois University. He had previously worked at Greenwich University, Hunter College of the City University of New York, and the University of Texas at Austin. His recent research has focused on the global Indymedia movement since 1999, and with Charles Husband of Bradford University on a comparative analysis of racism, ethnicity and media, forthcoming in 2005 *Representing 'Race'*, Sage, London.

**Catherine Eschle** is Lecturer in the Department of Government at the University of Strathclyde, where she teaches International Relations and Feminism. She is author of *Global Democracy, Social Movements and Feminism* (Westview 2001, Boulder, USA) and of several journal articles on feminism, social movements and 'anti-globalisation' politics. She is co-editor (with Bice Maiguashca) of *Critical Theories, World Politics and 'The Anti-Globalization Movement* (Routledge, forthcoming).

**Ivor Gaber** began his professional life as a television journalist with the Visnews television news agency (now Reuters TV). From there he moved on to the UK's leading commercial television news organisation ITN where he worked as a producer and reporter and then to BBC TV current affairs. He then established his own independent production company, and also entered academe as a lecturer, in television production at Goldsmiths College, University of London. He was appointed Britain's first Professor of Broadcast Journalism at Goldsmiths in 1994 and was made Emeritus Professor six years later. He is now a freelance journalist, researcher and consultant. His current production work involves producing documentary series for BBC Radio's World Service and for Channel Four Television in the UK.

**Wilma de Jong** is a Lecturer in Media Theory and Production at the University of Sussex. As an independent film producer/maker, she owned a film company for twelve years and produced many films on social/cultural/ political subjects. She won several national and international prizes. Her research interests include pressure groups and the media, civil society and the media and documentary theory and practice She has taught at Kent Institute of Art and Design and Goldsmiths College.

**Anastasia Kavada** is a doctorate student at the School of Media, Arts and Design of the University of Westminster. Her research interests include the impact of the internet on social movements, civil society organisations and the process of political mobilisation.

**Ronnie D. Lipschutz** is Professor of Politics and Associate Director of the Center for Global, International and Regional Studies at the University of California, Santa Cruz. His most recent books include *Global Environmental Politics: Power, Perspectives and Practice* (2004, Albany: State University of New York Press), *Cold War Fantasies – Film, Fiction and Foreign Policy* (2001, Lanham, MD: Rowman and Littlefield), and *After Authority – War, Peace and Global Politics in the 21st Century* (2000, Albany: State University of New York Press).

**Marianne Maeckelberg** is a doctoral student at the University of Sussex. She worked in the World Social Forum office in Mumbai leading up to and during the WSF gathering in 2004 and was a member of the UK coordinating committee for the European Social Forum held in London in Autumn 2004.

**Kate O'Riordan** is a lecturer in Media, Culture and Communication Studies in the department of Continuing Education at the University of Sussex. Her previous publications have addressed issues of gender and sexuality in visual digital culture, the internet, computer games and mobile telephony.

**Pollyanna Ruiz** was born in Mexico in 1971. She lived and was educated in England before moving first to Portugal and then Brazil. Her general support of the anti-globalisation movement developed into a more analytical interest in 1998 when the Movemento Sem Terra began successfully to impact on the Brazilian mainstream. She returned to England in order to develop these interests further and is currently completing a PhD on the anti-globalisation movement and its promotional strategies at Sussex University.

**Martin Shaw** is Professor of International Relations and Politics at the University of Sussex. A sociologist of war and global politics, he has written on social movements, media and civil society. He was an activist in the student movement of the 1960s and the nuclear disarmament movement of the 1980s. His books include *Dialectics of War*, London: Pluto, 1988; *Post-Military Society*, Cambridge: Polity, 1991; *Global Society and International Relations*, Cambridge: Polity, 1994; *Civil Society and Media in Global Crises*, London: Pinter, 1996; *Theory of the Global State*, Cambridge University Press, 2000 and *War and Genocide*, Cambridge: Polity, 2003. He is currently working on *The New Western Way of War* (to be published by Polity in 2005). His website is www.martinshaw.org.

**Colin Sparks** is Professor of Media Studies and Director of the Communication and Media Research Institute at the University of Westminster. He has written extensively on the political economy of the media, on media and democracy in societies in transitions, and on aspects of globalisation.

**Neil Stammers** is Senior Lecturer in Politics at the University of Sussex. His research interests lie in the fields of social movements, globalisation, power and human rights. He is currently writing a book on 'Social Movements and Human Rights'. Recently published work includes: 'Social Democracy and Global Governance' in L. Martell et al (eds), *Social Democracy: Global and National Perspectives* (2001); *Rights, Movements, Recognition – Papers in Social Theory 6* (2001) (ed.), Papers in Social Theory 6, Brighton, Warwick Social Theory Centre/Sussex Centre for Critical Social Theory) 'Social Movements and the Challenge to Power' in M. Shaw (ed.), *Politics and Globalization: Knowledge, Ethics and Agency* (1999, London: Routledge); 'Social Movements and the Social Construction of Human Rights' in *Human Rights Quarterly* (1999).

**Dave Timms** has been the Press Officer of the World Development Movement since May 2000. In this capacity he has attended a number of international summits including those of the G8, IMF and World Bank and WTO. He is co-editor of *After Seattle: Globalisation and its Discontents* (with Barbara Gunnell, The Catalyst Trust, 1999) and was a member of the programme working group for the first European Social Forum, held in Florence in November 2002. From 1995 to 1998 David was publicity officer for *Red Pepper* magazine.

**Peter Waterman** has been a researcher and senior lecturer at the Institute of Social Studies (ISS) in The Hague (The Netherlands) on unions, social movements and internationalism. He carried out research on union and labour rights strategies by dockworkers and port authority workers in Lagos (Nigeria) in the 1970s and by Spanish dockworkers in European context in the 1980s. He was the author of academic papers, books and articles, both in English and Spanish, on issues such as the succession of trade union internationalism by a more general modern international labour rights solidarity in a global economy, requiring new communication methods connecting workers at the base of the unions.

**Alice Wynne Willson** is head of media relations for the international development charity ActionAid. Previously editorial director of *Network Photographers*, one of the world's leading photojournalism agencies, she cut her teeth at the *Independent Saturday Magazine* and also worked for the *Daily Telegraph* and *Reportage*. She is on the steering committee of Positive Lives – an international project that uses photography exhibitions to raise awareness about issues surrounding HIV/AIDS and to campaign against stigma and denial.

# Index

*Compiled by Sue Carlton*